Education for Democratic Intercultural Citizenship

Moral Development and Citizenship Education

Series Editors

Fritz Oser (*University of Fribourg, Switzerland*)
Wiel Veugelers (*University of Humanistic Studies, Utrecht, The Netherlands*)

Editorial Board

Nimrod Aloni (*Kibbutzim College of Education, Tel Aviv, Israel*)
Marvin Berkowitz (*University of Missouri-St.Louis, U.S.A.*)
Maria Rosa Buxarrais (*University of Barcelona, Spain*)
Helen Haste (*University of Bath, U.K./Harvard University, U.S.A*)
Dana Moree (*Charles University, Prague, Czech Republic*)
Clark Power (*University of Notre Dame, U.S.A.*)
Jasmine Sim (*National Institute of Education, Singapore*)
Kirsi Tirri (*University of Helsinki, Finland/Stanford University, U.S.A.*)
Joel Westheimer (*University of Ottawa, Canada*)

VOLUME 15

The titles published in this series are listed at *brill.com/mora*

Education for Democratic Intercultural Citizenship

Edited by

Wiel Veugelers

BRILL
SENSE

LEIDEN | BOSTON

This is an open access title distributed under the terms of the CC-BY-NC 4.0 License, which permits any non-commercial use, distribution, and reproduction in any medium, provided the original author(s) and source are credited.

All chapters in this book have undergone peer review.

The Library of Congress Cataloging-in-Publication Data is available online at http://catalog.loc.gov

Typeface for the Latin, Greek, and Cyrillic scripts: "Brill". See and download: brill.com/brill-typeface.

ISSN 2352-5770
ISBN 978-90-04-41192-0 (paperback)
ISBN 978-90-04-41193-7 (hardback)
ISBN 978-90-04-41194-4 (e-book)

Copyright 2019 by Koninklijke Brill NV, Leiden, The Netherlands.
Koninklijke Brill NV incorporates the imprints Brill, Brill Hes & De Graaf, Brill Nijhoff, Brill Rodopi, Brill Sense, Hotei Publishing, mentis Verlag, Verlag Ferdinand Schöningh and Wilhelm Fink Verlag.
Koninklijke Brill NV reserves the right to protect the publication against unauthorized use and to authorize dissemination by means of offprints, legitimate photocopies, microform editions, reprints, translations, and secondary information sources, such as abstracting and indexing services including databases. Requests for commercial re-use, use of parts of the publication, and/or translations must be addressed to Koninklijke Brill NV.

This book is printed on acid-free paper and produced in a sustainable manner.

Contents

List of Figures and Tables   VII
Introduction   VIII

1 Education for Democratic Intercultural Citizenship (EDIC)   1
   Wiel Veugelers

2 Theory and Practice of Citizenship Education   14
   Wiel Veugelers and Isolde de Groot

3 Ethical Competences for Democratic Citizenship at School, University and in Family   42
   Maria Rosa Buxarrais, Elena Noguera and Francisco Esteban

4 Social and Educational Inclusion in Schools and Their Communities   61
   Ghazala Bhatti

5 Teachers' Moral Competence in Pedagogical Encounters   81
   Elina Kuusisto and Kirsi Tirri

6 Educational Activities in Civil Society   107
   Dana Moree and Terezie Vávrová

7 Educational Policy and Leadership to Improve Democratic Citizenship Education   124
   Eve Eisenschmidt, Triin Lauri and Reet Sillavee

8 Preparing Educators and Researchers for Multicultural/Intercultural Education: A Greek Perspective   148
   Anastasia Kesidou

9 Experiencing Democratic Intercultural Citizenship: EDIC Intensive Programmes   166
   Elina Kuusisto, Dana Moree and Reet Sillavee

10 Students' Experiences in EDIC+ Intensive Programmes   184
   Ghazala Bhatti

11 The Future of EDIC+   191
   Wiel Veugelers

Figures and Tables

Figures

5.1   Teachers' support in ethical sensitivity.   99
7.1   Efficiency and equity in education (Source: Lauri & Põder, 2013).   130
7.2   The process of raising proactive citizens.   135
7.3   Concept of the module.   136

Tables

5.1   Schedule of the module.   90
5.2   Instructions for the course tasks.   91
5.3   Evaluation criteria for the learning diary and the mini-study.   93
5.4   Topics of the mini-studies, research questions, related articles, instruments, data analysis, and discussion.   94
5.5   Ethical sensitivity group: Dimensions of ethical sensitivity.   98
5.6   Ethical sensitivity group: Teachers' ways of showing support.   99
5.7   Moral dilemma group: Teachers' and students' perceptions of moral dilemmas in schools.   100
5.8   Mindset group: Categories, subcategories, and examples from the data.   102
5.9   Purpose group: Categories, subcategories, and examples from the data.   103
7.1   The main characteristics of ideal-typical governing modes in educational policy and school choice (Source: Lauri, 2013).   128
7.2   Outline of the module.   137
9.1   Schedule of the EDIC Intensive Programmes in Prague and Tallinn-Helsinki.   171
9.2   Individual and group tasks.   179

Introduction

Future societies need critical, engaged, democratic and intercultural citizens. Education has an important role to fulfil in cultivating such citizens. Erasmus Strategic Partnerships enable universities to work together, to develop new initiatives and to learn from each other. The topic of Education for Democratic Intercultural Citizenship is very interesting for such a partnership, given the differences in ideas, policy and practice between countries and universities. These differences, within a common democratic and intercultural framework, can challenge teachers, researchers and students to cooperate and act as a professional learning community. The first chapter of the book describes the goals, strategy and envisioned outcomes of our strategic partnership Education for Democratic Citizenship. We call it EDIC+, where the + refers to Erasmus+.

The seven universities already had longstanding collaborations but could extend these in the Strategic Partnership EDIC+. The focus in the Strategic Partnership, running from September 2016 until September 2019, was on curriculum development. Each university, applying their particular field of expertise, developed an international module within the theme of Education for Democratic Intercultural Citizenship. Each module is comparative, research-oriented and linked with schools and institutions in society. Chapters 2 to 8 detail the seven modules: their theoretical framework, their curriculum guidelines, their concrete activities and organisation, and the participating students' experiences. We start with the module of the leading university in EDIC+, the University of Humanistic Studies in Utrecht, followed by the other universities in alphabetic order.

One important element in the collaboration concerns the annual intensive programmes in which teachers and students of the seven universities meet for a try-out of crucial elements of their own module, to exchange experiences with the different modules, and to learn about the local context of intercultural democratic citizenship. You can read about the intensive programmes of Prague 2017 and Tallinn/Helsinki 2018 in Chapter 9, with a particular focus on the local context. Chapter 10 reports on how the students experienced these intensive programmes. We will complete the book at the end of February, shortly before our intensive programme in Thessaloniki: on time to present the book at the final EDIC+ conference in Utrecht on June 19–20. The last chapter of the book is about the future of EDIC+.

CHAPTER 1

Education for Democratic Intercultural Citizenship (EDIC)

Wiel Veugelers

1 Why an EDIC+ Project?[1]

Europe and its participating countries need a strong democracy, an inclusive society, and active citizens. Intercultural and democratic competences are crucial for the future of Europe, its countries and its citizens. Education can play a central role in developing the necessary knowledge, skills and attitudes among young people.

Universities have a double role to play: they need to educate academics who can and want to contribute to such an inclusive and democratic society, and university-educated teachers, educational researchers and curriculum developers can work in schools and other educational institutions on empowering young people for active citizenship participation.

The pedagogical role of teachers in contributing to a more inclusive and democratic society is very important in this period of European history in which an increasing globalisation challenges traditional values. Strengthening international cooperation in all parts of Europe is very relevant to broadening the horizon of students, teachers, and academic researchers. A more inclusive and democratic society is as relevant for the future of Europe as economic growth. Education, and in particular teachers, can contribute to this moral enterprise. As research shows, attention for democratic and intercultural issues is currently not very strongly embedded in the curricula of teacher education and educational science.

1.1 Why an Erasmus Strategy Partnership on EDIC?

This strategic partnership aims to support democratic intercultural citizenship education in different ways, for instance by developing a joint curriculum and through the professional development of academic staff. The project will have a direct influence on students in the different modules and in intensive programmes. Strategic work will be done in own universities, through the cooperation between our universities, and with partners in civil society. The outcomes of this project will also be transferred to other universities and ultimately to

© KONINKLIJKE BRILL NV, LEIDEN, 2019 | DOI: 10.1163/9789004411944_001
This is an open access chapter distributed under the terms of the CC-BY-NC 4.0 License.

the society in each country. The project hopes to boost the social responsibility of universities and other institutes for higher education, and to contribute to active and engaged citizenship in Europe.

Through inter-university cooperation and the development of joint curricula, EDIC+ tries to contribute to a direct increase in social inclusion in partner countries and to the promotion of intercultural and civic competences among students. The quality and relevance of higher education will be improved, as the partner universities will have the opportunity to learn from each other's best practices and in this way to strengthen the field of Education for Democratic Intercultural Citizenship. The interdisciplinary nature of cooperation is addressed by including a broad range of partners representing social sciences, humanities, as well as teacher education.

By offering holistic Education for Democratic Intercultural Citizenship, the curricula developed during this project will support the future education of teachers and educational professionals, training them in how to promote European values, for example by preventing violent radicalisation, fostering social integration, and enhancing intercultural understanding (see Erasmus+ Guide 2016). The teaching/learning activities envisaged by this project (as well as educational activities continuing after the end of this project) will help participants build a sense of belonging to a European community. Further, the project seeks to develop social capital among future teachers and educational professionals, and to empower them to participate actively in European society by including a variety of international as well as local students and teachers.

The values of democracy and tolerance are currently strongly supported by the European Commission and the European Parliament. Education should play a central role in developing these values. (See European Commission, 2016: Promoting citizenship and the common values of freedom, tolerance and non-discrimination through education: overview of education policy developments in Europe following the Paris Declaration of 17 March 2015. Also see the Motion for a European Parliament resolution on the role of intercultural dialogue, cultural diversity).

1.2 *Education for Democratic Intercultural Citizenship*

Education prepares young people for the labour market, for living in society and for their personal well-being. For Europe and its countries it is very important that young people are prepared well for living and participating in a democratic and inclusive society. This preparation for society is called 'citizenship education'. Citizenship goals are formulated at the national, European and global level. Active or participatory citizenship of people, also young people, is considered to be crucial for the sustainability of future democracy in nation states and in Europe. Inclusiveness of different social and cultural groups and social and political integration at the national and European level is important for a peaceful future for all human beings, in Europe and worldwide.

Active and involved participation of citizens is not only the foundation for the well-being of society, but also for the spirit of entrepreneurship in our societies. Economic, social and cultural entrepreneurship and citizenship are interlinked and necessary for a sustainable, dynamic and future-oriented society. Cooperation, dialogue and intercultural communication between people and groups are a source of creativity and diversity, and can stimulate possibilities for many people to live a good life and to contribute to a humane and flourishing society. A strong educational focus on democratic and intercultural citizenship development in all areas of education is very relevant for the future of Europe and its citizens.

The objectives of the project are to develop an international curriculum at the university level that supports (future) teachers and educational scientists in creating curricula and practices for Education for Democratic Intercultural Citizenship (EDIC) at all levels of education to cultivate future European citizens. Until now, citizenship education, particularly with a focus on democracy and intercultural dialogue, has not received much attention in teacher education and educational studies (for review studies Veugelers, 2010; Bhatti & Leeman, 2011; Tirri, 2011; Sanger & Osguthorpe, 2013; Teodoro & Guilherme, 2014).

University educational programmes, especially teacher training curricula, currently lack sufficient practice with regard to teaching topics related to democratic intercultural citizenship education. At the same time, developments in European society are adding urgency to the need for these competences among teachers and educational specialists. We think that a strong stimulus is needed in this area of education. Future Europe needs a democratic and inclusive society with critically engaged citizens, and education can contribute to this.

2 Strategy of EDIC+

The educational programme we will develop during the three project years will consist of different modules in different universities and joint intensive programmes for teachers and students. The programme will be research-oriented, comparative, and linked with civil society. Most importantly, the project will be transnational: universities from the south (Barcelona, Thessaloniki), the north (Helsinki and Tallinn), the west (Bath, Utrecht) and the east of Europe (Prague) are participating. The programme will express European inclusiveness, with attention for national, regional and local differences. The modules developed will give Master students the opportunity to make choices and to develop a personal profile within the field of democratic intercultural citizenship education. The programme will be open to all students. In particular, we want to include prospective teachers (of all school subjects), educational researchers and curriculum designers.

The intensive programmes will be international educational activities in themselves and the motor for the development of modules. In the intensive programmes, parts of the modules will be tried out and critically reflected on by peer-teachers and students from different universities and different parts of Europe.

The following seven modules have been agreed upon:

1.	University of Humanistic Studies	Theory and Practice of Citizenship Education
2.	University of Barcelona	Ethical Competencies for Democratic Citizenship at School and in Families
3.	University of Bath Spa	Social and Educational Inclusion in Schools and their Communities
4.	University of Helsinki	Teachers' Moral Competence in Pedagogical Encounters
5.	Charles University Prague	Educational Activities in Civil Society
6.	University of Tallinn	Education Policy and Citizenship in Education
7.	Aristotle University Thessaloniki	Multicultural/Intercultural Education

In choosing these seven topics, we are drawing on the expertise of the different universities and have compiled a relevant combination of topics that together cover the broad area of Education for Democratic Intercultural Citizenship.

2.1 *Objectives of EDIC+*

The concrete objectives of the project are:

1. To develop a curriculum for Education for Democratic Intercultural Citizenship (EDIC), formally recognised and supported by seven universities in different parts of Europe.
2. To stimulate student exchange in this area and gather collective experiences in intensive programmes.

EDUCATION FOR DEMOCRATIC INTERCULTURAL CITIZENSHIP (EDIC)   5

3. To promote the professional development of teachers in this field (and a professional development programme).
4. To stimulate a more complex, critical and engaged concept of citizenship that combines social, political, intercultural and entrepreneurial components.
5. To strengthen the cooperation between universities and civil society.
6. To develop a partnership between European universities that stimulates cooperation between researchers, teachers and students in this field.
7. To develop curriculum materials and student products with open access and on the EDIC website.
8. To educate a new generation of teachers, curriculum developers, and researchers.

In an intensive cooperation, the group of experts of the seven universities will develop a European curriculum, in which the national level, the European level, and the global level are included. The curriculum will be research-oriented, will use the experiences and expertise of the participating countries in a comparative way, will link the universities with civil society institutions, and will create possibilities for Master students to gain international experiences.

The project aims to educate a new generation of teachers, educational scholars and practitioners who are oriented towards the needs of a future global world, and Europe in particular. It will lead to the inclusion of more dynamic, intercultural, comparative and research-oriented learning in the curriculum of universities.

2.2 *From EDIC to EDIC+*

Most universities involved in this project participated with their students and teachers in the highly successful Erasmus Intensive Programmes in May 2013 in Utrecht and May 2014 in Barcelona. These universities see the development of a common curriculum as the next complementary step. The intensive programmes demonstrated the specific expertise of the participating universities and teachers, stimulated the connection of different theories, and shared interesting teaching methods. In this way, the programmes have contributed to closer cooperation between the involved universities in teaching and research.

This Erasmus Strategic Partnership gives the opportunity to build a platform, a network, a curriculum and experts in the field of Education for Democratic Intercultural Citizenship. It takes the cooperation between the involved universities to a higher level. The new EDIC+ project can advance curriculum development, teachers' expertise, and student exchange. On the inter-institutional level, there will be a joint curriculum and an organisational structure that can support the project, stimulate knowledge transfer to other universities, and develop new initiatives in the field of citizenship and intercultural education.

2.3 Task of Participating Universities

Each partner is responsible for the development and teaching of one module. Further, each partner will have an EDIC coordinator and one assistant coordinator, although more teachers and researchers will be involved in the local team. Both the coordinator and assistant coordinator will have a teaching task in the module. Each partner also has to stimulate student exchange and contribute to the joint activities such as the intensive programme, and on the curriculum level to ensure a fit between the modules and the formal procedures to develop a joint certificate. Each partner communicates regularly with their cooperating civil society organisations. Once a year, they will each have a meeting with all these civil organisations to exchange experiences and develop new initiatives.

Each year in autumn there is a transnational project meeting of the EDIC+ coordinators of the seven universities. Herein, management policy, finance, and coordination of the curriculum development and the supporting research activities will be addressed.

Each year in spring there will be an intensive transnational programme of 10 days. Students and teachers of the involved universities will participate in this intensive programme. The programme will hold educational value for the students and professional development potential for teachers. During this programme, curriculum development will be assessed, research and design activities will be coordinated, and the exchange of students will be monitored.

To stimulate further cooperation between the universities, the module developed at each university will also host a visiting professor from one of the other partners. This scholar will give a lecture and workshop in the module and will inquire into the theory and practice of the module as a 'critical friend'.

2.4 Outcomes of the Project

These 12 results are envisioned over a period of three years (September 2016–August 2019):

1. The joint development of a curriculum for Education for Democratic Intercultural Citizenship (EDIC+), a network structure, and an intensive programme.
2. The development of one 7.5 ECTS (Master level) module (in English) by each participating university. The seven modules will together constitute

EDUCATION FOR DEMOCRATIC INTERCULTURAL CITIZENSHIP (EDIC)

the integrated curriculum EDIC+. All materials will be published (in an open-access book and on the EDIC+ website).

3. The recognition of all seven modules by all EDIC universities. All universities will offer the entire EDIC+ curriculum to their students.

4. Signing of an agreement by all EDIC universities for student exchange with other participating universities through Erasmus grants.

5. Participation of students from these seven universities and students from other universities in these modules. Students can use Erasmus exchange grants for participating in modules at other universities.

6. Awarding of an EDIC+ certificate to students after completing two or more modules of the EDIC curriculum. (For students of the EDIC universities this can be a module at their own institute and a module at one of the other universities. The intensive programme can be part of one of the modules).

7. All modules will have the following methodological elements:
   a. Combination of theory and practice
   b. Link with civil society institutions (site visits, guest lectures)
   c. Research and change orientation
   d. International and comparative orientation through the use of data and examples from other countries, in particular the EDIC+ participants
   e. A visiting professor in each module from one of the other EDIC universities to give a lecture and act as a critical friend during the process of curriculum development.

8. Creation of a team of scholars who can function as experts, co-supervisors or members of a Master or PhD-tribunal in the other participating universities.

9. An academic international e-journal offering students the opportunity to publish their research, their curriculum material and their educational experiences. (We had to drop this goal because an Erasmus Strategic Partnership cannot finance such an activity.)

10. An annual intensive programme (IP) of ten days for students and teachers. After the project period, other resources, such as Erasmus exchange grants, will be used to continue with the IP.

11. Dissemination of activities in all participating countries; at the European level presentations will be given at leading educational conferences (ECER, EARLI, ATEE).

12. Setting-up of a proper management structure to ensure the sustainability of the EDIC+ curriculum after the EDIC+ project is completed.

2.5 Developmental Process

1. First year: develop an outline for own module, carry out comparative research, and teach a number of essential components of the modules at own university.
2. Second year: first try-out of prototype modules.
3. Third year: second try-out of modules, with focus on assessment and sustainability/implementation.
4. Each year: an intensive programme of ten days with the following components:
   a. A try-out of elements of the modules
   b. Gathering ideas and feedback of the students to improve the modules (students as co-constructors of the modules). From each university, two teachers and three students can participate.
5. Each year: three-day management and curriculum meeting of the coordinators of each university to work on the curriculum development, in particular on connections between the modules, to guide comparative research activities, to monitor the quality of modules, and to arrange institutional conditions (recognition of modules, exchange contracts between the universities). Also, the organisation and financial situation will be evaluated and monitored.
6. Set up internet platform: internal (in first year) for participating teachers and students, and external (with open access) (by third year) for other interested scholars, students, policy-makers, etc.
7. Prepare and publish (open access) book and curriculum material.

Students of (teacher) education programmes in the participating universities and other universities will be the main beneficiaries of this project. The target group consists of future teachers and other educationalists, curriculum developers, and academic researchers. The purpose is to educate a new generation of engaged, competent and entrepreneurial educators involved in making society more democratic, intercultural, inclusive and future-oriented (in Europe and in a global world).

By developing this programme we aim to contribute to creating university curricula that are research-oriented, comparative, civic-embedded, and society-linked. Because of their multidisciplinary approach and focus on active and dialogic learning, the developed curricula can serve as an example for future curriculum development in (other) universities.

Both own students at the respective universities and exchange students can benefit from the developed modules. They will participate in a module that is international, research-based, and linked to society. The idea is that the curriculum stimulates connections with civil society, and a critical engagement

EDUCATION FOR DEMOCRATIC INTERCULTURAL CITIZENSHIP (EDIC) 9

with democracy and with the role education can play in building a more inclusive society.

The specific tasks leading to the production of the intellectual output are as follows:

- Analysing possible target groups who would be interested in participating in this module.
- Defining the aims of the module according to the goals of EDIC+ and the needs of the target groups.
- Collecting data from other EDIC+ countries through comparative research.
- Describing the content of the module according to its aim, and analysing and incorporating new changes brought on by field experience and the results of latest research findings.
- Making agreements with civil society organisations and schools for guest lectures and field visits.
- Describing the learning outcomes and assessment criteria.
- Piloting parts of the module in the EDIC+ intensive programmes and at own universities.
- Discussing the programme and its practice with the visiting EDIC+ teacher.
- Improving the module.
- Producing a final version of the module.

3 Results of the Erasmus+ Strategic Partnership EDIC+

3.1 *Developmental Process*

The strategic partnership gave the opportunity to intensify the cooperation between the seven European universities. The project started in September 2016 and ended on August 31 2019. We are writing this result paragraph already in January 2019, so not all developments in the third project year can be included. However, we wish to have this results paragraph in the book that will be presented at the final international multiplier event held in Utrecht on 19–20 June.

The *Intensive Programmes* could be continued and now serve as a motor for the curriculum development in each university, an international learning site for students, a professional development environment for teachers, and a platform for new initiatives. During each Intensive Programme, there was always a meeting of all teachers on the curriculum development in which we discussed the progress of the modules.

The *module development* in each university focused on the embedding of EDIC+ elements in the curriculum of the participating universities and on the development of a specific module for the joint inter-university EDIC+ curriculum grounded on the own expertise. All the universities could organise try-outs of the modules or at least crucial and new elements of it.

Critical friends attended another university, gave a lecture in the EDIC+ module and reflected on the curriculum development. The critical friend was in the second and third year a powerful instrument to collaborate at the teaching level itself. Both the critical friend and the receiving university were positive about it.

Meetings of the *executive committee* were held during the Intensive Programmes and one in the autumn of each year. At this meeting, the organisation of the whole project, the organisation in the different universities, the progress of the deliveries, implementation and dissemination, and new initiatives were discussed. We could attend as executive committee of EDIC+ all participating universities. This was also very helpful to understand the specific expertise and context of each university and to support the implementation of EDIC+ in the university by meeting relevant officials of the university.

3.1.1 Link with Teaching Common Values Research

At the same time that the Erasmus Strategic Partnership EDIC+ started, the European Parliament asked us to perform a comparative research on the policy and practice of teaching the common values democracy and tolerance in all 28-EU Member States (Veugelers, De Groot, & Stolk, 2017). In all 28 EU Member States, academic experts collected data on the policy and practice of teaching democracy and tolerance. Additional data were collected through case studies in 12 countries. These 12 countries included the seven countries involved in EDIC+. This research was a great stimulus for getting data, doing comparative research and building a network of academic experts on citizenship education in all EU Member States.

3.2 *Intensive Programmes*

The 10-day Intensive Programmes (IP) are always held in spring. In 2017 the IP was in Prague, in 2018 in Tallinn and Helsinki, and in 2019 in Thessaloniki. Three students of each university participated. At all the universities, there were more students with an interest in the programme. In 2018 there were two students who rejoined the IP, now covering their own costs directly.

One interesting aspect was the participation of several students from outside Europe (Iran, China, Columbia, Chile, Venezuela, Ghana). Their experiences with intercultural citizenship and education expanded the view and made the programme more global.

EDUCATION FOR DEMOCRATIC INTERCULTURAL CITIZENSHIP (EDIC)   11

In each IP, all the teachers presented parts of their module in a lecture or workshop. Students also had the opportunity to talk with them more informally in round table sessions. School visits were made that allowed students to observe lessons and to talk with principals, teachers and pupils. Guest lectures were given by representatives of NGOs, and guided tours were made in the city with a focus on citizenship (you can read more about the IPs in Chapter 9).

The students always stayed for the full 10 days; teachers between 4 and 6 days. The schedules of the teachers were arranged around the curriculum meeting and the meeting of the executive committee. Teachers were responsible for the selection, guiding and assessment of the students of their university. Students could actively participate in the programme by presenting their research, their analyses of Education for Democratic Intercultural Citizenship in their country, through dialogues with teachers and other students, and through the many joint formal and informal meetings during their stay (Students' experiences in the IPs are presented in Chapter 10).

3.3   *Module Development*
In the first year, all the universities made a first draft of their module. The topic was chosen with a view to the expertise of the university and their participating staff. The drafts were discussed in the curriculum meeting during the IP in Prague. In the second year each university planned a try-out of the module (or central parts of it).

The organisational embedding of the module was quite a challenge. Two models emerged: modules that take a long time, 8–10 weeks with weekly activities (Tallinn; Thessaloniki) or intensive modules of one or two weeks (Helsinki, Utrecht, Bath). Some modules also had an in-between structure (Barcelona, Prague). In the first year Barcelona and Prague could only organise try-outs of small parts of the module because they could not find enough students to participate.

All the universities could develop their module within the theoretical topic they had chosen. Connections with schools and civil society were made. Students also had the opportunity to get actively engaged in the programme. As said before, the critical friends in the module were really an addition to the content of the module and to the dialogues about the programme.

The experiences with the modules, the reflection on these experiences and the renewed plans were discussed in the curriculum meeting during the IP in Tallinn. In that meeting, a first draft of the chapters of the book was discussed. A second draft was discussed in the executive committee in autumn 2018 in Barcelona.

3.4 Teacher and Student Participation and Exchanges

Much has been said about the participation of teachers and students in the Intensive Programmes. This was close to perfect. All participants see the value of the Intensive Programme in itself and as a motor of the curriculum development and the professional development of the teachers. We hope we can continue these Intensive Programmes!

The critical friendship element was also perceived as positive; unfortunately, three visits could not be arranged in the first year. For the third year all friendship visits could be arranged. Some arrangements to continue these visits in the future have already been made, for example by using Erasmus teacher exchange grants.

Getting Master students to participate in the modules at the different universities was not so easy. We do not yet have all the data for the third year, but can already make the following two comments:

- EDIC+ focuses on Master and PhD students. Most of their programmes are very structured and do not leave not much room for flexibility and choices. Most universities became more aware of this bonding of students to their own programme and are searching for more choices and flexibility in Master and PhD-programmes.
- Erasmus exchange grants for students require a period of at least three months. For Master and PhD students, this period is often too long (see first point). Having grants for say two weeks would strongly facilitate student exchange and participation in full-time programmes.

Nevertheless, nearly all modules had enough students to run the programme, either because they actually had a group of 15–20 students (Helsinki; Thessaloniki), or a small group of eight students (first year Utrecht) in which four Dutch and four exchange students worked intensively together; or because the module was included in a regular course with interested foreign students attending (Tallinn).

3.5 Implementation and Dissemination

All seven universities continue their curriculum work and try to include the EDIC+ module and crucial elements in their regular programme. Working on the EDIC+ modules has stimulated a stronger focus on society, international developments and on the role of intellectuals in it. Democracy and intercultural developments are getting more attention at the involved universities.

Students that participated in the Intensive Programmes still have many contacts with each other and are really EDIC ambassadors. In each country a national multiplier event has been organised in May in which colleagues of other universities, policy-makers and NGOs learn about the outcomes of

EDIC+. This book will be presented at the final international multiplier event June 2019.

Note

1 Parts 1 and 2 of this chapter are strongly based on the submitted proposal.

References

Bhatti, G., & Leeman, Y. (2011). Convening a network within the European conference on educational research: A history of the social justice and intercultural education network. *European Educational Research Journal, 10*(1). 129–142.

Sanger, M., & Osguthorpe, R. (Eds.). (2013). *The moral work of teaching and teacher education*. New York, NY: Columbia University.

Teodore, A., & Guilherme, M. (2014). *European and Latin America Higher Education between mirrors*. Rotterdam, The Netherlands: Sense Publishers.

Tirri, K. (2011). Holistic school pedagogy and values: Finnish teachers' and students' perspectives. *International Journal of Educational Research, 50*, 159–165.

Veugelers, W. (2010). Moral values in teacher education. *International Encyclopedia of Education, 7*, 650–655.

Veugelers, W., De Groot, I., & Stolk, V. (2017). *Research for Cult Committee – Teaching common values in Europe*. Brussels: European Parliament, Policy Department for Structural and Cohesion Policy. Retrieved from http://bit.ly/2pm5Yh9

CHAPTER 2

Theory and Practice of Citizenship Education

Wiel Veugelers and Isolde de Groot

1 Introduction

Education has an important task in preparing young people for their participation in society. Citizenship is now the central concept for scholars and practitioners who engage in this educational task. It concerns both legal rights and obligations, and how people live together in communities, nations, and in the global world. People can, and often do, have different ideas about what makes a good citizen and what are good ways of living together. They may also have different ideas about how education can contribute to citizenship development.

This EDIC+ module of the University of Humanistic Studies focuses on different ideas about citizenship and citizenship education in theory, policy and practice. In the first part of the module, students use a comparative approach to examine commonalities and differences between nations in Europe and in the non-Western world. In the second half, students evaluate educational practices and policies of schools and NGOs in light of key theoretical concepts, and develop an educational activity.

1.1 *Broadening and Deepening the Concepts of Citizenship and Citizenship Education*

The concepts of citizenship and citizenship education are now central concepts in the theory, research, policy and practice of education. Citizenship education refers to how education can support students' development of identity. In the last few decades the concept of citizenship has been both broadened and deepened (Veugelers, 2011a). 'Broadened' means that citizenship is no longer just linked with the national state, but also with regional arrangements (e.g. European citizenship), and even with the whole world through the concept of global citizenship. 'Deepened' means that the concept of citizenship has been extended from the political level to the social and cultural level. It is about living together in a particular society. As a result of this deepening, citizenship has strengthened its connection with moral development. Citizenship is now the central concept in both policy and research when examining the role of education in developing students' identity.

© KONINKLIJKE BRILL NV, LEIDEN, 2019 | DOI: 10.1163/9789004411944_002

This is an open access chapter distributed under the terms of the CC-BY-NC 4.0 License.

In many countries the policy of citizenship education has intensified recently: in Europe, in other parts of the Western world, in Asia, but also in Latin America. It is a paradox that in an era dominated by neo-liberal policy with a strong market orientation and limited government interference, education policy now focuses so strongly on citizenship education. The identity development of a person is not left to the autonomy of the free individual, but is made the target of a direct socialisation effort by schools, coordinated by the national government.

From a positive perspective, one may argue that educational policy is a democratically chosen manner of socialising human beings into a democratic way of life and into a lively civic and political engagement. However, even within such a democratic framework, different ideological articulations are possible, and the specific articulation depends on the embedded configuration of moral values like adaptation, individualisation, and social concern.

This EDIC+ module of the University of Humanistic Studies aims to provide students with knowledge of different theoretical approaches to citizenship education, an in-depth understanding of policies at the national and European level, and skills to design and evaluate practices of citizenship education. The module will be theoretical, comparative and practice-oriented.

2 Transitions in Citizenship Education Research

As research on citizenship education is becoming a solid academic sub-discipline, it is interesting to examine key transitions in the academic field of citizenship education over the past five decades. Traditionally, the academic field of citizenship and citizenship education was part of the discipline of political science. In the post-war period, Marshall (1964) in particular shaped the modern thinking about political systems, institutions and rights and duties. In the seventies, sociologists like Isin and Turner (2002) and Bourdieu (1984) entered the field, making the connection between the political arena and society stronger. During this period, the focus in the sociology of education was on the reproduction of society, that is, on social and political power relations and positions.

Critical pedagogy emerged as a novel field of research with the work of Freire (1985) and was expanded by Giroux (1989) into a more comprehensive theory of building democracy through education, making citizenship theory and research more dynamic and transformative (Veugelers, 2017a). Apple and Beane (2005) focused on democratic schools and Mc Laren (1989) on 'life in schools' of underprivileged students.

Political psychologists like Torney-Purta (2002) initiated attention for the cognitive and affective processes involved in youngsters' social and political development. Philosophers, for example McLaughlin (1992), Nussbaum (1997) and Crick (1999) entered the debate about what citizenship and in particular democracy and participation means, and how education can or cannot contribute to citizenship development. This has been followed more recently by the more political philosophy of Mouffe (2005), which emphasises contradictions (agonism) in citizenship and democracy.

Within education studies, related disciplines started to use the term citizenship as well. In social studies research, for example, scholars have focused on curriculum content (Kerr, 1999), on classroom activities like deliberation (Parker, 2003), and on teaching about controversial issues (Hess, 2009). Scholars on multicultural education have argued that learning about, through and for diversity and plurality is at the very heart of citizenship education (e.g. Banks, 2004, 2017). At the same time, human rights scholars (Osler & Starkey, 2010) have focused attention on individual rights and common human values. Within the field of educational studies and pedagogy, Westheimer and Kahne (2004) examined learning in in-service education activities and developed a typology of citizenship education. Biesta (2011a, 2011b) explored 'subjectification' in relationship to citizenship education and on how students actively give meaning to life and find their way in the world. School effectiveness research resulted in comparative studies like the International Civic and Citizenship Study (ICCS, 2010, 2017). About 30 countries participated in these comparative studies on practices and effects of citizenship education.

In research on moral education, Haste (2004) and Oser and Veugelers (2008) linked morality with society and the political domain: moral values are not considered as abstract notions but as embedded in societal contexts and political power relations. The moral and political must be linked more closely together: the moral must become more political and the political more moral (Veugelers, 2017a).

Post-colonial studies (Andreotti, 2011; Torres, 2017) went beyond a Western perspective on citizenship and citizenship education and emphasised social justice and societal transformation (Veugelers, 2017b). A specific Asian perspective has been examined by scholars like Kennedy, Lee and Grossman (2010) and Sim (2011). They showed that an 'Asian' perspective has a more positive view on being social and of attachment to local and regional traditions.

More recently, the concept of citizenship has also been used in countries with strong internal conflicts, for instance by Reilly and Niens (2014) in relation to Northern Ireland and Goren and Yemini (2016) with regard to Israel. The concern for sustainability has also become part of citizenship: the citizen

THEORY AND PRACTICE OF CITIZENSHIP EDUCATION 17

and his surroundings should become not only democratic but also sustainable (Gaudelli, 2016).

All these extensions of citizenship have made the concept very complex. All these researchers, with their own knowledge base, specific articulations of concepts and research methods, have contributed to what we can now call the academic sub-discipline of citizenship education studies. It is a dynamic field with different social, moral, cultural and political perspectives.

3 Different Political Orientations of Citizenship

Traditionally, distinctions in citizenship have been made in terms of for instance weak and strong (Barber, 1984), making citizenship appear as a linear construct. However, citizenship can have different ideological articulations. The academic (Western) scholarship on citizenship is closely related to especially the concept of democracy, but citizenship occurs just as well in non-democratic societies, in the form of an authoritarian citizenship. Citizenship is a concept that pertains to participation in a nation and society, without defining the type of participation. It is in fact an ideologically neutral concept.

Even regarding democracy, there are many different ideas (see e.g. Gutman, 1987; Touraine, 1997; Mouffe, 2005; Veugelers, 2007; Biesta, 2011a; De Groot, 2013). Scholars have developed different positions on, for example, the way people need to contribute in order for democracy to thrive, the influence that people can have on politics, and the societal and civil domains that can be part of democratic processes like labour organisations, educational institutions, and the role of non-governmental organisations (NGOs). The debates are essentially about the balance of two elements of democracy: freedom and equality (Mouffe, 1998, 2018). Freedom refers to being entitled to have and express one's own opinions and the possibility to participate in democracy. Equality refers to the opportunity to participate in democratic processes and the possibility of equal power relations in democracy. Freedom and equality together form part of a political vision on democracy.

3.1 Different Educational Goals and Types of Citizenship

Educational systems, schools within a system and teachers within a school; they can all have different educational goals, also with regard to citizenship and citizenship education. In several research projects (with both quantitative and qualitative instruments), we asked teachers, students and parents which educational goals they find important. Statistical analyses showed three clusters of educational goals: discipline, autonomy, and social involvement

(Veugelers & De Kat, 2003; Leenders, Veugelers, & De Kat, 2008a, 2008b, 2012). (See for more conceptual explorations of these clusters Veugelers, 2007, 2017b.) Each cluster expresses a clear and different political articulation.

- *Discipline*, for example, has to do with listening and behaving well. These are goals that are emphasised especially in the educational movement that is called 'character education' (Lickona, 1991). It is about promoting good behaviour and following norms. In socialisation research, as in the work by the sociologist Durkheim (1923), disciplining is considered an educational task: education teaches you how you should behave.
- *Autonomy* refers to personal empowerment and formulating your own opinion. These goals are central to the moral development tradition of Kohlberg (Power, Higgins, & Kohlberg, 1989) but also in the structural sociology of Giddens (1990), with the emphasis on 'agency'. Autonomy can be defined as the experience of freedom, and giving meaning to your own life. In the Western world and in modernity more generally, people's development of autonomy is considered very important.
- The third cluster, *social involvement*, shows a broad spectrum of social goals: from an instrumental coexistence, a social-psychological empathy, to a social justice-based solidarity and combating inequality in society. In this social spectrum, different scientific orientations can be found: the justice approach by Rawls and Kohlberg, the concept of care by Noddings (2002), and the concept of empowerment by the Brazilian pedagogue Freire (1985). Social involvement can vary greatly in its political orientation.

Our research, with both quantitative and qualitative instruments, shows that these three clusters of discipline, autonomy and social involvement are important educational goals for teachers, students and parents.

3.1.1 Types of Citizenship

Further analysing our data (with person-centred factor analyses), we could construct three types of citizenship, expressing different orientations:

- The first type is *adaptive* citizenship. This type scores high on discipline and social involvement. Socially involved not in a political sense, but in a moral commitment to each other, especially your own community. For autonomy, the scores are not so high for the adaptive type.
- The second type, *individualised* citizenship, scores high on autonomy and fairly high on discipline but relatively low on social involvement. This type has a strong focus on personal development and freedom, not on the social.
- The third type, *critical-democratic* citizenship, scores high on social involvement and on autonomy. On discipline this type scores low. We call this type critical-democratic because of its focus on the social and on society,

THEORY AND PRACTICE OF CITIZENSHIP EDUCATION

a critical engagement with the common good, and a democracy that leaves room for individual autonomy and personal articulation.

In a survey of Dutch teachers in secondary education, with a representative sample, we could conclude that 53% of teachers pursue a critical-democratic citizenship, 29% an adaptive type, and 18% an individualising type. This variety is not the same for the different levels of education: in pre-university secondary education we see more support for the individualised type and in the pre-vocational education, for the adaptive type. Support for a critical-democratic type was the same for both levels. A reproduction of social class positions and power relationships supported by differences in schooling becomes visible in these citizenship orientations (Leenders, Veugelers, & De Kat, 2008a).

3.1.2 Types of Citizenship and Civic Education Practice

These three types of citizenship each correspond, in an ideal way, to a specific practical operationalisation of citizenship education with an own methodology and a focus on certain goals:

- *Adaptive*: strong transmission of values, in particular adaptive values, and attention for standards and norms. Teacher-directed education, and students seated in rows. Values are embedded in the hidden curriculum.
- *Individualised*: strong focus on developing students' independence, and on critical thinking. Students work a lot individually. Values are a personal choice.
- *Critical-democratic*: focus on learning to live together and to appreciate diversity, and on active student participation in dialogues. Cooperative and inquiry-oriented learning is practiced often. Attention for social values and critical reflection on values.

Of course, the types of citizenship and the corresponding practical classroom interpretations are ideal-typical constructions. In people's views and in educational practice we find many hybrid forms of citizenship and citizenship education. But these three types of citizenship and citizenship education clearly demonstrate that citizenship is not a matter of bad or good citizenship, and that different orientations in the political nature of citizenship and citizenship education are possible. It also shows that nations, schools and teachers can make choices in their educational goals and in their practice of citizenship education.

3.2 *Differences between Goals, Practices, and Experiences of Citizenship Education*

The curriculum can be approached in different ways (Goodlad, 1979): the ideal curriculum (or, the abstract level), the interpreted curriculum (what teachers personally want to do), and the operationalised curriculum (the curriculum as practiced in education). At all curriculum levels different articulations of citizenship and citizenship education can be found.

In the previous section, we reported insights from empirical studies on the goals that Dutch teachers pursue. In the following section we focus on education practice: on Dutch teachers' views on the extent to which they realise these goals. Our studies revealed that teachers often find themselves unable to realise these objectives entirely. This is particularly true of the goals of autonomy and social involvement. It is striking that in the Netherlands, teachers as well as parents indicate that discipline in education still receives relatively a lot of attention and is also fairly well developed in students. They realise that it is much more difficult to develop strong autonomy, where students take real responsibility for their own actions and deliberate on alternatives in a grounded manner. The social orientation, and especially the attitude in it, receives even less attention in educational practice and is also more difficult to achieve (Veugelers, 2011a, 2017a).

3.2.1 Adaptation, Individualisation, and the Social: Cultural and Political Differences

In traditional education, the disciplinary adapting mode of citizenship gets a lot of attention. In modern teaching methods with a focus on self-regulating learning and in child-centred pedagogical perspectives, the individual citizenship is more central. This individual orientation is further strengthened in education, in the 'hidden curriculum', by the competition and selection that is strongly embedded in many educational systems. This performativity becomes even more important in an ideology and policy of accountability. Students have to compete with each other and are made responsible for their own educational success. This individual competitive orientation has grown stronger in the Western world in the past decades, and the Netherlands offers a good example. However, Asian countries like South Korea, Singapore and Taiwan are also strongly competitive-oriented.

The social orientation depends largely on cultural and political traditions. The social, in its positive sense of collaboration and social justice, seems to be less embedded in the practice of Western educational systems. Countries with a social democratic political orientation, such as the Scandinavian countries, have a stronger social orientation (Green & Janmaat, 2011). This also applies for some Latin American countries, as the result of strong social movements focusing on empowerment (Teodoro & Guilherme, 2014; Veugelers, De Groot, Llovomate, & Naidorf, 2017; Veugelers, 2017a). In some East Asian countries, there is a social orientation as part of a more collective culture, often infused by Confucianism (Kennedy, Lee, & Grossman, 2010; Sim, 2015).

THEORY AND PRACTICE OF CITIZENSHIP EDUCATION

The concept of global citizenship transcends the nation, but this concept shows differences as well (Oxley & Morris, 2013). In our own theoretical and empirical research on global citizenship, we distinguish an open, a moral, and a social-political global citizenship (Veugelers, 2011b, in press). A social-political orientation stresses the injustice of inequality and seeks more transformation of power relations: it is more political than appealing in general to moral values like in the moral global citizenship. The open global citizenship is presented as neutral, but in fact it is a neo-liberal market orientation.

International comparative studies like the International Civic and Citizenship Education Study (2010, 2017) reveal how adolescents think and act in the area of citizenship. Many youngsters support democracy and individual freedom on an abstract level. However, these studies also show that in many Western countries the social and political involvement and the future envisioned involvement of youngsters is not very strong. For example, in Northwest European countries like the Netherlands, the UK and Belgium, youngsters indicate a lack of interest in being involved in politics and the common good. On the other hand, they do express certain political opinions such as restricting rights and state support for immigrants.

In our own research with the three types of citizenship, we find among youngsters a strong focus on autonomy, and a social involvement which is more psychological and focused on their own communities rather than global and social justice oriented (Leenders, Veugelers, & De Kat, 2008b, 2012). De Groot (2013) studied adolescents' view on democracy and found that many students are not interested in participating in democratic practices, often because they feel that they cannot have any influence.

3.2.2   Distinguishing Types of Citizenship and Citizenship Education

The relevance of the distinction between types of citizenship and citizenship education is that it shows how choices can be made at the different policy levels, that these choices have consequences for practices of citizenship education, and that these differences are grounded in different ideologies. Other scholars similarly make distinctions in types of citizenship (see for a review Johnson & Morris, 2010). Westheimer and Kahne (2004) distinguish between a personally responsible, a participatory, and a social justice oriented citizen. Our distinction emerged from research on teachers' pedagogical goals, which showed that teachers can have different ideas about citizenship. Westheimer and Kahne did their research in a research project about in-service learning. They examined what students actually did in these projects and which goals were set for the projects. Therefore, their focus was more on how people can contribute to society and less on politics. A strong point of the Westheimer and Kahne typology, however, is the focus on social justice and on contributing to society.

In our typology, the focus is on people's participation in the societal and political processes and power relations, and on the ideological orientation that people express in their conceptualisation of citizenship: is the focus on adaptation to norms, on developing and arguing one's individual views, or on acting as a critical and engaged participant in democratic processes. The typology is about the social and political way people participate in society and the ideology they use to substantiate their position. It is important to show in educational research and in teaching that different political and ideological articulations of citizenship are possible. Education should challenge youngsters to study different perspectives and to develop their own position in response.

4 Teaching Common Values Democracy and Tolerance

So far we have looked at the theory and practice of citizenship and citizenship education. However, educational policy can also express different articulations of citizenship. A country's education policy can address citizenship education in different ways and can emphasise different moral values. Between countries there can be commonalities and differences. This EDIC+ module focuses strongly on citizenship and citizenship education, in particular in Europe. The European Union has always stressed the relevance of the values of democracy and tolerance for Europe as a community as well as for its Member States.

At the request of the European Parliament we conducted a study on how, in all 28 EU Member States, attention is devoted to the values of democracy and tolerance, both in policy and practice (Veugelers, De Groot, & Stolk, 2017). This research focused on the policy of teaching the common values of democracy and tolerance in secondary schools, and how this policy is implemented in practice. Further, it covered how teachers, local communities and NGOs influence the teaching of common values. The education policy of all 28 European Union Member States was analysed by national academic experts, and in-depth curriculum studies were performed in 12 Member States. The EDIC+ universities participated in the study and the study was a starting point for the curriculum development in EDIC+.

In the theoretical framework of the study, three components of democracy were distinguished: participation, democratic politics, and democratic society; as well as three components of tolerance: interpersonal relations, tolerance towards different social and cultural groups, and an inclusive society. Further, a distinction was made between a national and an international orientation.

A review of existing relevant studies (e.g. CDP, 2005; ICCS, 2009) shows some evidence that students' value development is stimulated by a 'whole school approach' that incorporates the teaching of values in four ways:
- A specific value-oriented subject.
- Integration of values into related subjects.
- Cross-curricular activities that build links with the community.
- A democratic school culture, involving:
  - more dialogical methodologies of teaching and learning,
  - active participation of students in schools,
  - inclusive education in bringing together different groups of students and teachers.

In this research, we investigated whether these elements are part of the education policies of the EU Member States, and whether schools and teachers are able to realise these elements in practice. We first present the main conclusions and then the recommendations.

Conclusions

Policy

Greater attention to the teaching of values, including democracy and tolerance, is evident in the education policies of all EU Member States. Although Teaching Common Values (TCV) is fairly important in half of the EU Member States, compared to other topics and subject areas the attention given to TCV is very meagre.

An analysis of the practice of TCV in 12 EU Member States shows that there are only a few Member States where the different components of teaching for democracy and tolerance receive systematic attention across schools. TCV is often not strongly implemented in education policy in terms of concrete curriculum instruments and supporting measures. This results in practices that do not always devote real attention to TCV. There is not only a gap between policy and practice, there is also a gap within policy: between general ideas and concrete measures. Moreover, the EU Member States differ in the extent to which they steer TCV policy.

In several EU Member States, there is a strong tendency to separate students into different groups based on different learning capacities. This reduces opportunities to learn about social and cultural differences. A second element that limits diversity among students is the prevalence of private or religious schools.

Curriculum

In most EU Member States, there is a focus on political participation within the attention devoted to democracy. However, attention should also be given to two other elements of democracy: to democracy as a process of deliberation and consensus-building, and to the creation of a democratic society that is just and inclusive and values freedom of speech and equality. Education practices that relate to all these different components of democracy are scarce.

Tolerance is mostly addressed at the interpersonal level and to a larger extent at the level of cultural groups, but very little at the level of an inclusive society. While national orientation receives abundant attention in education policy, attention for the international dimension is not very strong, although it is growing. Teaching about national issues is mostly not very critical, however.

Recommendations

Based on the outcomes of the research we formulate recommendations at the different levels: EU, nation states, curriculum, schools.

Policy

Both the EU and each EU Member State has to take responsibility to support democracy and tolerance as common societal values and to support the sustainability of such a society. An intensive dialogue in society on what constitutes the common values and the role of education in promoting them is an expression of a lively democracy, and is a challenge for tolerance. EU Member States and the EU should support such dialogues. The EU can challenge its Member States to develop their own educational vision on Teaching Common Values like democracy and tolerance, stimulate the development of innovative practices, promote teacher and student exchange to help them experience different political and educational practices, and stimulate comparative research.

At the national level, education policy steering should target aims, guidelines for content and subjects, as well as activities. Further, education policy should challenge schools to use their relative autonomy to demonstrate their own vision and practice of TCV.

Curriculum

Greater attention should be given in education policy and practice to all three components of democracy. TCV also has to address all three elements of value development, namely knowledge, skills, and a democratic attitude. Besides tolerance, concepts with more positive attitudes such as appreciation, pluralism, and respectful engagement should be used. All three levels of tolerance (interpersonal relations, social and cultural groups, inclusive society) need more attention in education policy and practice.

Learning democracy and tolerance can be strengthened by cultivating social and cultural diversity in schools and classrooms. Education policy should stimulate diversity in education (among both students and teachers). Each country has to find the right balance in education between national and international orientation, so as to strengthen democracy and tolerance both nationally and internationally and to address both levels in a critical way.

Before the EDIC+ module starts, the participating students read the research report and analyse the case study of their own country, or the country of their university, and formulate concrete suggestions on how to improve the policy and practice of teaching democracy and tolerance.

5 Curriculum Guidelines EDIC+ University of Humanistic Studies

In this module, students study different theories and concepts of citizenship and citizenship education. They learn to analyse national and local policies and practices of citizenship education. National (Dutch), comparative (focusing in particular on the participating countries), European, as well as global perspectives on citizenship and citizenship education will be covered. Intercultural aspects such as unity and diversity, psychological elements like engagement and emotions, and sociological variables such as social class, gender, religion and ethnicity will be included in the presented theories and analyses.

5.1 Curriculum Framework

In curriculum development it is important to formulate curriculum guidelines and a curriculum framework to steer the concrete programming of the module. In the *theoretical* part of the module, students learn about different theories of citizenship, citizenship education, moral education, intercultural education, and the possible links between these theories (see next section).

The *comparative* part of the module starts with in-depth analyses of the Dutch context of citizenship and citizenship education. After that, each student gives a critical presentation of citizenship and citizenship education in their own country (this presentation has to include small, personally-made video recordings). These presentations will be analysed jointly using national, European, and global perspectives. Interesting future-oriented theoretical, policy and practical directions will be delineated. The students analyse the Teaching Common Values report, paying particular attention to their own country, and how the recommendations in the report can improve teaching democracy and tolerance in educational policy, the curriculum, the schools, and the classroom in their country.

In this comparative part of the module, links are made with citizenship education outside Europe and the Western world: in Asia (Beijing, Singapore and Indonesia/Yogyakarta) and Latin America (Mexico and Argentina). The University of Humanistic Studies cooperates with these universities. Analyses and comparisons of these non-Western concepts and practices are made. In Skype meetings, students have dialogues with scholars outside Europe.

The third part of the module is more *practice-oriented*. Here students will apply theoretical concepts and comparative knowledge gained during the earlier part of the module. Students will study the citizenship curriculum practised at different levels of Dutch education (primary schools, secondary schools, and vocational schools). We try to include traditional schools, progressive schools, and multicultural schools. Groups of students will visit these schools, talk with teachers and pupils and will observe classes. The EDIC students will also give a short presentation to pupils about their own country and its citizens.

The second type of visit will be made to civil society organisations, e.g. Prodemos, Amnesty International, Anne Frank House, 'Fortress of Democracy', and the Humanist Ethical Association. Students will talk with staff members of these organisations about their educational activities. Experiences from both visits (schools and civil society) will be exchanged among students and analysed.

The module will be characterised by a research-oriented comparative approach (the place of citizenship education in schools and civil society in the different participating countries) and a linking of theory with practice. The final form of *assessment* will be a paper in which the students use the theory and the experiences gained from the module to design an educational policy and/or activity for a particular group of students in their own country.

THEORY AND PRACTICE OF CITIZENSHIP EDUCATION   27

The innovative didactical aspect of this EDIC+ module is a stronger comparative approach that is more practice-oriented and is linked with civil society. It should enforce the knowledge, skills, and attitudes of (future) teachers, researchers and curriculum designers. Regarding the content, attention for the concepts of citizenship, democracy and intercultural society will be increased in educational studies.

Teachers in our past research projects often mentioned a lack of professionalism regarding citizenship education, particularly in diverse classrooms and with controversial issues. With this module we want to address these concerns and support future teachers in their pedagogical work.

The module will be open to all university students since citizenship education is a responsibility for every citizen, in particular every intellectual. Nevertheless, teachers, curriculum designers and educational researchers have a special role in this.

5.2   *Lectures and Visits*

In the module we focus on theory, policy and practice of citizenship education. We start the module with a presentation and discussion of the research on citizenship and citizenship education as outlined above. Other lectures are given by faculty members of the University of Humanistic Studies and by guest lecturers.

5.2.1   Stories and Super Diversity

Yvonne Leeman uses stories to prepare student-teachers for teaching in an inclusive society and for social justice: for living together in diversity and inclusivity. It is a means to identify differences and commonalities. Stories can provide for a safe encounter, help develop empathy, broaden one's view of the world, enable deep learning, stimulate the imagination, and offer multi-perspectivity. Stories confront a person with his/her process of identity development (confrontation with own culture, developing new orientations, reflexivity on own biography, narrative imagination). It is crucial to be touched by emotions, real encounters, experiences of being an outsider, and learning new cultural codes. Teachers can use stories in their classrooms and in their own professional development.

5.2.2   Cultivating Political Spaces in Schools

Isolde de Groot (2018) discusses how politics and political questions enter the classroom. How can political spaces be cultivating? For instance by having a mix of student voices, through influence in school on substantial components, meta-conversations, an appreciation of disruption and conflict, and through opportunities for 'democratic' student participation. As part of this approach: how can schools organise mock elections? By integrating more critical elements of democratic citizenship in mock-related education, and by contributing to a democratic school culture by increasing student involvement in the organisation of mock elections. Increasing room for such activities in the curriculum and the professional development of teachers in this respect are important conditions to enhancing the contribution of mock elections to democratic citizenship education.

5.2.3　Strengths and Limitations of Democratic Experiences in Schools

Isolde de Groot argues that "In many democratic societies, schools are expected to prepare their students for participation in democratic societies. (Self)assessment frameworks, designed by scholars and curriculum developers, support the development of school-initiated democratic experiences. Existing frameworks, however, are not designed to capture the interplay between the practices organised, related educational activities, and the types of aims pursued in education programmes. I present an eight-sectored framework that intends to capture the multiplicity of democratic education and participation in schools, and I discuss extreme cases and cases that sit at the intersection of the eight boxes. To explore the viability of the framework, I demonstrate how the framework can be used to identify strengths and limitations of how mock elections are organised in Dutch high schools".

5.2.4　Democracy and Learning/Subjectification

Gert Biesta (2011a, 2011b) challenges the notion of democracy. A community needs a wall: who is in, and who is out. Democracy is a political project. It is about what should have authority in our collective lives. Democracy is not 'flourishing' but limiting, not a common identity but political relationships; it is common world, not a common ground.

Democracy is not driven by individual desires but by what can collectively be considered desirable. It is not telling children what they should desire and what not, but making the question 'is what I desire desirable' into a living question. Educational work is about arousing the desire for a democratic way of life. Democracy is the condition of possibility for the existence of a plurality of values. Democracy is a fountain rather than a wall.

5.2.5　Philosophical Reflections on Tolerance

Political philosopher Filimon Peonidis of our EDIC+ partner Aristotle University Thessaloniki gave a lecture in which he presented a historical-philosophical

THEORY AND PRACTICE OF CITIZENSHIP EDUCATION

analysis of the concept of tolerance. He showed that the concept refers to accepting otherness and that tolerance is in fact a quite recent phenomenon. It started, in the Western world, in the 16th century by accepting people who shook off traditional religious bonds. Tolerance is growing all over the world and is now considered to be part of human rights. However, human beings still have a long way to go to really live with tolerance and to change tolerance into appreciation.

5.2.6   Citizenship Education in Mexico

In a Skype session with Benilde Garcia-Cabrero of Autonoma University of Mexico, we discussed citizenship education in Mexico. Benilde clearly showed how social and political developments influence the kind of citizenship and citizenship education that is addressed in schools. After a period in which a conservative government emphasised national identity and adaptation and which created a loss of trust, the new more progressive government stimulates more active participation, rights and democratic engagement. Benilde argues for a better inclusion of emotions in citizenship education. Emotions have a great effect on changing moral values and attitudes. Benilde cautions against a too direct influence of politics on citizenship education: keep the good things and pay more attention to implementation.

5.2.7   Citizenship and Moral Education in China

In another Skype session, we discussed developments in moral and citizenship education with Chuanbao Tan and Lin Ke of the Center for Citizenship and Moral Education at Beijing Normal University. They explained that in China, moral education has traditionally been influenced strongly by Confucianism and that politically the focus was on responsibility and national identity. More recently there is attention for human rights and critical thinking as well. Modernisation in China requires citizens that respect human rights, cultural differences and can think critically in all domains of society: in economy, technology, politics, in social and cultural life, and in the natural environment. The challenge for China is to find the right balance between critical thinking, responsibility and social concern for the family, the nation and the global world. And also, between the national and the local, and the national and the global. Higher education and intellectuals have an important role in these societal developments.

5.2.8   Student Participation in Curriculum Development

Jeroen Bron is the coordinator of citizenship education at SLO, the Netherlands Institute for Curriculum Development, and the secretary of the taskforce for citizenship education of 'curriculum.nu'. In his PhD thesis, Bron (2018) focused on student participation in curriculum development. In his theoretical study he formulated five rationales for including a student voice in curriculum design: normative, developmental, political, educational, relevance. He developed a method to include all students in curriculum design and explored the method in six case studies. The studies showed that students can formulate topics to study and can make the curriculum more relevant, and that by exercising the method they can develop and demonstrate democratic citizenship qualities like communicating, cooperating and negotiating.

5.2.9 Multicultural Secondary Education School

We visited a multicultural school in Amsterdam and talked with the vice-principal, a teacher and students. The school really wants to be multicultural but for them it is difficult to attract native Dutch students. The free school choice in the Netherlands hinders the school in becoming truly multicultural. Many students and parents in the Netherlands choose a school that is not diverse but similar to their own milieu.

The students were very engaged with the school and with their own future, but they were not happy with the fact that is very difficult for them to meet native Dutch youngsters, either in their school or outside school. They want to integrate into Dutch society, but Dutch society and Dutch people should give them more opportunities.

5.2.10 Vocational Education

Another school we attended was a school for secondary vocational education (ROC) in Utrecht. We spoke with the vice-principal, a teacher of citizenship education and students. Schools in Dutch education are required to pay attention to citizenship education, but it are the schools themselves (or even a specific department) that makes the actual programme. This department finds citizenship education very important, with a focus on moral reasoning, political participation and becoming engaged. Students have two hours a week of citizenship education, in addition to special projects at times. Citizenship education should develop critical thinking: 'to learn to think about how others view' and 'from outside to inside'. Students were very positive about these lessons, and in a lesson that we attended they learned about moral, social and political dilemmas.

5.2.11 Fortress of Democracy

As an example of an NGO that contributes to citizenship education we attended the 'Fortress of Democracy'. The fort was part of the 'waterlinie' (water defence

THEORY AND PRACTICE OF CITIZENSHIP EDUCATION 31

system) built to protect Holland in case of war. During the cold war it served as an atomic bunker. Now it is a place where students can learn about democracy. Annually about 6000 students visit the Fortress. There is a permanent exposition with nearly 100 questions and dilemmas relating to society and democracy. We were impressed by the creativity in the activities involved and the many different topics addressed. Examples of activities are questions about what contributes to democracy and what hinders democracy, knowledge about the Second World War, Dutch Jews in the Second World War, privacy, the 'Zwarte Piet' issue ('Black Peter'), facts and opinions, own moral values, power relations, etc. (www.fortvandedemocratie.nl).

6 Organisational Context Now and in the Future

The long-term aim is to develop a module of 7.5 ECTS. The regular format of a module at the University of Humanistic Studies is 10 weeks half time. In the future we hope to realise a joint international master (and PhD) programme in the field of moral and citizenship education of at least 10 weeks. This programme will consist of the EDIC+ module, an additional module and writing a short essay. Together it should be 12 weeks (20 ECTS). Such a programme gives students the possibility to apply for an Erasmus exchange grant. As part of the EDIC+ Erasmus strategic partnership, the University of Humanistic Studies has already concluded Erasmus agreements with the other six participating universities. Now, in the developmental stage, we opt for what we call in EDIC+ the Intensive Programme format: a full-time week, with a preparation period and an essay afterwards. Three students of the University of Humanistic Students can combine this module with participation in the international Intensive Programme.

7 Programme Try-Out

(We present the text for the students.)
The central part of the module is one week full-time at the University of Humanistic Studies Utrecht: from January 29 until February 2 2018 (February 18–22, 2019). The preparation and the paper can be done in Utrecht or at the home university (guidance if necessary will then be given by Skype meetings). The minimum ECTS for the module is 5, if your university requires another amount we can increase the student's activities.

7.1 Schedule

January	20 hours	Preparation: reading and making presentation
January 29–February 2	40 hours	One week full-time in Utrecht
March–April	80 hours	Paper (5 ECTS, can be max. 7.5 ECTS)

8 Schedule EDIC+ Course University of Humanistic Studies Utrecht

8.1 Theory and Practice of Citizenship Education
Moderator Wiel Veugelers
Assistant Daniëlle Drenth

Monday January 29

9.30–10.30	*Introduction*
	Of the participants. Of the programme. Practical information
10.30–12.30	*Teaching Common Values Democracy and Tolerance*
	Presentation of research Wiel Veugelers. Discussion, see task 1
12.30–13.30	Dutch lunch together
13.30–16.00	Presentations of each participant: Moral and Citizenship Education in own country and/or in own research/study. See task 2
16.00–17.00	Skype meeting with Benilde Garcia, University of Mexico
	Moral and Citizenship Education in Mexico and Latin America
17.30	Drinks in university cafeteria

Tuesday January 30

9.30	Reflection
10.00–11.00	*Different Concents of Citizenship and Citizenship Education*
	Lecture of Wiel Veugelers
11.00–11.45	Practical preparation of visits Wednesday
12.30–14.30	*Finding, Making and Using Stories for and about Living in Superdiversity*
	Lecture/workshop Yvonne Leeman
15.00–16.45	*How to Slow Down Life without Stagnating Society: Resonance in an Accelerating World*
	Lecture by visiting German sociologist Hartmut Rosa

Wednesday January 31

9.00	Travel to Amsterdam
10.00–12.30	*Visit to School*
	A school for secondary education in a multicultural surrounding
	Talks with teachers and students

Thursday February 1

9.30–10.00	Reflection on programme Wednesday
10.00–12.00	*Cultivating Political Spaces in Schools: The Case of Mock Elections*
	Lecture/workshop Isolde de Groot
13.30–15.30	Guided tour in Utrecht, focus on Philosophical and Humanist topics
	By Jules Brabers, Humanist Historical Centre
16.00–18.00	Visit to Fortress of Democracy, Peace education

Friday February 2

9.30–10.00	Reflection on programme Thursday
10.00–12.30	*Subjectification and Citizenship Education*
	Lecture by Gert Biesta
13.30–15.00	Discussing follow-up activities (finishing the module)
15.00–16.30	Evaluation

In the second year we made some small changes, so that we could try out some other activities.

9   Part of Schedule EDIC+ Course University of Humanistic Studies Utrecht 2019

9.1   *Theory and Practice of Citizenship Education*

Wednesday February 20

9.30	*Philosophical Reflection on Tolerance*
	Prof. Filimon Peonidis, Aristotle University Thessaloniki
12.00–12.30	Lunch
12.30	Travel to school (bike or bus)
13.00–16.00	Visit to ROC Utrecht, a school for higher vocational education
	Presentation and talks with teachers and students

Thursday February 21

9.30–12.00   Visit to Fortress of Democracy
This is an NGO that organises activities for students on democracy and peace

13.30–15.30   Presentations of students about their own research

16.00–17.00   *Moral and Citizenship Education in Mexico and Latin America*
Skype meeting with Prof. Benilde Garcia, University of Mexico

Friday February 22

9.30–10.30   *Moral and Citizenship Education in China*
Skype meeting with Prof. Tan and Dr Lin, Beijing Normal University

11.00–13.00   *Enhancing Students' Participation in Citizenship Education*
Lecture by Dr Jeroen Bron SLO (National Institute of Curriculum Development)
Dr Bron coordinates the national curriculum development on citizenship education

13.00–13.30   Lunch

13.30–15.00   Finishing the module: conclusions and evaluation

10   Tasks for Students

10.1   *Task 1 Study Teaching Common Values Report*

Read the Teaching Common Values report (pp. 9–32 and pp. 181–202). And study three country case studies (1 North-Western Europe, 1 Eastern Europe, 1 South Europe): the case study reports of three countries and what is written about them in Chapters 4 and 6.

Questions:

1.   What do you think are interesting and good examples (in policy and in practice)?
2.   What needs improvement (in policy and practice)?
3.   Which idea(s) will you use in your future educational practice?

Prepare some input for the discussion. The study can be downloaded at: http://bit.ly/2pm5Yh9

10.2   *Task 2 Personal Presentation*

Each participant gives a short presentation about moral and citizenship education in his/her own country and/or in the own research or other educational activities. Try to give a personal touch. Perhaps you can use some short video material.

Each participant has maximum 15 minutes (if possible with some time for questions).

10.3 Literature for Module

Biesta, G. (2011). The ignorant citizen: Mouffe, Ranciere, and the subject of democratic education. *Studies in Philosophy of Education, 30*, 141–153.

Conde-Flores, S., Garcia-Cabrera, B., & Alba-Meraz, A. (2017). Civic and ethical education in Mexico. In B. Garcia-Cabrero, A. Sandoval, E. Trevino, S. Diazgranados, & M. Perez (Eds.), *Civics and citizenship* (pp. 41–66). Rotterdam, The Netherlands: Sense Publishers.

De Groot, I. (2018). Political simulations. *Democracy and Education, 16*(2), 1–11.

Johnson, L., & Morris, P. (2010). Towards a framework for critical citizenship education. *The Curriculum Journal, 21*(1), 77–96.

Print, M., & Tan, C. (2015). Educating "good" citizens for a globalized world. In M. Print & C. Tan (Eds.), *Citizens in a global world for the twenty-first century* (pp. 1–10). Rotterdam, The Netherlands: Sense Publishers.

Veugelers, W. (2011). The moral and the political in global citizenship education. *Globalisation, Societies and Education, 9*(3–4), 105–119.

Veugelers, W. (2017). Education for critical-democratic citizenship. Autonomy and social justice in a multicultural society. In N. Aloni & L. Weintrob (Eds.), *Beyond bystanders* (pp. 47–59). Rotterdam, The Netherlands: Sense Publishers.

Veugelers, W., De Groot, I., & Stolk, V. (2017) *Research for cult committee – Teaching common values in Europe.* Brussels: European Parliament, Policy Department for Structural and Cohesion Policies. Retrieved from http://bit.ly/2pm5Yh9

11 Students' Experiences in the Module

Students offered written feedback at the end of the EDIC+ week, and they also formulated experiences and suggestions to improve the programme in their essay afterwards.

11.1 Format and Organisation

Students appreciated the intensity of the programme: one week full-time. They also appreciated the diversity in activities and the many teachers and other educational professionals with a lot of expertise that were involved in the programme. The visits to the multicultural school and the 'Fortress of Democracy' showed them critical practices.

The group was quite small, four Dutch students and four foreign students. However, the students saw this as an advantage. They could communicate a lot and had good contact with each other and the teachers. Some of them even argued in favour of keeping it this size.

11.2 Content

The students found it very relevant to focus on theory, policy and practice of citizenship and the relationships between them. They realised that there are differences and that educators can make different choices in theory, strategies and practices. The school visit was to a secondary school with nearly only migrants. The experiences of these students, in the school system and in society, made them aware of the fact that the Netherlands is not yet an inclusive society and that school choice and early determination separate different social and cultural groups. The visit to the 'Fortress of Democracy' showed them how an NGO can challenge pupils to think about society, democracy and their role in it.

The lectures focused on different elements and perspectives on citizenship and citizenship education. Students appreciated this diversity and the opportunity to have many dialogues with the teachers and among themselves.

11.3 Experiences in the Second Try-Out

When finishing this chapter we had just completed our module for the second try-out. We had six Dutch students and six international students (Belgium, Italy, UK, Pakistan, USA, Zambia). Here are some of their experiences.

> One of the most important things I became especially aware of during this week is the importance of national/local history and context when it comes to the local implementation of citizenship education. This became apparent as we discussed citizenship education in a variety of different countries through the participant presentations, readings and guest lectures. We can learn a great deal from sharing good practices across countries, but cannot simply 'copy and paste' a certain practice without taking into account the specific local context and history.

> I really appreciated the variety of learning methods used during this module (participant presentations, discussion sessions, lectures, field visits, etc.), the diversity among the participants and lecturers as well as the combination of sessions focused on citizenship education in theory and citizenship education in practice. Most importantly, I have the feeling I am going home as a member of an empowering community of researchers and practitioners who share the common objective of making sense of and promoting citizenship education.

> I found this week immensely enriching and enjoyed exploring complexities of moral philosophy, citizenship and the role of the citizen. I am leaving this week with a renewed commitment to a global critical democratic

form of citizenship. I was particularly interested to learn from our colleagues from out of Europe (Zambia, Pakistan, China and Mexico) and was reminded of things we take for granted about our curriculums in Central/Western European countries.

It was emphasised that good citizenship education is not the transmission of a static set of values nor an adherence to a strict set of criteria. It was communicated that citizenship education, when undertaken well, is a reflexive, empathetic and transformative discipline that has a lot to offer young people across the world. It made me realise that, if we want more emphasis on a European/global citizenship education, we may have to fight for it!

I greatly enjoyed the presentations of my classmates. I found that I had a lot to learn from my classmates and was very appreciative of the fantastic mixture of practices, disciplines, nationalities and inclinations of the other students. We worked well as a group and my classmates stimulated a lot of critical thinking, which I am very grateful for.

I learned how the Netherlands took humanism seriously and the pride the residents had in being humanists. I learned how openly the topic of diversity and religion was discussed in Netherlands.

I learned that there are many different views on citizenship and moral education and it can be done right and wrong in many ways, and everything in between.

I found the lectures very interesting as they offered me new standpoints and new perspectives on how to approach history and how to design more inclusive lessons, where pupils have the possibility to express their voice and be more active during decision making.

I learned how different European countries approach citizenship education when I read the Teaching Common Values case studies and we discussed it. We also learned how Mexico approaches citizenship education and how their policies are affected with the change in governments. I found the conversation with Mexico very interesting for the reason that she was able to show that training works when you are in the field with the teachers and not when you deliver superficial workshops. We learned how China was now starting to discuss human rights. We also learned that they want to progress in their ideas towards citizenship education.

The teachers were great at creating an open, relaxed, and inclusive environment.

Overall, I can say I undoubtedly learned a substantial amount about the manifestation of civic and moral education around the world, the best practices for this form of education, and the role of the state in civic and moral education. The module also helped me refine my own conception of moral and civic education and how I feel that I would put it into practice in the classroom.

The visits were appreciated a lot:

Fortress of Democracy provided me with many interesting ideas to stimulate discussion and practice with children I work with – I am interested in the ways that disabled children are often not expected to think critically despite often having the capability to do so. I would like to introduce some of the concepts explored at the Fortress in a gentle way.

My favourite activity was visiting the MBO school, and it was so interesting to see Dutch students participating in citizenship education and hearing their own (extremely well-spoken) experiences and opinions. It really made me want to go back into the classroom myself. I also loved visiting the Fortress of Democracy. It was interesting to experience firsthand how citizen education is attempted in schools, through NGOs.

Visiting the Fortress after the school was good. The school triggered to think about how to apply citizenship education for this target group. The Fortress provided some answers to it.

And the last quote:

The best thing was: meeting everyone and sharing ideas.

References

Andreotti, V. (2011). The political economy of global citizenship. *Globalisation, Societies and Education, 9*(3–4), 307–310.

Apple, M., & Beane, J. (Eds.). (2005). *Democratic schools*. Portsmouth, NH: Heinemann.

THEORY AND PRACTICE OF CITIZENSHIP EDUCATION   39

Banks, J. (Ed.). (2004). *Diversity and citizenship education: Global perspectives.* San Francisco, CA: Jossey-Bass.

Banks, J. (Ed.). (2017). *Citizenship education and global migration.* Washington, DC: AERA.

Barber, B. (1984). *Strong democracy.* Berkeley, CA: University of California Press.

Biesta, G. (2011a). *Learning democracy in school and society.* Rotterdam, The Netherlands: Sense Publishers.

Biesta, G. (2011b). The ignorant citizen: Mouffe, Ranciere, and the subject of democratic education. *Studies in Philosophy of Education, 30,* 141–153.

Bourdieu, P. (1984). *Distinction.* London: Routledge.

Bron, J. (2019). *Student voice in curriculum development.* Utrecht: University of Humanistic Studies.

Conde-Flores, S., Garcia-Cabrera, B., & Alba-Meraz, A. (2017). Civic and ethical education in Mexico. In B. Garcia-Cabrero, A. Sandoval, E. Trevino, S. Diazgranados, & M. Perez (Eds.), *Civics and citizenship* (pp. 41–66). Rotterdam, The Netherlands: Sense Publishers.

Crick, B. (1999). The presuppositions of citizenship education. *Journal of Philosophy of Education, 33*(3), 337–352.

De Groot, I. (2013). *Adolescents' democratic engagement.* Utrecht: University of Humanistic Studies.

De Groot, I. (2018). Political simulations. *Democracy and Education, 16*(2), 1–11.

Durkheim, E. (1971[1923]). *Moral education.* New York, NY: Free Press.

Freire, P. (1985). *The politics of education: Culture, power and liberation.* South Hadley, MA: Bergin & Garvey.

Gaudelli, W. (2016). *Global citizenship education: Everyday transcendence.* New York, NY: Routledge.

Giddens, A. (1990). *The consequences of modernity.* Cambridge: Polity.

Giroux, H. (1989). *Schooling for democracy.* London: Routledge.

Goodlad, J. (1979). *Curriculum inquiry.* New York, NY: McGraw-Hill.

Goren, H., & Yemini, M. (2016). Global citizenship education in context: Teacher perceptions at an international and a local Israeli school. *Compare, 46*(5), 832–853.

Green, A., & Janmaat, J. (2011). *Regimes of social cohesion.* London: Palgrave.

Gutman, A. (1987). *Democratic education.* Princeton, NJ: Princeton University Press.

Haste, H. (2004). Constructing the citizen. *Political Psychology, 25*(3), 413–440.

Hess, D. (2009). *Controversy in the classroom.* New York, NY: Routledge.

International Civic and Citizenship Education Study. (2010). *ICCS 2009 International Report.* Amsterdam: IEA.

International Civic and Citizenship Education Study. (2017). *ICCS 2010 International Report.* Amsterdam: IEA.

Isin, E., & Turner, B. (Eds.). (2002). *Handbook of citizenship studies.* London: Sage Publications.

Johnson, L., & Morris, P. (2010). Towards a framework for critical citizenship education. *Curriculum Journal, 21*(1), 77–96.

Kennedy, K., Lee, W., & Grossman, D. (Eds.). (2010). *Citizenship pedagogies in Asia and the Pacific.* Dordrecht: Springer.

Kerr, D. (1999). Citizenship education in the curriculum: An international review. *The School Field, 10*(3–4), 5–31.

Leenders, H., Veugelers, W., & De Kat, E. (2008a). Teachers' views on citizenship in secondary education in the Netherlands. *Cambridge Journal of Education, 38*(2), 155–170.

Leenders, H., Veugelers, W., & De Kat, E. (2008b). Moral education and citizenship education at pre-university schools. In F. Oser & W. Veugelers (Eds.), *Getting involved: Global citizenship development and sources of moral values* (pp. 57–74). Rotterdam, The Netherlands: Sense Publishers.

Leenders, H., Veugelers, W., & De Kat, E. (2012). Moral development and citizenship education in vocational schools. *Education Research International.* doi:10.1155/2012/901513

Lickona, T. (1991). *Educating for character.* New York, NY: Random House.

Marshall, T. H. (1964). *Class, citizenship and social development.* Chicago, IL: University of Chicago Press.

McLaren, P. (1989). *Life in schools.* New York, NY: Longman.

McLaughlin, T. (1992). Citizenship, diversity and education: A philosophical perspective. *Journal of Moral Education, 21*(3), 235–250.

Mouffe, C. (2005). *On the political.* London: Routledge.

Mouffe, C. (2018). *For a left populism.* London: Verso.

Noddings, N. (2002). *Educating moral people.* New York, NY: Teachers College Press.

Nussbaum, M. (1997). *Cultivating humanity.* Cambridge, MA: Harvard University Press.

OECD. (2016). *Netherlands 2016: Foundations for the future.* Paris: OECD.

Oser, F., & Veugelers, W. (Eds.). (2008). *Getting involved. Global citizenship development and sources of moral values.* Rotterdam, The Netherlands: Sense Publishers.

Osler, A., & Starkey, H. (2010). *Teachers and human rights education.* London: IOE Press.

Oxley, L., & Morris, P. (2013). Global citizenship: A typology for distinguishing its multiple conceptions. *British Journal of Educational Studies, 3*, 301–325.

Parker, W. (2003). *Teaching democracy.* New York, NY: Teachers College Press.

Power, F., Higgins, A., & Kohlberg, L. (1989). *Lawrence Kohlberg's approach to moral education.* New York, NY: Columbia University Press.

Print, M., & Tan, C. (2015). Educating "good" citizens for a globalized world. In M. Print & C. Tan (Eds.), *Citizens in a global world for the twenty-first century* (pp. 1–10). Rotterdam, The Netherlands: Sense Publishers.

Reilly, J., & Niens, U. (2014). Global citizenship education as education for peacebuilding in a divided society. *Compare, 44*(1), 53–76.

Sim, J. (2011). Social studies and citizenship for participation in Singapore: How one state seeks to influence its citizens. *Oxford Review of Education, 37*(6), 743–761.

Teodore, A., & Guilherme, M. (Eds.). (2014). *European and Latin American Higher Education between mirrors.* Rotterdam, The Netherlands: Sense Publishers.

Torney-Purta, J. (2002). Pattens in the civic knowledge, engagement, and attitudes of European Adolescents. The IEA Civic Education Study. *European Journal of Education, 37*(2), 129–141.

Torres, C. A. (2017). *Theoretical and empirical foundations of critical global citizenship education.* New York, NY: Routledge.

Touraine, A. (1997). *What is democracy.* Boulder, CO: Westview Press.

Veugelers, W. (2007). Creating critical-democratic citizenship education: Empowering humanity and democracy in Dutch education. *Compare, 37*(1), 105–119.

Veugelers, W. (2011a). Theory and practice of citizenship education: The case of policy, science and education in the Netherlands. *Revista de Educacion, 209*–224.

Veugelers, W. (2011b). The moral and the political in global citizenship education: Appreciating differences in education. *Globalisation, Societies and Education, 9*(3–4), 473–485.

Veugelers, W. (2017a). The moral in Paulo Freire's educational work. *Journal of Moral Education, 46,* 412–421.

Veugelers, W. (2017b). Education for critical-democratic citizenship. Autonomy and social justice in a multicultural society. In N. Aloni & L. Weintrob (Eds.), *Beyond bystanders* (pp. 47–59). Rotterdam, The Netherlands: Sense Publishers.

Veugelers, W. (in press). Different views on global citizenship. In D. Schugurensky & C. Wolhuter (Eds.). *Global citizenship education and teacher education.* London: Routledge.

Veugelers, W., De Groot, I., Llomovatte, S., & Naidorf, J. (2017). Higher education, educational policy and citizenship development. *Education and Society, 35*(1), 27–42.

Veugelers, W., De Groot, I., & Stolk, V. (2017). *Research for cult committee – Teaching common values in Europe.* Brussels: European Parliament, Policy Department for Structural and Cohesion Policy. Retrieved from http://bit.ly/2pm5Yh9

Veugelers, W., & de Kat, E. (2003). Moral and democratic education in secondary schools. In F. Oser & W. Veugelers (Eds.), *Teaching in moral and democratic education* (pp. 193–213). Bern: Peter Lang.

Westheimer, J., & Kahne, J. (2004). What kind of citizen? The politics of educating for democracy. *American Educational Research Journal, 41*(2), 237–269.

CHAPTER 3

Ethical Competences for Democratic Citizenship at School, University and in Family

Maria Rosa Buxarrais, Elena Noguera and Francisco Esteban

1 Introduction

We live in a pluralistic world, in a democratic society, where different ways of seeing and coping with life coexist. The evolution of society is complex and uncertain, and people must face great challenges, confusion and disorientation that do not help them to find their way forward in life.

Moreover, the multiculturalism of our societies, especially the most advanced ones, requires learning how to live together. It is not only living side by side during a specific stage of life, with individuals of different characters, intellectual levels, ethnicity or religion. We will have to set in childhood and youth the fundamentals of this coexistence so that these persist into adulthood.

What kind of education is appropriate to build a democratic society? We define a democracy as a form of social organization in which individuals can exercise their autonomous and participatory character, remembering in a meaningful way the aims of politics and of all the spheres of civil society that, mainly, are the service of the affected by the decisions that are made in them (Cortina, 1993). Therefore, a democratic society will be based on values such as autonomy, solidarity and dialogue between cultures.

Citizenship education in pluralistic and democratic societies implies a process of personal and autonomous construction that takes place thanks to the coexistence and the interrelation with the other people of the community. We propose an education that promotes the acceptance of others, active tolerance and respect, knowledge of the other, involvement in collective projects, factors that contribute to propose an intercultural education model (Hoyos & Martínez, 2004).

Educating citizens who are critical and committed to the reality of their time has become one of the tasks most demanded by today's society. In spite of its importance it is not being attended as it would correspond, so it is urgent to help build the figure of the citizen in this time of change. One of the most pressing challenges facing education today is how to prepare citizens to respond to what will come in the near future.

© KONINKLIJKE BRILL NV, LEIDEN, 2019 | DOI: 10.1163/9789004411944_003
This is an open access chapter distributed under the terms of the CC-BY-NC 4.0 License.

ETHICAL COMPETENCES FOR DEMOCRATIC CITIZENSHIP

In Spain, citizenship education consists of an area that is promoted in schools with the aim to fostering the harmonious co-existence and mutual beneficial development of individuals and of the communities they are part of (Buxarrais, 1997). In democratic societies citizenship education supports students in becoming active, informed and responsible citizens, who are willing and able to take responsibility for themselves and their communities at the local, regional, national and international level.

We want to mention some empirical inputs collected as part of a comparative, international study involving 28 State Members of the European Union (Veugelers, De Groot, & Stolk, 2017). The aim of this effort was to analyse the policies related with the teaching of core civic values (democracy, participation, tolerance) in secondary education, and how were those policies spelled out in practice, in terms of curricula, methods and school culture. We were also interested in the role of the different actors involved in the teaching of those values: teachers, students, local communities, NGOs and other civil society organizations.

For that purpose, we adopted an exploratory, qualitative approach (Stake 2010) and employed an intentional sample that included an Official from the Education Ministry, two experts working with NGOs, and four teachers from the secondary (or high school) level. All of them were pleased to participate and expose their views answering an ad hoc questionnaire. As first step, it was employed a written questionnaire about the following subthemes: educational policies, educational contents, school culture, participation, history and future of the educational policies. Each country had a key-informant (an university professor) selected because his/her expertise in this field. The first author of this chapter was the Spanish representative or key informant.

As second step we prepared another questionnaire for consulting other types of key-informants: high schools' teachers, officials in charge of educational policies and NGOs representatives. Since 2012, the Spanish public curriculum does not demand teaching about citizenship values. Thus, one might assume that both teachers and educational institutions would have renounced to bother themselves with this apparently superfluous task. Nothing, however, could be further from the truth. As our interviewees explained, citizenship education survives among us because a number of teachers and schools insist on promoting an active, critical and responsible citizenship, as well as democratic values, through very diverse educational practices.

In short, most schools considered by us reported, in one way or another, to work on the following themes: (1) identity and dignity of persons; (2) understanding and respect toward interpersonal relationships; and (3) coexistence and social values. But beyond those common themes there are few shared theoretical frameworks or practical guidelines. The Ministry of Education consults, occasionally, to some NGOs about designs and practices of Values Education. However, only a few schools use the didactic materials prepared by the NGOs, since ultimately these decisions belong to the schools Head Teachers.

Citizenship education needs to help students develop knowledge, skills, attitudes and values in four broad competence areas (Buxarrais, 1997): (1) interacting effectively and constructively with others; (2) thinking critically; (3) acting in a socially responsible manner; and (4) acting democratically.

We need an education that allows us to understand critically our world, to be interested in knowing more about those controversial issues socially and ethically, to recognize the value of diversity, to argue with quality, to be persevering in the defence of our rights, to accept the limitations of personal and community life, to value the common good and participate collaboratively and actively in its achievement. Citizenship education is not only teaching to estimate certain specific values of our culture, or those that base the Declaration Universal of Human Rights or the democratic constitutions of the countries, is also and above all, providing cognitive resources to people so that they can learn ethically throughout their lives and so that they have illusion and are able to participate in the collaborative construction of a citizenship active and democratic.

Citizenship education involves not only teaching and learning of relevant topics in the classroom, but also the practical experiences gained through activities in school and wider society that are designed to prepare students for their role as citizens. Teachers and school leaders play a key role in this learning process. The training and support provided to them is therefore central to the effective implementation of citizenship education.

2 Theoretical Background

A mature civic and democratic behavior does not only depend on the ideals and moral purposes of a person, but also and above all on their ability to apply those ideals to their daily life in a consistent and differentiated way. In that sense, our proposal of intervention in citizenship education has been called: Model of Construction of Moral Personality (Buxarrais, Martínez, Puig, & Trilla, 1995). We understand that citizenship education is a variety of moral education, based on the conviction that morality is not something given in advance, assumed, or simply decided or chosen; instead, morality must be generated by a complex effort in the processing or reprocessing of lifestyles and values that are considered correct and appropriate for each situation.

Therefore, citizenship education involves a constructive task: ethics is not discovered, but it is built. In this way, it should be understood as a task of building or rebuilding personal and collective valuable moral ways. Therefore, it is not a construction alone, nor is it devoid of past and outside any historical context. On the other hand: it is a socially influenced task, which also has precedents and cultural elements of value that undoubtedly help shape their results. The moral is ultimately a cultural product whose creation depends on each subject and whole.

But how and through what elements and dynamics can the teachers develop these ideas in the classroom? To answer these questions, we must start from the premise that a proposal for citizenship education cannot consist only of proposed values to teach, but consists mainly in proposing what conditions educational institutions, schools, colleges or universities must meet in order to be an optimal scenario in which childhood, adolescence and youth could develop all the human dimensions that allow them to evaluate, estimate, accept and build values.

Educating from the moral point of view is, above all, providing conditions, generating climates and helping recreate values, creating new ways of being, valuing their lives and guiding the ones who are learning to be able not only to find their place in the world but also be the author and master of their actions, to achieve an ethical learning.

The kind of ethical learning that we wish to defend draws upon a theoretical and practical model known as 'the construction of moral personality'. This model has been used for many years in our pre-university education and it brings together ideas from other models that focus on development and moral reasoning (Kohlberg 1981, 1984; Colby & Kohlberg, 1987; Gibbs, 2003), emotion and sensation (Noddings, 2008; Prinz, 2009) and moral character (Hartshorne & May, 1930; Berkowitz, 2002; Lapsley & Clark, 2005; Carr, 2008; Doris, 2008; Nucci & Narváez, 2008).

The moral personality model also takes on board the contributions of integrated models in moral developmental theory (Turiel, 1984; Rest, 1986). The goal of our ethical learning model is to provide students with a firm moral grounding, both as private individuals and as members of collectives (Tirri & Nokelainen, 2011; Veugelers, 2011).

The model is based on the following premises: (1) knowledge, as the cognitive-behavioural tradition proposes, must favour the use of communicative rationality and dialogue in dispute resolution; (2) in accordance with Kantian ethics (Kant, 1785/2008), people must be treated as ends in themselves and their freedom and individuality must be respected; (3) in accordance with Aristotle (1998) we must, in the notion of our future as virtuous individuals, recognize a teleological dimension; and (4) again with reference to Aristotle, students should be called upon as individuals to act within and exert influence upon their community (Aristotle, 1962).

This ethical learning model stems from educational work carried out in eight areas of development that together constitute what we call ethical learning (Puig & Martín, 1998): self-knowledge; autonomy and self-regulation; dialogue; the ability to transform the environment; empathy or social perspective; social skills; critical understanding of reality; and finally, reasoning. These eight areas are further assigned to three basic learning categories: the construction of self, learning in fellowship, and socio-moral reflection.

Construction of self entails: self-knowledge, autonomy and self-control. This category involves individuals learning to be autonomous within their communities, acquiring an understanding of who they are through their relationships with others, being able to evaluate this understanding, and, finally, learning how morally- and ethically-challenging scenarios require them to weigh up or temper the way they behave. Construction of self thus involves the formation of our way of being and everything that encompasses our intrapersonal sphere at what has been called a 'microethical' level (Apel, 1985). Within this category, ethical and moral teaching must ensure that students reflect on the kinds of professionals and citizens they aspire to be. Finally, construction of self also teaches students to acquire a series of values: the importance of effort, perseverance, personal growth, the acceptance of one's own vulnerability and of setbacks, and freedom.

Learning in fellowship entails ability in dialogue and the acquisition of empathy or social perspective, as well as of social skills. Primarily, this category trains individuals in the skills they need to live with others. It involves learning and defending norms or standards that are recognized as socially beneficial, whether or not they are the result of formal legislation and requires individuals to acquire a set of abilities and social skills ranging from openness and transparency to sensitivity with regard to the principles of community value. Finally, it also means learning to assess knowledge in terms of its social value and understanding that knowledge gained for example at the university is not an end in itself but the means by which to return to the community what rightfully belongs to it. Insofar as it helps individuals to be aware of ethical and moral issues at local, national and international levels of community life, this category can be said to provide teaching at a 'mesoethical' level (Apel, 1985). It also touches on the fourth component in the Four-Component Model: moral character or courage (Rest, 1986). In addition, learning in fellowship challenges certain existing notions such as otherness, as well as topics in values education such as civility, hospitality, brotherhood and dialogue. It does this by reiterating the idea that twenty-first century European educational systems students

ETHICAL COMPETENCES FOR DEMOCRATIC CITIZENSHIP

should behave as an 'elite' in the etymological sense of this term, defined not as an exclusive group but as a set of individuals who are actually involved in the community because they are responsible for their actions and omissions (Steiner, 2004).

The third category, socio-moral reflection, entails a critical understanding of reality and an ability to engage in moral and ethical reasoning. This category trains people to consider real and hypothetical scenarios in which there is controversy or conflict and to be able to anticipate conflict as the potential outcome of a given situation. It helps students learn the importance of reflecting before acting or of acting according to a process of reasoning. Learning in socio-moral reflection is therefore a way of experiencing knowledge in its ethical and moral dimensions, of questioning that knowledge and of making objective, ethically-informed decisions. This category operates at what can be called a 'macroethical' level (Apel, 1985). Some of the values that underpin socio-moral reflection are justice, human dignity, respect, hope, interest, rigour and criticism.

3 Aims of the Module and Curriculum Guidelines

Our proposal for ethical competencies does not only consist of proposing a set of values to be fostered, but also to condition the social milieu on a series of requirements so that it becomes a fertile moral soil. We expect that students acquire knowledges and strategies in order they can promote and cultivate democracy as a way of living, understand participation in collective projects and practice the search for the common benefit agreements. These are goals that can only be achieved by creating an atmosphere based on caring relationships among all. This also implies the alignment of the educational institutions with the family in order to contribute to the general process of moral human development, and to the development of specific ethical abilities: to recognize, understand, select, build, assess and apply moral values. But as every area has their own identity we will treat them independently, unless we find common dimensions and aspects.

On completion of this module, the student should be able to be aware of the current level of ethical competences in school, university and family, and to analyse real life and hypothetical moral situations relevant for those contexts

3.1 At School
3.1.1 Aims
- To analyse ethical competencies for a democratic citizenship that we should foster in schools and investigate the possible pros and cons of them.

- To learn about different educational strategies for the development of ethical competences, and to examine which ones seem the best suited for their classrooms or schools.

3.1.2 Curriculum Guidelines

At least four education scenarios in values and moral development can be highlighted in school: (1) peer interaction, (2) teacher action, (3) the moral climate of the institution and (4) the double transversality of its contents. Peer interactions and the direct action of teachers are the two most natural settings in which we form our personality. Teachers, through the exercise of their duties, should provide conditions to appreciate values, knowledge management, mediate conflicts and positively catalyse human expression through verbal and nonverbal forms that allow our artistic, physical, emotional and affective manifestations.

However, the school as a whole and the double transversality of the contents of specific values education programs are also particularly relevant scenarios for the construction of the moral personality of students: the moral climate of the school is a development factor and can be of moral progress and the double transversality of the contents shows us again how contents are not only informative but also procedures and attitudes that shape our behaviours and feelings. The school must be effectively impregnated with those contents or values that are intended to be appreciated by its students. To promote and cultivate democracy as a way of living, to understand participation in collective projects, and to practice the search for common good agreements are goals that can only be achieved by creating an atmosphere that represents these values, and particularly caring relationships between teachers, the students and ultimately, of all who take part in the school life.

We bet on a curriculum in relation to reality and context, and for active educational and social interventions in our community in favour of community development. We consider that service-learning could be a good example, a pedagogical proposal that combines learning processes and community service in a single well-articulated project in which participants are trained by working on the real needs of the environment with the aim of improving it (Puig, Batlle, Bosch, & Palos, 2006). It is a typology of projects that links all kinds of learning to carry out actions that respond to social demands. It is characterized by being socially useful, flexible and adapted to the recipients; for performing a service where you learn by collaborating within the framework of reciprocity; by entering into a process of acquiring knowledge and skills for life; for requiring active and reflective participation; for needing parliamentary networks and instances of collaboration and support; and for having a

ETHICAL COMPETENCES FOR DEMOCRATIC CITIZENSHIP 49

formative and transformative impact (Puig, 2012). Thus, Service Learning requires contact with other entities that could provide spaces for action – a type of institutional collaboration we call "educational experience's partnerships" (Graell, 2015).

A basic definition of the partnership proposed by Glendinning (2002) stipulates that the partnership constitutes a joint work agreement between organizations, institutions or independent groups that decide to collaborate in pursuit of common objectives; they need to create organizational processes to achieve this goal; implement their action program together; and share risks, responsibilities and benefits. The partnership that we would call educative arises from social and educational responsibility towards citizenship: an education that is socially committed to the reality in which it is located. Social transformation arises from social actions spurred by educational projects.

We have the option of visiting the following non-governmental organizations:
- Fundació Solidaritat UB http://www.solidaritat.ub.edu/
- Institut Diversitas http://www.institutdiversitas.org/
- Oxfam Intermón https://www.oxfamintermon.org/es
- Fundació MigraStudium http://www.migrastudium.org/

3.1.3 Examples of Activities

ACTIVITY 1: Recognizing the group

The facilitator informs the group that he or she will suggest some labels or categories to visualize common and divergent aspects of the group. This, in order to promote the awareness of belonging to a group with different individual profiles or personalities, but nevertheless with possible common interests or projects to be developed taking advantage of the different capacities of its members.

Examples of labels or categories:
- Year/month of birth
- Place of birth (neighbourhood, city, country, etc.)
- Languages spoken
- School/course
- Extracurricular activities
- Instruments played
- Pet animals
- Profession to be exercised
- Types of positions carried out in different contexts and institutions
- Types of participation in projects
- Topics that concern them about their city (or their school)

After each label or slogan, the participants are grouped and then a small debate is opened aloud to analyse what has happened and express some anecdotes or remarks. Once the instructions have been made, the participants are asked to think of labels that interest them. Once this phase of the activity is finished, the participants are asked to group again according to a label or category that facilitates the division of the large group into small groups of more or less five participants.

Then they are asked to make some balance, to think about what "group photography" has emerged from the activity and write a definition that specifies their feelings about belonging to the group. The different groups share their results and a debate is opened. Then the "secretaries" of each group come together to write a single definition as an element of collective memory, and to summarize in three points what everyone would have to contribute to the collective so that it could be considered a true group.

ACTIVITY 2: Intercultural dialogue and democracy
- Answer the following unfinished questions and unfinished phrases about the intercultural dialogue and democracy.

First it is answered individually or in pairs and then they will be read, comparing and commenting on the answers to each unfinished question or phrase.

1. The intercultural dialogue is ...
2. Democracy is ...
3. Intercultural dialogue is positive if ...
4. What difficulties do we find when we talk with other people? ...
5. When we talk, should we always be sincere? Why? ...
6. What would you demand from a person who would like to talk to you? ...
7. What would you demand of yourself? ...
8. The objective of the intercultural dialogue is ...
9. Think about situations in which the intercultural dialogue favoured the solution of a situation and in others in which its lack harmed it ...
10. Say what you think about this statement: "Dialogue is impossible, the strongest party always wins" ...
11. Can there be a correct realization of a participation project if the conditions of a good dialogue are not followed?

A few options for incorporating to the filling of uncomplete sentences activity for elementary schools:
- Have you ever wished to live in a different country? Why or why not?
- Do you know people from other countries or cultures?
- Do you have friends or relatives from other countries or cultures?

ETHICAL COMPETENCES FOR DEMOCRATIC CITIZENSHIP   51

- What would you say are the main differences between them and us?
- A bad thing of the school having people from different countries or cultures is ...
- A good thing of the school having people from different countries or cultures is ...
- Some time ago only Italians used to eat pasta and pizza, only Japanese used to eat sushi, and most people around the world had never eaten a hamburger. Now all this has changed a lot. Are these kind of changes are good or bad? Why?

ACTIVITY 3
An option, for high school or university students could be:
Read the following explanation about the differences between the meaning of the words "multicultural" and "intercultural".

> Multicultural education uses learning about other cultures in order to produce acceptance, or at least tolerance, of these cultures. Intercultural Education aims to go beyond passive coexistence, to achieve a developing and sustainable way of living together in multicultural societies through the creation of understanding of, respect for and dialogue between the different cultural groups. (UNESCO, 2006, p. 18)

Given this explanation, do you think the education you have received until now is mostly monocultural, multicultural, intercultural? Why? Can you offer an example?

ACTIVITY 4: Educational telecommunication networks
The Educational telecommunication networks aims at the improvement and the promotion of ICT-based innovation of education.
It attempts to achieve its aims by:
- Promoting collaboration and cooperation between pupils, students, educators and researchers.
- Availing access to international networks.
- Promoting and supporting professional development of teachers and educators.
- Developing innovative concepts, instruments and content.
- Performing research.
Here you have some links to the Educational telecommunication networks:
- International Education and Resource Network, iEARN.
  http://www.iearn.org

- ESP European School Project
  http://www.espnet.eu/
- GS Global Schoolhouse de la GSN, Global Schoolnet Foundation
  http://www.gsn.org
- Kidlink
  http://www.kidlink.org

Think individually and share with others about the areas and moral dimensions that these networks and projects can help to develop.

3.1.4 Assessment

1. Active participation in face-to-face classes. Attendance at seminars with professors and students in order to present and share ideas and discuss readings (20% of the final grade).
2. To analyse suggested readings and writing essays about them (40% of the final grade).
3. Analysis of case studies in group (30% of the final mark).
4. NGOs and schools' visits (10%).

The evaluation of this proposal has a formative meaning, to improve attitudes and acquisition of intercultural and democratic values (tolerance, recognition and acceptance of other cultures, citizenship and democratic conscience, solidarity, etc.) It is important to have an auto-evaluation exercise, so students can think about their own opinions and attitudes. It is interesting to share them with other students and the professor, so the group will know more about the class.

Preparation of one-page essay on the ideas worked on this part of the module.

3.2 *At University*

3.2.1 Aims

- To know the history and tradition of university education, its genesis and evolution from the 12th century to the present day.
- To know the philosophical and pedagogical principles that give meaning to the idea of university education, as well as the different ways in which they are interpreted.
- To interpret the different positions around the idea of university education, its epistemological foundations, as well as the pros and cons of each of them.
- To analyse the idea of university education in a prospective and speculative way, that is, considering contemporary circumstances.

ETHICAL COMPETENCES FOR DEMOCRATIC CITIZENSHIP

3.2.2 Examples of Activities

Activities that will be worked with students both face-to-face and virtual:

ACTIVITY 1. In the famous metaphor of Bernardo de Chartres (circa 1130), the intellectuals are represented as those men who were standing on the shoulders of the ancients, in order to see beyond them. What do you think that representation means for the first universities?

ACTIVITY 2. Hardly had the first universities consolidated, when already could be heard complaints like those of the eminent chancellor of the University of Paris (1218 and 1236) Philippus de Grevia: "In another time, when each master taught independently and when the name of the university was unknown, there were more lessons and discussions and more interest in the things of knowledge. However, now when you have met in a university, the lessons and discussions have become less frequent; everything is done hastily, little is learned, and the time necessary for the student is wasted in meetings and disputes. While the old men debate in their meetings and establish statutes, the young people organize base plots and plan their night attacks". Think about this quote based on what was explained and worked on in this part of the module.

ACTIVITY 3. Erasmus writes in Familiarum colloquiorum formulae (1512-22): "not only to teach students a refined language but also and above all to educate them for life". Relate the said statement with the ideas considered in this module.

ACTIVITY 4. Reflect on the following quote from Humboldt: "The human can only develop in the form of cooperation ... so that the fruits achieved by some satisfy others, and all can see the general, original force that in the individual only reflects in a concrete way or derivative ...".

ACTIVITY 5. Comment on the following quote from Humboldt: "The State must keep in mind that, in reality, its intervention does not stimulate nor can it stimulate the achievement of the university's own aims, which, far from it, its interference is always disturbing; that without him things would in themselves go infinitely better", and continues: "The State must have the intimate conviction that, inasmuch as universities comply with the ultimate goal that corresponds to them, they also fulfil their own purposes, and also, from a higher point of view, from a point of view that allows a much greater concentration and an agglutination of forces that the State cannot put in motion".

ACTIVITY 6. Comment on the following quote from Richard Sennet (Corrosion of Character) in relation to university education: "How can a human being develop the story of his identity and personal history in a university made of episodes and fragments?"

3.2.3 Assessment

1. A review of between 4 and 5 pages of each of the following texts:
   - Laredo, P. (2007). Revisiting the third mission of universities: Toward a renewed categorization of university activities. *Higher Education Policy, 20*(4), 441–456.
   - MacIntyre, A. (2009). The very idea of a university: Aristotle, Newman and Us. *British Journal of Education, 57*(4), 347–362.
2. Participation in a virtual forum on some aspect of university education that will be proposed by the professors of the module.
3. Preparation of a final 3-page essay on the ideas worked on in this part of the module.

3.3 *At Families*

3.3.1 Aims

1. To promote and collaborate in organized actions for enhancing the contribution of families to citizenship development.
2. To analyse in a critical way the most important factors currently impinging upon family education: mass media, gender and intergenerational relationships, multiculturality, sustainable development, mass consumption, etc.
3. To design and to implement a support program for families about how to foster moral values in children and youngsters.

3.3.2 Contents

1. Family and families
   1.1. Origins and concepts.
   1.2. Familiar diversity.
   1.3. Families in the Information and Technology Society.
2. Why and how to educate in values in the family context.
   2.1. Family paper in values development.
   2.2. Familiar culture: dimensions.
   2.3. How values are learned and constructed in the family.
   2.4. Relation between family and school.
3. Controversial situations in the family context.
   3.1. Using technologies and social media.
   3.2. Responsible consumption: the value of austerity.
   3.3. Conciliation of familiar, personal and working life: the value of responsibility.
   3.4. Leisure management.
4. Pedagogical proposals in the family context related to values education.

3.3.3 Examples of Activities

ACTIVITY 1: Analyse the underlying family model in a movie. The teacher provides a list of 20 films where various family models appear.

ACTIVITY 2: Carry out an interview with parents of different types (nuclear, single-parent, reconstituted, etc.), to know what kind of family practices they carry out in order to educate in values.

ACTIVITY 3: Read one of the following articles and propose a set of recommendations for families to educate in values.

Dunn, J. (2006). Moral development in early childhood and social interaction in the family. In M. Killen & J. G. Smetana (Eds.), *Handbook of Moral Development* (pp. 331–350). Mahwah, NJ: Lawrence Erlbaum Associates.

Halstead, J. Mark (1999). Moral Education in Family Life: The effects of diversity. *Journal of Moral Education, 28*(3), 265–281.

3.3.4 Assessment

1. Final project that will be worked on throughout the course. The project consists of, firstly, to answer some global questions and, secondly, to list a glossary of concepts related to the learning outcomes of the Master. The project will gather 16 contributions taking in account the question-answer part and the glossary (60% of the final mark).

2. Attendance and the participation in class: Student may choose to expose any content related to the subject in class, proposing some debate, or to organize a talk with families. Teachers will choose the speech topic (40%).

4 Process and Conclusions

The actual module will run spring 2019. So at this time no evaluation can be presented.

We present here the evaluation of one of the students who attend the Intensive Programme. Having the opportunity to know different countries and learn from their education system was an extraordinary experience. As a Chilean student at the University of Barcelona, who was studying the Master's Degree in Education in Values and Citizens, to be able to participate in the Erasmus experience was like a dream come true. In the first place, sharing the day to day with students of different nationalities was really enriching, because I could learn from each one of them his way of contributing to society, from his own studies and realities of life. In addition, the teachers who participated in each presentation, exposed topics related to what I was studying, which was much more significant. The topics addressed were mainly related to citizenship, interculturality, inclusion, civic participation, and democracy, respect for human rights, the ethics of care, education in values, ethical sensitivity, moral and ethical virtues that educators should have, as well as the importance of fighting against violence and the different ways in which it manifests itself. In addition, each student had the opportunity to present the culture and educational system of their country of origin, and that exercise was quite positive for knowing more about each other.

The first seven days we were in Tallinn, they were quite intense from 9 a.m. until 6 p.m. in classes, where every day we had a different activity, either linked to the themes or to the recreational activities, which generated a space of confidence and relaxation for all. Every day we could be in a new place in the city, which opened the doors to us to know a completely different culture.

The three days we spent in Helsinki were very intense, although academically we didn't learn as much as in Estonia. In any case, it was a very rewarding experience. In both cities we had the opportunity to go to a public school, where they treated us very kindly and we knew superficially their educational system. Visiting both schools freely and understanding the way in which they develop topics such as freedom, human rights, autonomy, interculturality, democracy, values education, respect and everything that it involves, was a space of knowledge and openness towards different ways of educating.

To summarise I consider that this experience changed a part of me, as a person and as an educator, since it expands your mind and your way of seeing the world, learning, exchanging, knowing realities, ideas and key topics to transform society, such as:

- The way to eradicate the stereotypes and prejudices that exist towards cultures or people in general and how harmful they are.
- How citizenship and democracy are worked at the educational level.
- How schools can be truly inclusive and intercultural spaces.
- The ethical competences in the school, the conditions and strategies to address them.
- The construction of the moral personality applied to the classroom.
- The importance of the ethics of care and how to apply it in schools.
- Work participation at all times, highlighting that students are already citizens with the right to freely express their opinions.
- Among many other subjects, but what really stands out is the cultural exchange that I had the chance to live, in a friendly and welcoming academic environment.

ETHICAL COMPETENCES FOR DEMOCRATIC CITIZENSHIP 57

There are several topics that could be sequenced and scheduled not interesting for the students of the Master, but necessary for a better understanding of citizenship and multiculturalism. In short, the assessment of the visit and activities is very positive. Moreover, it is even recommended to extend this activity to other contexts and realities due to its high training value.

References

Apel, K. (1985). *La transformación de la filosofía* [The transformation of philosophy]. Madrid: Taurus.

Aristotle. (1962). *The Politics.* London: Penguin Books.

Aristotle. (1998). *The Nicomachean ethics.* New York, NY: Oxford University Press.

Bauman, Z. (2005). *Postmodern ethics.* London: Blackwell.

Berkowitz, M. (2002). The science of character education. In W. Damon (Ed.), *Bringing in a new era in character education* (pp. 43–63). Standford, CA: Standford University Press.

Biesta, G., & Lawy, R. (2006). From teaching citizenship to learning democracy: Overcoming individualism in research, policy and practice. *Cambridge Journal of Education, 36*(1), 63–79.

Burroughs, M. R. (2017). Educating the whole child: social-emotional learning and ethics education, *Ethics and Education, 12*(2), 218–232.

Buxarrais, M. R. (1997). *La formación del profesorado en educación en valores. Propuestas y materiales* [Teachers' formation in values education. Proposals and materials]. Bilbao: Desclée de Brouwer.

Buxarrais, M. R., Martínez, M., Puig, J. M., & Trilla, J. (1995). *La educación moral en primaria y en secundaria* [Moral education in elementary and secundary education]. Barcelona: Edelvives.

Buxarrais, M. R., & Zeledón, M. P. (2006). *Las familias y la educación en valores democráticos. Retos y perspectivas actuales* [Families and education in democratic values. Current challenges and perspectives]. Barcelona: Claret.

Carr, D. (2008). Character education as the cultivation of virtue. In L. Nucci & D. Narvaez (Eds.), *Handbook of moral and character education* (pp. 99–116). New York, NY: Routledge.

Colby, A., & Kohlberg, L. (1987). *The measurement of moral judgment.* Cambridge: Cambridge University Press.

Cortina, A. (1993). *Ética aplicada y democracia radical* [Applied ethics and radical democracy]. Madrid: Tecnos.

Davis-Kean, P. (2005). The influence of parent education and family income on child achievement: The indirect role of parental expectations and the home environment. *Journal of Family Psychology, 19*(2), 294.

Doris, J. (2010). *Lack of character. Personality and moral behaviour.* New York, NY: Cambridge University Press.

Dunn, J. (2006). Moral development in early childhood and social interaction in the family. In M. Killen & J. Smetana (Eds.), *Handbook of moral development* (pp. 331–350). Mahwah, NJ: Lawrence Erlbaum Associates.

Epstein, J. (2018). *School, family, and community partnerships: Preparing educators and improving schools.* New York, NY: Routledge.

Gibbs, J. (2003). *Moral development and reality: Beyond the theories of Kohlberg and Hoffman.* Thousand Oaks, CA: Sage Publications.

Graell, M. (2015). Los centros educativos y las entidades sociales deben establecer relaciones de colaboración. In J. M. Puig (Ed.), *11 ideas clave ¿Cómo realizar un Proyecto de aprendizaje servicio?* [11 Key ideas. How to realize a service-learning project], (pp. 65–76). Barcelona: Graó.

Greenhaus, J., & Powell, G. (2006). When work and family are allies: A theory of work-family enrichment. *Academy of Management Review, 31*(1), 72–92.

Halstead, J. (1999). Moral education in family life: The effects of diversity. *Journal of Moral Education, 28*(3), 265–281.

Hartshorne, H., & May, M. (1930). A summary of the work of the character education inquiry. *Religious Education, 25*(7), 609–611.

Henderson, A., & Mapp, K. (2002). *A new wave of evidence: The impact of school, family, and community connections on student achievement* (Annual Synthesis, 2002). Austin, TX: Center of Family and Community Connections with Schools.

Hoyos, G., & Martínez, M. (2004). *¿Qué significa educar en valores hoy?* [What does it mean to educate in values nowadays?]. Barcelona: Octaedro.

Kant, I. (1785/2008). *Fundamentación de la metafísica de las costumbres* [The groundwork of the metaphysics of morals]. Madrid: Espasa-Calpe.

Kohlberg, L. (1981). *The meaning and measurement of moral development.* Worcester, MA: Clark University Press.

Kohlberg, L. (1984). *Essays on moral development. The psychology of moral development.* San Francisco, CA: Jossey-Bass.

Kozma, R. B. (2011). A framework for ICT policies to transform education. In R. Kozma (Ed.), *Transforming education: The power of ICT policies* (pp. 19–36). Paris: UNESCO.

Kymlicka, W. (1989). *Liberalism, community and culture.* Oxford: Oxford University Press.

Lapsley, D., & Clark, F. C. (2005). *Character psychology and character education.* Notre Dame, IN: University of Notre Dame Press.

ETHICAL COMPETENCES FOR DEMOCRATIC CITIZENSHIP 59

Laredo, P. (2007). Revisiting the third mission of universities: Toward a renewed categorization of university activities? *Higher Education Policy, 20*(4), 441–456.

MacIntyre, A. (2009). The very idea of a university: Aristotle, Newman and us. *British Journal of Education, 57*(4), 347–362.

Noddings, N. (2008). Caring and moral education. In L. P. Nucci & D. Narvaez (Eds.), *Handbook of moral and character education* (pp. 161–174). New York, NY: Routledge.

Nucci, L., & Narváez, D. (Eds.). (2008). *Handbook of moral and character education.* New York, NY: Routledge.

Osler, A., & Starkey, H. (2006). Education for democratic citizenship: A review of research, policy and practice 1995–2005. *Research Papers in Education, 21*(4), 433–466.

Oxley, L., & Morris, P. (2013). Global citizenship: A typology for distinguishing its multiple cownceptions. *British Journal of Educational Studies, 61*(3), 301–325.

Pérez, A. (2007). Principales modelos de socialización familiar [Main models of family socialization]. *Foro de educación, 5*(9), 91–97.

Pigozzi, M. (2006). A UNESCO view of global citizenship education. *Educational Review, 58*(1), 1–4.

Prinz, J. (2009). *The emotional construction of morals.* New York, NY: Oxford University Press.

Puig, J. (2012). *Compromís cívic i aprenentatge a la universitat. Experiències de l'aprenentatge servei* [Civic commitment and learning in the university. Service-learning experiences]. Barcelona: Graó.

Puig, J., Batlle, R., Bosch, C., & Palos, J. (2006). *Aprenentatge servei. Educar per a la ciutadania* [Service-learning. Educating for citizenship]. Barcelona: Octaedro.

Puig, J., & Martín, X. (1998). *La educación moral en la escuela. Teoría y práctica* [Moral education in schools: Theory and practice]. Barcelona: Edebé.

Rawls, J. (1971). *A theory of Justice.* Cambridge, MA: Harvard University Press.

Rest, J. (1986). *Manual for the defining issues test.* Minneapolis, MN: Center for the Study of Ethical Development.

Rüegg, W. (Ed.). (1996). *A history of the University in Europe. Vol II. Universities in the Modern Europe.* Cambridge: Cambridge University Press.

Sennet, R. (2000). *La corrosión del carácter* [The corrosion of character]. Barcelona: Anagrama.

Steiner, G. (2004). *The idea of Europe.* Tilburg: Uitgeverij Nexus.

Tirri, K., & Nokelainen, P. (2011). *Measuring multiple intelligences and moral sensitivities in education.* Rotterdam, The Netherlands: Sense Publishers.

Turiel, E. (1984). *El Desarrollo del Conocimiento Social. Moralidad y Convención* [The development of social knowledge: Morality and convention]. Madrid: Debate.

UNESCO. (2006). *UNESCO guidelines for intercultural education.* Paris: Author. Retrieved from https://unesdoc.unesco.org/ark:/48223/pf0000147878

Veugelers, W. (Ed.). (2011). *Education and humanism. Linking autonomy and humanity.* Rotterdam, The Netherlands: Sense Publishers.

Veugelers, W., De Groot, I., & Stolk, V. (2017). *Research for cult committee – Teaching common values in Europe.* Brussels: European Parliament, Policy Department for Structural and Cohesion Policy. Retrieved from http://bit.ly/2pm5Yh9

Walker, J. L., & Taylor, J. H. (1991). Family interactions and the development of moral reasoning. *Child Development, 62,* 264–283.

Williams, A. L., & Merten, M. J. (2011). iFamily: Internet and social media technology in the family context. *Family and Consumer Sciences Research Journal, 40*(2), 150–170.

CHAPTER 4

Social and Educational Inclusion in Schools and Their Communities

Ghazala Bhatti

1 Introduction

This chapter is about inclusion and inclusive education. It looks at how sociologists have defined inclusion and how educationalists have sought to develop ideas which have implications for students' academic and professional development. The EDIC + project helped to create learning spaces for individuals in educational institutions, such as schools and universities. Shared learning experiences provided opportunities for working with diversity and difference and for professional networking. Participating students came from diverse backgrounds and from many countries across the world. This chapter considers the theoretical background which led to the development of the module at Bath Spa University. It also presents student evaluations of the module trialled before the final schedule of the Masters level module was put together.

2 Democracy and Human Rights

Although education has been declared a basic human right for quite some time now, 262 million children and youth were not in school in 2016 (UNESCO, 2016). According to the United Nations 57 million children in poor countries have no schools. These are shocking figures. When some children living in poverty do manage to access basic schooling, it does not mean they will acquire adequate life skills which lead either to educational fulfilment or decent employment. The developing world faces challenges mostly because of economic reasons and the capability people have to achieve what is best for them (Sen, 1980).

Economically advanced countries also struggle with inclusion, when for example they consider the education of the gypsy, Roma, traveller and indigenous communities (Gobbo, 2009; Levinson & Hooley, 2014). In some countries such as in England there are faith-based schools – the Catholic, Jewish and Muslim schools. Questions have been raised about their contribution to society and role in inclusion/exclusion (Short, 2002; Jackson, 2006). Is it the shortcomings

© KONINKLIJKE BRILL NV, LEIDEN, 2019 | DOI: 10.1163/9789004411944_004

This is an open access chapter distributed under the terms of the CC-BY-NC 4.0 License.

of the state school system or society's failure to include *everyone* that lead to the setting up of different types of schools? Often those who are not fluent in the dominant language of a country are at risk of being excluded from engaging in school and the wider society (McEachron & Bhatti, 2015). Researchers have documented the connection between heritage, culture, identity negotiation and the important role language acquisition and language maintenance play in the lives of children and young people. Blackledge and Creese (2010) have looked at the negotiation of language in institutional settings. Teacher training courses may not routinely heighten teachers' awareness, and not all teachers are knowledgeable about this important aspect of children's identities. Osler and Starkey (2010) have raised the issue of teachers and human rights education.

All of these examples show that there are many dimensions and layers of exclusions. Inclusive education aims to work for *all* in a way that can help society develop. How to do this successfully is a serious concern for many educationalists. So what does equity really mean in different contexts and what can inclusive education achieve? Can decisions arrived at through international consensus (e.g. UNICEF, UNESCO) be agreed upon as democratic decisions which are enforceable because they benefit a majority of people educationally? The answers are not easy. Inclusion remains an aspiration, and Inclusive Education is the means through which that aspiration can be realized. Its role is pivotal for present and future educational endeavours.

Julie Allan (2005) has named Inclusion 'an ethical project'. Not to be inclusive is to be unethical. Osman (2015) comments on values in education which offer 'pedagogies of hope' resulting in a

> growing interest in inclusion and inclusionary practices (...) fuelled by the increasing criticism of tokenism in inclusion accompanied by significant advances in our knowledge about inclusive philosophies and pedagogies. (Osman, 2015, pp. ix–x)

Although this quotation is about past injustices and indifference to the educational destinies of children and young people in South Africa, this is not true *only* of South Africa. Marginalized communities and excluded children and young people exist everywhere, as demographic changes ensure a constantly shifting landscape. One current example of this is the education of refugees in Europe and how that is being handled in different countries. The local situation matters, as do policy and structural issues at the national level. Political will, resources and capability (Sen, 1993) for positive change must decide whether a school or a community responds to the need for inclusion. This is a matter for social justice in its broadest sense.

SOCIAL AND EDUCATIONAL INCLUSION IN SCHOOLS 63

> Social justice for educationalists is not just about advancing theoretical knowledge and analytical understandings. It is also about interrogating practice in real educational settings which challenge prior assumptions (Griffiths, 2003). For social justice in education, the social, cultural, emotional and political contexts are as relevant as social structures and institutional practices. (Bhatti & Leeman, 2011, p. 131)

How can social justice be made to work for the many? Young (1990, 1996) states that there can be no justice unless structural inequalities are questioned and the idea of a homogeneous public is challenged to include culturally plural groups. An inclusive participatory framework which looks critically at the white male norm would make spaces for others to contribute to the social and public good. This is a reminder of the chasm between good intentions and everyday realities for many people. Unless challenged, institutional practices will continue to reinforce and reinvent inequalities in education because of many factors such as ethnicity, social class and gender. Most societies would aim to maintain certain values and a certain standard of what is desirable for the public good.

Should each country teach its own special values to children? Are these different from the values being taught everywhere else? In Britain the advice issued by the Department of Education to all maintained schools asked them to 'promote the fundamental British values' (DfE, 2014, p. 4).

This has caused much discussion among educators and academics. It is seen as

> ... a response to fears of extremist religious Ideologies, terrorism and Muslim sharia law, and on page 5 of the guidance a reference is made to the reissued 'Prevent' strategy (Home Office, 2011) which actually defines extremism as 'vocal or active opposition to fundamental British values, including democracy, the rule of law and mutual respect and tolerance of different faiths and beliefs' (...) At a time when the United Kingdom is threatened with break-up, and a possible withdrawal from the European Union, and with the 'end of Empire' (...) what actually constitutes British values is highly debatable and cannot be reduced to a three-line slogan. (Tomlinson, 2015, p. 10)

For Vini Lander

Whilst there may be popular and political consensus with this list of values, the claim that they are wholly British is troublesome and in an

> attempt to forge cohesion, the unintended effect, but some (Hoque, 2015) would argue intentional effect, has been to create notions of insider–outsider citizen, or as Taras (2013, p. 420) notes, 'the subaltern internal others' or the stranger within, a stratification of citizenship into those who really belong, namely the indigenous majority, those who can belong, namely those of minority ethnic heritage who have assimilated or integrated and those who really do not quite belong, or those we tolerate up to a point, namely the Muslim 'other'. (Lander, 2016, p. 275)

This overt politicization of educational spaces has caused researchers to look more deeply at the meaning and implications of these values. Janmaat reports 'levels of support for fundamental British values (FBVs) among 23 year olds are already very high and do not differ between the white British majority and various minority ethnic groups' (Janmaat, 2018, p. 251). Sant and Hanley (2018) suggest that teachers' own positions will affect how they teach. This will depend on educators' understanding of the nation as an entity or as a social construct, and it will also depend on whether their own understanding of national identity is open or closed to other interpretations.

Panjwani (2016) summarised four inter-related strands of criticisms against FBVs which show the complexity facing educators and researchers. Documenting what Muslim teachers make of FBVs, he found that despite their criticisms of FBVs

> Muslim teachers did not see any incompatibility between FBVs and their conception of Islamic values ... teachers' responses reflect Rawls 'overlapping consensus' and situates the roots of this consensus in contemporary Muslim intellectual history and the modernist reforms ... teachers' responses problematise the essentialised understanding of terms such as 'Islam' and 'the West' and indicate the interpretive and open-ended nature of cultures. (Panjwani, 2016, p. 329)

Are children of minority ethnic or mixed-race or Muslim backgrounds seen as outsiders? Which other countries teach 'fundamental values' in the same way? At a time when Brexit is being debated in a climate of national soul searching about 'what does it mean to be British?' is it reasonable to expect a national consensus about 'FBVs, what they mean and how they should be taught to young children and then tested in schools? It is not easy to find quick answers which all teachers and parents would agree upon.

SOCIAL AND EDUCATIONAL INCLUSION IN SCHOOLS   65

3   Inclusion and Disability Studies

Studies about disability often emphasise the need for Inclusion. Sometimes it is assumed that 'inclusion' is about including disability, and is concerned mainly with addressing the educational rights of children and young people who 'have special educational needs'. Discussions about disability in this context include physical disability and also learning differences. This highlights the opposite positions suggested by the medical and social models of disability (Smith, 2008). Disabled people have not been given the respect and rights they deserve, and it can be seen that so many years after the Salamanca Agreement (UNESCO, 1994), although attitudes are changing, they are changing extremely slowly. The question of accepting disability and special needs as part of a whole range of normal human experience has not been resolved. This dilemma emerges in debates about whether or not children with special educational needs should be included in main stream classes, or educated separately (Cigman, 2006). Questions such as whose rights are more important, and whether segregation based on disability should be acceptable to everyone in society, are still being debated.

Barton's insightful sociological contribution to the field of inclusion challenges over-simplification and reductive thinking.

> Len (Barton) argued that social exclusion, of which disablism is one element, (1) has many compounding forms of differing exclusions, (2) is not a natural but a socially constructed process, (3) has no single factor that can remove it and (4) it is in constant need of conceptual analysis. (Goodley & Runswick-Cole, 2010, p. 273)

The above points defy superficial solutions for challenges to social and educational exclusions. They consider the whole child/young person, rather than identifying someone by their disability alone. This field is contested and politicized. The way schools deal with inclusion can influence democratic processes in what (Slee, 2010) has called the 'politics of possibility' for the whole of the school community.

Writing about disability, and against segregation based on 'ability' Sally Tomlinson (2010) asserts that

> Inclusive education is part of the effort to counter the often pointless global struggles for economic dominance, and the encouragement of seemingly endless competition between institutions, teachers, parents and young people. Whatever the cultural, political, social or economic

> differences between countries, every society that aspires to create a decent, humane and effective system of education should think in terms of inclusion. Inclusion is an issue of equity and ethics, human rights and social justice, and also economic improvement. (Tomlinson, 2010, p. 544)

She suggests that there is an argument here not about special educational needs but special educational rights which are deeply embedded in the social model of disability.

> A social interpretation of disability argued that whatever a person's perceived impairment, they were further disabled by society's failure to accommodate to their needs. (Tomlinson, 2010, p. 543)

There is an Equalities Act in place now which incorporates previous acts in UK

> In UK The Equality Act 2010 legally protects people from discrimination in the workplace and in wider society. It replaced previous anti-discrimination laws with a single Act, making the law easier to understand and strengthening protection in some situations. It sets out the different ways in which it is unlawful to treat someone. (https://www.gov.uk/guidance/equality-act-2010-guidance)

The extent to which this can be realized in practice, and in the field of education in particular, is open to question and must remain under scrutiny.

3.1 Intersectionality

Some groups in society experience multiple forms of disempowerment and oppression and this can lead to higher levels of exclusions. Crenshaw (1989) defines intersectionality as the structures that make certain identities become consequences and the vehicle for vulnerability. Individuals get caught up and are at the receiving end of the way injustices built into the structure of institutions work together to bring about inequality. According to Gillborn (2015) intersectionality is 'multiple forms of inequality and identity and how they inter-relate in different contexts over time'. Conceptually, intersectionality works with the ideas presented above. It works against selecting just one factor e g. gender or ethnicity. Instead, it takes account of how all of these come together to cause inequality in society, and this inequality must be challenged.

Collins' (2017) definition of intersectionality includes many axes of social divisions, how they act together and influence each other through

(1) racism, sexism, class exploitation and similar systems of oppression are interconnected and mutually construct one another; (2) configurations of social inequalities take form within intersecting oppressions; (3) perceptions of social problems as well reflect how social actors are situated within the power relations of particular historical and social contexts; and (4) because individuals and groups are differently located within intersecting oppressions, they have distinctive standpoints on social phenomena. (Collins & Bilge, 2016, p. 25)

This explains how some people live at the 'intersection' of many kinds of oppressions which are not of their own making. If we fail to recognize these intersections we will effectively marginalize, ignore and silence those who are most at risk of exclusion. Children and young people from families which live at the intersections of many forms of oppressions are to be found in schools and in other social institutions and organisations.

4   Social and Educational Inclusion Module

Taking into account the complex and competing definitions of inclusion and their impact on education and society as defined above, a module on Social and Educational Inclusion was designed at Bath Spa University. This module aims to provide post graduate students with the tools to question and explore inclusion and inclusive education with reference to their own professional and personal experiences. In reality, while trying out ideas and putting this module together at Bath Spa University we found ourselves working face to face with students who had come directly from countries such as Columbia, Ghana, Pakistan, Syria, Venezuela and Zambia. We were also working with students of local British heritage, as well as students whose parents had migrated from countries such as Somalia. They were the first in their families to attend a British university. So the module had to respond to the questions raised from many perspectives and in voices which shared the experiences of living and being educated in many countries. A purely "British" module which only discussed examples of research from Britain just would not work. Students wanted to contribute and learn with their peers through sharing their educational trajectories and life experiences and their own lived realities.

In order for the module about Inclusion and Inclusive Education to be successful and relevant for all our students, it would *have* to engage with global and international issues. Not to do so would exclude the participation of students and their voices, and that would be counter-productive to the overall aims of this module. The questions which formed a fundamental part of this module were of scholarly and research interest to a group of academics. The module was therefore designed to include contributions from more than just one or two academics. This enriched the quality of discourse within the module. We also wanted to work with colleagues outside the university, including charities and NGOs, and to develop other non-university collaborations. The idea would be to invite colleagues to the university for guest lectures, as well as taking students outside the university to become familiar with the ways in which NGOs and other charitable organizations work against exclusion.

A full description of the module which was approved at the university is as follows:

Education for Democratic Intercultural Citizenship

Social and Educational Inclusion in Schools and their Communities Bath Spa University

This is an optional module for Masters and Doctoral students. It is a complementary module for ERASMUS+ students enrolled on EDIC+ (Education for Democratic Intercultural Citizenship) Programme. Students can study one 7.5 ECT module in their own university, plus another 7.5 ECT module in one of the other participating universities. Students might also like to take another optional module in Bath Spa University as well, which may be on offer at the same time as the EDIC module. (Students are normally asked to have 6.5 IELTS – in English to participate in Masters level teaching in the English language at Bath Spa University). IELTS (International English Language Testing System) indicates the level of acceptable competence in English. The level varies according to the academic expectations of a programme. As a Masters level module the IELTS reflect the basic standard of English language required to ensure that the course is easily accessible to all students.

4.1   *Aims*

After completing this module students will be able to
- Demonstrate an understanding of the key ideas about social justice, human rights and social and educational inclusion with particular reference to education. These concepts include exclusion and inclusion, identity, diversity and equity.

SOCIAL AND EDUCATIONAL INCLUSION IN SCHOOLS 69

- Engage with sociological and educational debates concerning key notions which have British, European and global implications.
- Become aware of the 'bigger picture' – the challenges and barriers to inclusion socially and educationally and in terms of policy.
- Acquire an understanding of the psychology of social exclusion and inclusion.
- Understand the development of identity and belonging among young people.
- Develop strategies to overcome prejudice and social and educational exclusion.
- Learn from educational professionals who research/work successfully with excluded and marginalised groups, or those with special or additional educational needs, such as minority ethnic groups, refugees, excluded children, gypsy and traveller children.
- Develop inter-disciplinary understanding and a multi-professional approach to encourage inclusion.
- Enhance an understanding of inclusive education with a view to developing a link between conceptual understanding and professional and practical outlook.
- Develop skills of intercultural communication and the ability to work with diversity on an individual basis and with peers from other countries.

4.2 *Teaching*

This module will be taught through lectures, seminars and tutorials. Students will be expected to work collaboratively, and to present their work together in small groups after each section of the module has been taught. The presentations will be based on students' own learning and reflections on what they have gained from reading, lectures, discussions in class and from their own research. The module will have three sections. These are: (i) sociological enquiry, (ii) school/organization-centred approach and (iii) students' own investigation of a topic of personal and professional interest to them.

Students will be expected to write a learning journal throughout the module in which they can record and reflect on ideas obtained from their reading as well as those gained from lectures and seminars with tutors and guest speakers. Formative feedback will be provided for individual presentations in class. This will help students to do a poster presentation which will receive further formative feedback and discussion before they submit their final essays or research-based texts for assessment. The final summative assignment is an essay of 3500 to 4000 words. Students can choose to write either (a) a conceptual paper exploring inclusion or (b) use examples from research and their own experiences to explore an aspect of social and educational inclusion in a particular setting/context within their own country or (c) a comparative account of two countries if they have comparative experience and wish to develop a comparative research perspective.

4.3 Prior Knowledge

There is no expectation of previous knowledge about this topic. It is assumed that post graduate students will come from diverse backgrounds, and possibly from different countries.

4.4 Module Content

This module will look critically at social and educational inclusion, opening up assumptions about the questions of rights, equity and inclusion with regard to many factors such as race/ethnicity, gender, social class and disability. The broad aim of the module is to look at human rights, social justice and the value of intercultural understanding and dialogue, providing students with opportunities to develop social and educational understanding of complex issues. Students will be invited to engage in debate and argument about the dilemmas faced by teachers, their students and the community, to think of ways forward, and to connect these to curriculum-based experiences. These will be considered with reference to policy and practice in a country with which students are familiar. We will work with the professional and personal experiences which students bring, whether these are school based, or youth work/community based, and will consider civic engagement.

The module comprises of three sections:

1. The first section will cover sociological and policy issues. It will encourage debate and develop an understanding of the key concepts – ideas about empowerment, entitlement to education, rights and responsibilities.
2. The second section will focus on the educational and organizational aspects of social and educational inclusion related to research-based findings. These will consider emancipatory research, action research and ethnography.
3. Thirdly, the module will focus on practical skills related to social and educational inclusion. This will mean meeting people who work in the field and visiting voluntary organizations to see how they engage in problem solving in their day-to day work.

4.5 Context

Identity is important for all students. Why is it that in some countries e.g.UK those young people who might have considered themselves 'European citizens'

SOCIAL AND EDUCATIONAL INCLUSION IN SCHOOLS

or 'global citizens', may have to re-configure their identity after Brexit? Is this a real or imagined identity? Where do settlers, new migrants and refugees/asylum seekers fit in European cities? Are schools helping them to have high aspirations and to make a positive future contribution to society? How can teachers and other education professionals become culturally responsive and equip their students to work confidently with the dominant language? The module will be further enhanced by contributions from visiting speakers. These include local organizations which work with excluded children (Black family support initiatives) statutory organizations and individuals who are responsible for educating children in care for example, and charitable organizations which work with young homeless people and have successfully helped them to obtain admissions in university courses. These professionals will share professional and personal experiences of working creatively with the challenges of inclusion and diversity, and help develop a deeper understanding of social and educational inclusion.

4.6   *Assessment*

Formative Assessment will involve individual presentation in class which will receive feedback. This will help students to produce a poster based on reading and experience of education in their own country/a country with which they are familiar OR they can choose to present a comparative account of two countries if they have relevant experience they wish to develop further. Students can explore how organizations are working to include young people socially and educationally. Feedback will be provided to help with summative assessment.

Summative Assessment will be an essay or a short empirical research based study of what is happening in the field, either with individuals or in an organization which is trying to work in an inclusive and innovative way with groups who find themselves on the margins of society. These can be for example refugee families, people with disabilities, young people who have English as an additional language, and are therefore educationally disadvantaged. More recently the needs of children of school going age and young people with mental illness have been acknowledged in UK and are receiving attention.

The Module at Bath Spa University is a collaboration between several academics. Their joint contribution will strengthen what the module has to offer future post graduate students.

4.7   *Students' Perceptions and Feedback on the Module*

Before being finalized the module was trialled in the university. We thought it would be useful to find out how students reacted to the try out module, and to see what they made of what we were trying to do in the class. What could we do better next time? Was there something we should do differently, and if so, what and how? Should we find a better way to connect different sessions? Was it a good or bad idea to involve many academics in the teaching of this module rather than just one or two people? We had to reassure all students that they could say anything they liked and that their critical feedback would be used to improve the final shape of the module as it appears below. Of course they did not have to take part if they did not want to. When introducing the idea of research and seeking informed consent and inviting students to take part in evaluation one of the key readings used in the IP in Charles University Prague was Morwenna Griffith's (2003) essay on empowerment. Other students in subsequent IPs were also informed of this text which explains *why* their voices are important and how their ideas would be shared. The students in the try out module were asked to read Griffith's text as a starting point for a conversation before they began to evaluate it. This text seems to work whenever it is used with students. They realize what they have to say really matters, and that it will be taken seriously.

The questions students were invited to respond to were about each session and also how the whole course held together for them. Did it hold together well, and if not, then what more should we do to make it better?

At the very outset students were invited to write a daily learning journal in which they could address the following questions as prompts. They could write about other related matters as well in addition to these questions which were initially developed to document students' experiences of IPs held at Charles University Prague in 2017 and then used again at the Universities of Tallinn and Helsinki in 2018.

1. What were the 2 things (enjoyable and different) to what I'm used to?
2. What I found challenging and why?
3. What did I learn from my peers?
4. What did I contribute?
5. What did I learn about myself as a student and a researcher?

We received feedback from two trials of try out modules in Bath Spa University which were held in June 2018 and then again in January 2019. Different students attended these try out modules each time. This was because the Masters students who attended in June 2018 had completed their degrees by the time the second try out module ran. Some had left the university. Some of the doctoral students who attended the try out module in June 2018 were either busy doing field work, or they had other commitments. All the students who attended the January 2019 try out module were Masters students. On both occasions students were taught by at least six academics. The feedback from the students has helped to shape the module, which is planned to be offered

SOCIAL AND EDUCATIONAL INCLUSION IN SCHOOLS

at Bath Spa University in the future. The schedule of that module can be found after the presentation of students' feedback.

4.7.1   Summary of Student Feedback

The students appreciated and enjoyed learning about the different topics related to Inclusion and Inclusive Education. Some had heard or read about Inclusion before, whereas others had not. So the class had to create a level playing field for all students where no one would feel excluded, nor feel that they did not know enough, or that they did not belong in the group. In this situation the opening session was quite important as it set the ground rules and made it possible for the students to be introduced to each other. The teaching by different lecturers was highly valued, as it provided the students with an opportunity to interact with academics they had not met before. It also inspired students to read the research these colleagues were doing, or had done in the past. One criticism was that the students would have liked to meet all the lecturers again some three or four weeks later, so that they could continue the conversations after they had read more about the topics introduced by each speaker. This would have been difficult to arrange after the end of the course, though we did think about the possibility of organising IP style roundtables in the future, and also introducing a social event bringing all academics and students together in the last session.

International students added a lot to the modules because they questioned Eurocentric research and sometimes the data which was different from what they might have found if they researched the same topic in their own schools or in their own countries. On the whole they were happy to share the experiences from their own perspectives and their own countries. However, this was more likely to happen if there was a group of students who knew each other from another programme and had previous knowledge about each other's professional background or research interests. Some students had not met each other and initially they thought all the other students were more knowledgeable about Inclusion than they themselves were.

Some of the comments from the students are as follows:

4.7.2   Personal Knowledge and Course Content

> I was very moved to hear about the journey of a lecturer from where he started to where he is now. Leadership and equity is a very complicated thing.

> I had never thought seriously about how some children face so much bullying and that is why they don't go to school. This is because of their accent, or colour or social class. That the difference between home and school can break a child's wish to learn.

Critical race theory is something I knew nothing about. I am white I guess (Irish heritage) so I heard about white privilege for the first time and found it uncomfortable ... that it can cause inequality.

Issues about disability are very challenging. So, how kindly a society deals with disability tells us how civilized a society is.

4.7.3 Module Structure

It was good to have a lecture 10am to 12 and another one from 1 to 3pm. It kept us all together for lunch break. A longer gap would maybe lose some people?

I wish we could have some trips to go to outside Bath that were connected to the module ... like a cultural visit. A combination of work and fun?

A lecture each morning and a workshop every afternoon may work well. Two lectures a day are too much to study in a new topic.

Based on what the students said and what was possible we came up with the schedule of a module. This is presented below.

Schedule EDIC+ Course Bath Spa University

Social and Educational Inclusion

Module Leader: Ghazala Bhatti
Contributors: Prof Martin Levinson, Prof Charlotte Chadderton, Dr Mahmoud Emira, Dr Jim Hordern, Dr Chloe Yeh, Richard Parker, Caroline Kuhn & Shaun Taylor

Day 1
AM: Introduction – (ice breakers)
Dr Ghazala Bhatti – What is inclusion? An introduction to the module
Introducing different meanings of inclusion: social justice, intersectionality, human rights
PM: Case study – what does inclusion look like? (research evidence)

SOCIAL AND EDUCATIONAL INCLUSION IN SCHOOLS   75

Evidence presented in published research will be used in this session to interrogate the idea of inclusion and what has been reported about different topics which this module covers.

Day 2
AM: Prof Martin Levinson – Bridges and Barriers: the challenge of inclusion
This session will explore the interface between education and cultural identities, considering conflicting values/aspirations encountered in home and school contexts
PM: Richard Parker – Exclusion from school and society
PM: Specific examples of research about supporting different groups of vulnerable young people at school will be considered, such as potential and actual impact of approaches geared to improving schools' awareness of children and young people's needs. These include emotional needs around attachment, as well as critiques of such approaches.

Day 3
AM: Prof Charlotte Chadderton – Critical Race Pedagogies
This session will critically examine race and will consider its implications for education
PM: visit: Centre for Black Family support

Day 4
AM: Dr Jim Hordern – Pedagogic rights? Participation, enhancement and inclusion in education
This session will examine the issue of pedagogic rights (enhancement, inclusion and participation) as the basis for a democratic and inclusive society.
PM: Ghazala Bhatti – Language Matters
This session will look at the ways in which language and identity are linked, and how for example not knowing English can lead to disengagement with education in an English speaking country.

Day 5
AM: Dr Chloe Yeh – The Psychology of Prejudice and Inclusion
Prejudice is something which is age old. Why do we have prejudices and how do we make sense of the world?
PM: Workshop: Student led discussion on a topic about inclusion -formative assessment

This is planned to help students connect the theory of inclusion with their own particular topic of interest, which they can explore further in class to obtain critical and supportive feedback from their peers and tutor.

Day 6
Saturday – Cultural visit Pitt Rivers Museum of Anthropology, Oxford.
Sunday – No classes

Day 7
AM: Dr Mahmoud Emira – Leadership and Inequality in Education: problematising inclusion?
This session will discuss inclusion and inequality from a leadership perspective. It will highlight inequality that individuals from under-represented groups (e.g. disabled) experience when aiming to engage in leadership and how they can be supported.
PM: Student poster presentation in seminar – further development from Day 5 (formative assessment with feedback)
This is planned to help develop the initial ideas which were tried and tested during the workshop on Day 5. Students will be invited to put together a poster which represents their ideas, which they can present in class to their peers. They should be prepared to answer questions about the topic they are presenting. This is a formative assessment which should help the students to write the essays for the summative assessment after the end of the module.

Day 8
AM: Shaun Taylor – On social class & transitions
Transitions mark a change, a step in another direction. How do schools manage transitions and how do children experience them? Are some people excluded and others included?
PM: Workshop using real data gathered from home & school

Day 9
AM: Caroline Kuhn – Educational journeys and lifelong learning
This session will look at how inequality affects education systems: the case of Venezuela. Venezuela has the biggest reserve of natural gas in the world and one of the biggest reserves of oil. Yet 90% of the population lives in poverty. For a majority education is a luxury.

SOCIAL AND EDUCATIONAL INCLUSION IN SCHOOLS

Day 10
AM: Guest speaker from psychology department on vulnerability & artistic expressions
PM: Learning disability and inclusion lecture: dyslexia & autism
Not supporting students with learning difficulties can lead to their exclusion from school and exclusion from society. This session will look at learning disability /learning differences
AM: Round table with lead tutor
PM: Dr Ghazala Bhatti – tutorial support for summative assessment.

Day 11
AM: Library day
PM: End of course
The organizations which are linked to this module and which are located outside the university are as follows:
- mentoring plus, http://mentoringplus.net/
- supported housing – Bath based
- www.ndti.org.uk

4.8   *Literature for the Module*

Clough, P. & Corbett, J. (2006). *Theories of inclusive education.* London: Paul Chapman.

Emira, M., Brewster, S., Duncan, N., & Clifford, A. (2018). What disability? I am a leader! Understanding leadership in HE from a disability perspective. *Educational Management Administration and Leadership, 46*(3), 457–473.

Frandji, D., & Vitale, P. (2016). The enigma of Bernstein's pedagogic rights. In P. Vitale & B. Exley (Eds.), *Pedagogic rights and democratic education: Bernsteinian explorations of curriculum, pedagogy and assessment* (pp. 13–32). London: Routledge.

Gillborn, D. (2015). Intersectionality, critical race theory, and the primacy of tacism: race, class, gender, and disability in Education. *Qualitative Inquiry, 21*(3), 277–287.

Griffiths, M. (2003). *Action for social justice in education.* BuckinghAM: Open University Press.

Hamilton, P. (2018). School books or wedding dresses? Examining the cultural dissonance experienced by young gypsy/traveller women in secondary education. *Gender and Education, 30*(7), 829–845.

Hordern, J. (2019). Higher expertise, pedagogic rights and the post-truth society. *Teaching in Higher Education, 24*(3), 288–301.

Lucey, H. & Reay, D. (2010). Identities in transition: Anxiety and excitement in the move to secondary school. *Oxford Review of Education, 26*(2), 191–205.

Rogoff, B. (2003). *The cultural nature of human development.* Oxford: Oxford University Press.

5 Concluding Remarks: What Are the Challenges for Inclusion?

The field of education is constantly changing in response to the events that shape or question the meaning of inclusion. To return to the main topic of this chapter: how can we continue to work for inclusion and for inclusive education? This will be debated in the module offered at Bath Spa University to the students who will attend it to discuss social justice issues, and most importantly by the academics who teach it.

References

Allan, J. (2005). Inclusion as an ethical project. In S. Tremain (Ed.), *Foucault and the government of disability* (pp. 281–297). Ann Arbor, MI: Michigan: University of Michigan Press.

Bhatti, G., & Leeman, Y. (2011). Convening a network within the European conference on educational research. *European Educational Research Journal, 10*(1), 129–142.

Blackledge, A., & Creese, A. (2010). *Multilingualism: A critical perspective.* London: Bloomsbury.

Cigman, R. (Ed.). (2006). *Included or excluded? The challenge of the mainstream for some SEN children.* London: Routledge.

Collins, P. (2017). The difference that power makes: Intersectionality and participatory democracy. *Feminist Review, 8*(1), 19–39.

Collins, P., & Bilge, S. (2016). *Intersectionality.* Cambridge: Polity Press.

Crenshaw, K. (1989). *Demarginalizing the intersection of race and sex: A Black feminist critique of anti discrimination doctrine, feminist theory and antiracist politics.* Chicago, IL: University of Chicago Legal Forum.

DfE (Department for Education). (2014). *Promoting fundamental British values as Part of SMSC in schools.* London: Department for Education.

Gobbo, F. (2009). Moving lives: A reflective account of a three generation travelling attractionist family in Italy. In P. Danahar, M. Kenny, & J. Leder (Eds.), *Traveller, nomadic and migrant education* (pp. 13–28). London: Routledge.

Goodley, D., & Runswick-Cole, K. (2010). Len Barton, inclusion and critical disability studies: Theorising disabled childhoods. *International Studies in Sociology of Education, 20*(4), 273–290.

Gillborn, D. (2015). Intersectionality, critical race theory, and the primacy of racism: Race, class, gender and disability in education. *Qualitative Inquiry, 21*(3), 277–287.

Griffiths, M. (2003). *Action for social justice in education.* Buckingham: Open University Press.

Home Office. (2011). *Preventing extremism: The prevent strategy.* London: The Home Office.

SOCIAL AND EDUCATIONAL INCLUSION IN SCHOOLS

Hoque, A. (2015). *British-Islamic identity: Third generation Bangladeshis from east London*. London: ioE Press.

Jackson, R. (2006). Should the state fund faith-based schools: A review of arguments. *British Journal of Religious Education, 25*(2), 89–102.

Janmaat, J. (2018). Educational Influences on young people's support for fundamental British values. *British Educational Research Journal, 44*(2), 251–273.

Lander, V. (2016). Introduction to fundamental British values. *Journal of Education for Teachers, 42*(3), 274–279.

Levinson, M., & Hooley, N. (2014). Supporting the learning of nomadic communities across transnational contexts: Exploring parallels in the education of UK Roma gypsies and indigenous Australians. *Research Papers in Education, 29*(4), 373–389.

McEachron, G., & Bhatti, G. (2015). Teaching English as an additional language in the global classroom: A transnational study in the United States and United Kingdom. *Global Education Review, 2*(2), 59–83.

Osler, A., & Starkey, H. (2010). *Teachers and human rights education*. Stoke-on-Trent: Trentham.

Osman, R. (2015). Forward. In E. Walton & S. Moonsamy (Eds.), *Making education inclusive* (pp. ix–x). Newcastle-upon-Tyne: Cambridge Scholars Publishing.

Panjwani, F. (2016). Towards an overlapping consensus: Muslim teachers' views on fundamental British values. *Journal of Education for Teaching, 42*(3), 329–340.

Sant, E., & Hanley, C. (2018). Political assumptions underlying pedagogies of national education: The case of student teachers teaching 'British values' in England. *British Educational Research Journal, 44*(2), 319–337.

Sen, A. (1980). Equality of what? In S. Murrin (Ed.), *The Tanner lectures on human values*. Salt Lake City, UT: University of Utah Press.

Sen, A. (1993). Capability and well being. In M. Nussbaum & A. Sen (Eds.), *The quality of life* (pp. 1–6). Oxford: Clarendon Press.

Short, G. (2002). Faith based schools: A threat to social cohesion? *Journal of Philosophy of Education, 36*(4), 559–572.

Slee, R. (2010). Driven to the margins, disabled students, inclusive schooling and the politics of possibility. *Cambridge Journal of Education, 31*(3), 385–397.

Smith, S. (2008). Social justice and disability: Competing interpretations of the medical and social model. In K. Kristiansen, S. Vehmas, & T. Shakespeare (Eds.), *Arguing about disability* (pp. 1–15). London: Routledge.

Taras, R. (2013). Islamophobia never stands still: Race, religion and culture. *Ethnic and Racial Studies, 36*(3), 417–433.

Tomlinson, S. (2010). A tribute to Len Barton. *British Journal of Sociology of Education, 31*(5), 537–546.

Tomlinson, S. (2015). Fundamental British values. In C. Alexander, D. Weekes-Bernard, & J. Arday (Eds.), *The Runnymede school report: Race, education and inequality in contemporary Britain* (pp. 10–13). London: Runnymede Trust.

UNESCO. (1994). *Salamanca statement and framework for action on special needs education.* Paris: UNESCO.

UNESCO. (2016). *Sustainable development goals: leaving no one behind: How far on the way to universal primary and secondary education?* Paris: UNESCO.

Young, I. (1990). *Justice and the politics of difference.* Princeton, NJ: Princeton University Press.

Young, I. (1996). Communication and the other: Beyond deliberative democracy. In S. Benhabib (Ed.), *Democracy and difference: contesting the boundaries of the political.* Princeton, NJ: Princeton University Press.

CHAPTER 5

Teachers' Moral Competence in Pedagogical Encounters

Elina Kuusisto and Kirsi Tirri

1 Introduction

This chapter presents the Education for Democratic Intercultural Citizenship (EDIC) module called 'Teachers' moral competence in pedagogical encounters', which emphasises ethical sensitivity, a growth mindset in learning, and purpose in life. We explain the theories behind these three concepts and present empirical findings that show how these are needed to educate ethical professionals who promote intercultural and democratic education in schools.

In Finland, which is the context for this chapter, teachers are seen as autonomous and ethical professionals who have the pedagogical freedom to implement the values and educational goals of Finland's national core curriculum in their own way in their classrooms (Tirri, 2014). These values are (1) the uniqueness of each pupil and the right to a good education; (2) humanity, general knowledge and ability, equality and democracy; (3) cultural diversity as richness; and (4) necessity of having a sustainable way of living (Finnish National Board of Education, 2016, pp. 15–16). The core values acknowledge the importance of developing students as human beings and democratic citizens by emphasising equal opportunity for every student to learn, meeting students' individual needs, and engaging students in pro-social plans for their future. Basic education in Finland is based on respect for human rights, which in turn promote 'well-being, democracy and active agency in civil society' (Finnish National Board of Education, 2016, p. 16). School education is intended to support this kind of holistic growth, not only in the cognitive domain but also in the affective, moral, social, and behavioural domains.

School teachers instruct entire generations of children and young people in these common values. To do so, teachers must negotiate multiple views and student interests as well as the views and interests of parents, colleagues, school administrators and representatives of the society. Teachers thus need to be aware of the consequences of their actions; in other words, they need ethical sensitivity (Narvaez & Endicott, 2008). In Finland the importance of moral competence for teachers has been made more pressing by the increasing

© KONINKLIJKE BRILL NV, LEIDEN, 2019 | DOI: 10.1163/9789004411944_005
This is an open access chapter distributed under the terms of the CC-BY-NC 4.0 License.

numbers of students and families from a wide array of socio-economic and cultural backgrounds. Ethical sensitivity has been found to be the most critical of the ethical abilities, as without it the ethical dimensions of a situation may not even be recognised. Finnish teachers typically feel that their educational programmes do not provide sufficient tools for dealing with the moral dilemmas and conflicts that challenge democracy and tolerance in schools (Tirri, 1999, 2017; Veugelers, de Groot, & Stolk, 2017). Therefore, the first aim of the present module, 'Teachers' moral competence in pedagogical encounters', is to equip and educate future teachers with skills in ethical sensitivity so that they can develop democratic and intercultural citizenship proficiency and ethical attitudes in themselves as well as in their students.

In inclusive school systems such as Finland's, students at each grade level are taught together in the same classroom regardless of abilities until the age of 15 (Tirri & Laine, 2017). This creates natural opportunities to learn mutual respect and dialogue, which are important skills in creating a sustainable and tolerant society. Inclusive education means that students with learning and behavioural challenges as well as gifted and talented students are taught in the same group. Teachers are expected to differentiate their instruction to provide individualised tuition and learning processes for all students. The Finnish educational system can be described as especially active in promoting the values of equality and individualism (Tirri, 2017, p. 84). Studies have shown that, in order to individualise and thus promote every student's development in the best possible way, understanding the role of mindsets in learning is essential (Rattan, Good, & Dweck, 2012; Rissanen, Kuusisto, Hanhimäki, & Tirri, 2018a, 2018b; Rissanen, Kuusisto, Tuominen, & Tirri, 2019). Learning mindsets refer to implicit beliefs about whether or not human qualities such as intelligence, giftedness, and personality can be developed; a growth mindset (the incremental theory) holds that they can, while a fixed mindset (the entity theory) holds that these qualities are innate and fixed. A teacher's mindset has an impact on how, and even on whom, she or he instructs (Dweck, 2000; Rissanen et al., 2018a, 2019). Research indicates that teachers' implicit beliefs need to be identified and also challenged during teacher education (Rissanen et al., 2018a, 2018b, 2019). Teachers must learn to address their own belief systems and learn how to support growth mindset in their students, interfering when they notice fixed mindset-motivated behaviour with self-limiting patterns. It can be said that teachers' moral and professional responsibility in a democratic society is to have a growth mindset towards every student regardless of background or current competencies. Students with learning and behavioural problems as well as gifted students need to have tasks that provide sufficient challenges and opportunities to learn from their mistakes. Studies show that in intercultural societies students may face stereotyping, meaning that racial or gender stereotypes may unconsciously hinder the learning process (Aronson, Fried, & Good, 2002). However, knowledge about mindsets and how beliefs systems work is one of the best educational tools for cultivating intercultural and democratic citizenship so that every student is supported in developing their agency and becoming active citizens who realise their potential to the full.

In today's societies young people can choose among countless opportunities. Some students navigate and thrive in such an environment, but a growing number of students have problems in choosing, making decisions, and keeping commitments. It has even been stated that the stress from which many young people are suffering is not rooted in having too much to do, but rather in having expectations that are too low or having no long-term goals for their lives (Damon, 2008). Our goal is to educate teachers who can reflect on the educational purposefulness of their calling from different points of view and who can help their students find purpose in their lives (Bundick & Tirri, 2014). Democratic societies need citizens who are engaged in civic and political activities (Veugelers et al., 2017). Teachers can stimulate participation in civic activities as a means of promoting what will eventually be an effective democracy. This can achieved by building purpose, which includes beyond-the-self aspirations; in other words, supporting societal participatory skills and a responsible attitude towards the community and the future (Damon, 2008; Tirri, 2017, p. 85).

The EDIC module presented in this chapter approaches the topic from the perspective of three theories, which are believed to involve key factors in building teachers' moral competence, namely ethical sensitivity, growth mindset in learning, and purpose in life. These theories are presented in more detail in the next section.

2 Theoretical Framework

2.1 *Ethical Sensitivity*

We know from earlier empirical research that moral experts demonstrate holistic orientations and skill sets in four processes of ethical behaviour: ethical sensitivity, ethical judgement, ethical motivation, and ethical action (Bebeau, Rest, & Narvaez, 1999). Although all these skills and attitudes are essential, the most important is ethical sensitivity because it is needed in order to recognise and to understand ethical problems and their symptoms. Our previous studies on ethical sensitivity in Finland and Iran (Gholami, Kuusisto, & Tirri, 2015; Hanhimäki & Tirri, 2009; Kuusisto, Tirri, & Rissanen, 2012) have shown its importance in teaching and learning. Thus, we see ethical sensitivity as a possible key ingredient of teachers' moral competence for solving moral conflicts that threaten or challenge students' democratic and intercultural development.

Darcia Narvaez (Narvaez & Endicott, 2008) has operationalized ethical sensitivity with seven dimensions: (1) reading and expressing emotions, (2) taking the perspectives of others, (3) caring by connecting with others, (4) working with interpersonal and group differences, (5) preventing social bias, (6) generating interpretations and options, and (7) identifying the consequences of actions and options. These dimensions illustrate that ethical sensitivity is about *seeing* the ethical aspect of a situation. Ethical sensitivity means being aware of one's own and other people's feelings and knowing how to express and regulate these feelings appropriately in a given situation. Taking the perspective of others indicates being able to take into account alternative viewpoints and look at a situation from another person's position.

A study conducted among Finnish and Iranian teachers found significant differences, especially with regards to this dimension (Gholami et al., 2015). For Finnish teachers, taking the perspective of others was a prerequisite for caring by connecting with others; in other words, Finnish teachers show caring by considering the viewpoint of the other person. However, this was not the case with the Iranian teachers; minding others' perceptions was not associated with caring. The result can be understood by taking into account the cultural differences between Finland and Iran: Finland is a country that supports individualistic values, whereas Iran advocates collectivist ones, and specifically values connected with the Iranian interpretation of Islam. Therefore, in Iran 'in many social conflicts "individual agency" and people with secular values are ignored, while the "collective structure" and individuals with a sacred orientation are acknowledged' (Gholami et al., 2015, p. 902). The study by Gholami et al. also showed that caring by connecting with others is the central element in teachers' ethical sensitivity and a culturally invariant aspect of ethical sensitivity. Nevertheless, the manifestation of caring in terms of taking the perspective of others is dependent on culture.

Ethical sensitivity also means identifying, perceiving, and responding to diversity in a pro-social way, and understanding how one's own and others' positions, prejudices, and preconceptions are affecting an interaction. An ethically sensitive person shows compassion in generating interpretations, as one comprehends that people might make the same mistake over and over again because of automatic responses. And finally identifying the consequences of actions and options refers to the visualisation of and consideration given to multiple alternative strategies for proceeding in a given situation.

2.2 *Growth Mindset for Learning*

Carol Dweck's (2000) theory of mindsets refers to the set of beliefs concerning whether intelligence, personality, and morality can be developed (a growth mindset) or cannot (a fixed mindset). In the everyday life of schools, teachers encounter various moral dilemmas, and their solutions to these reflect their values and beliefs. Also in the context of teaching and learning, mindset seems to play a crucial role in moral education (see Rissanen et al., 2018b) and could be one of the essential elements of teachers' moral competence.

Dweck's (2000) studies have consolidated the foundational role that mindsets play in learning. Mindsets influence one's perceptions of goals, efforts, mistakes, and morality. The goal of a person who has a fixed mindset is to 'look smart' and perform in a way that confirms a high level of intelligence. Efforts or mistakes are not valued. Instead, they are understood as signs of inability, which in turn leads to lying and to hiding failures and flaws. The attitudes of those who have a growth mindset are quite the opposite. The goal is to learn, to become smarter, which means that efforts and mistakes are understood as essential steps in learning. With a growth mindset a person does not have to hide mistakes or lie about them, as mistakes are seen as a natural part of the learning process. The idea is that everyone can learn; however, we should realise that people have different possibilities and conditions for learning.

Mindsets are developed in encounters with parents, teachers, and the surrounding society and culture. The most important factor in forming mindsets has been found to be feedback (Mueller & Dweck, 1998). Praise and criticism should be directed towards processes, such as learning strategies and effort. In addition, the use of the phrase 'not yet' in expressing criticism allows room for improvement and motivates a person to carry on (Ronkainen, 2018). The focus on process can be regarded as the core of growth mindset pedagogy (Rissanen et al., 2019). Person-orientated praise and criticism should be avoided, as this kind of feedback consolidates a fixed mindset, which in turn promotes helpless responses and makes students vulnerable in coping with challenges and mistakes (Kamins & Dweck, 1998; Mueller & Dweck, 1998). Dweck's studies have shown that even though mindsets are relatively stable, they can be changed over a long period of time and even primed for a shorter period. Therefore, it is important that teachers learn about Dweck's theory so that they recognise how mindsets are actualised in everyday life in their classrooms. Teachers also need to learn how to support the development of a growth mindset in their students.

Beside process focus, growth mindset interventions illustrate that another key factor in supporting growth mindset has been teaching students about neurogenesis and neuroplasticity (Blackwell, Trzesniewski, & Dweck, 2007;

Schmidt, Shumow, & Cam-Kakar, 2015). Images of 'brains as muscles' have been found to help students visualise what is happening in their brains when they practise and put effort into learning. Understanding how brains function enables students to understand why learning can be challenging, and in fact must be challenging, and why repetition is crucial. Studies also show that in order to keep up the results of interventions, teachers need to be engaged in constantly reminding students about growth mindset practices (Schmidt et al., 2015).

3.3 Purpose in Life

The notion of 'purpose' is the most profound phenomenon of human experience, as it provides reasons not only for acting ethically but also for living. Research has found powerful links between the pursuit of positive purpose and life satisfaction (Damon, 2008). In the view of Damon, purpose promotes pro-social behaviour, moral commitment, achievement, and high self-esteem. Purpose has a social orientation; therefore, individualism or a strong orientation to one's own life is not considered to be a purpose. Instead, purposelessness is associated with such matters as depression, addictions, deconstructive behaviour, and lack of productivity. In 2002 the British government was the first to officially identify a growing phenomenon: young people who were neither in school nor in training nor employed (NEET) (Damon, 2008), suggesting an increasing number of youngsters who lack purpose in their lives and struggle to find a meaningful life. Given these findings, we argue that the ability of teachers to foster students' sense of purpose could also be one of the key elements of teachers' moral competence.

The interest in studying purpose and the meaning of life in fields of psychology and educational sciences peaked for the first time in the 1960s. Still, it should be noted that these topics were being discussed long before that time in philosophy and theology. The interest in the 1960s was generated by Viktor Frankl's *Man's Search for Meaning*, first published in 1958. In this book Frankl describes his experiences as a Holocaust survivor and how, during his imprisonment, he observed that those who had a purpose and those who were able to find meaning in suffering were the ones who were able to cope with the horrible conditions. He found that high levels of belief systems can enable human beings to endure life's hardships and that, regardless of circumstances and environment, we have the mental freedom to choose our attitude.

Based on Frankl's work, Damon, Menon, and Bronk (2003) have constructed a theory that defines purpose as a stable, long-term goal to contribute to the world beyond the self and is also meaningful to the self (Damon, Menon, & Bronk, 2003; Damon, 2008). This multi-dimensional conceptualisation indicates that real purpose is a concrete goal. Purpose is something that can be

TEACHERS' MORAL COMPETENCE IN PEDAGOGICAL ENCOUNTERS   87

identified and aspired to. Secondly, purpose is not only a dream, but also something that one is engaged in realising and actualising by making plans and choosing activities with which to reach the goal. Thirdly, purpose is meaningful to oneself. Purpose is something that one is impassioned about and finds to be profoundly important. Fourthly, purpose not only benefits oneself, but also others. This 'other' focus provides a pro-social aspect to the definition formulated by Damon et al. (2003).

Within this framework it is said that everyone can find a purpose, and moreover, purpose can be taught and its development supported (Tirri & Kuusisto, 2016). Purpose can be taught in schools with methods that are both explicit and implicit. Explicit methods help students to process their desires, values, and aspirations intentionally and learn and reflect on inspiring life histories, such as Viktor Frankl's. By discussing purposes, teachers model adults who are able to deliberate on the future orientation of students and who hopefully have found their own purposes in life. Implicit methods mean that students' purpose development is supported through all kinds of teaching, regardless of the subject matter or content, by enlightening students and helping them to understand the personal and societal relevance of the studied content. For example, in science classes students may be asked to write a brief essay describing how the materials studied that week could be applied in their lives (Hulleman & Hrackiewicz, 2009).

3.4   Aims of the Module and Curriculum Guidelines
In this module our objective will be to equip future teachers with moral competence so that they know how to support their pupils' holistic growth to become active citizens engaged in intercultural communication. The module will draw on Finnish research-based teacher education, the goal of which is to educate autonomous professionals who are committed to promoting values of equality, individualism, tolerance, and democracy (Tirri, 2017). In Finland teaching has a strong moral dimension, and teachers are considered to be moral professionals (Tirri, 2014). Thus, in this module student teachers will learn to cultivate their moral competence by participating in various ideological, pedagogical, and intercultural negotiations. In the course of the module, student teachers will collaborate in international teams while they jointly produce a mini-study and prepare a teaching session which they will hold. By conducting, learning, and following scientific conventions in doing small-scale research projects, students develop their critical thinking skills and learn to apply and evaluate theoretical and practical perspectives in moral competence.

In this module student teachers will learn about moral professionalism in teaching and holistic school pedagogy (Tirri, 2011). They will learn to identify and solve moral dilemmas and conflicts in schools and cultivate their ethical sensitivity by communicating and comparing their views with student teachers from different European and non-European countries (Hanhimäki & Tirri, 2009; Hedayati, Kuusisto, Gholami, & Tirri, 2017a; Tirri, 1999). They will learn how implicit theories about intelligence affect teaching and learning, and they will practise feedback styles, which have been found to improve learning outcomes significantly and reduce stereotype threat (Aronson et al., 2002; Dweck, 2000; Rattan et al., 2012; Rissanen et al., 2018a, 2018b, 2019; Schmidt et al., 2015). They will also study how to support their pupils' purpose in life (Bundick & Tirri, 2014), given that today, a general lack of purpose is associated with the stress that people are experiencing and with apathy in the young (Damon, 2008).

The module builds on the principle of 'We teach what we research, and we research what we teach', which captures the ethos of research-based Finnish teacher education (Tirri, 2014). The module is designed so that students learn the theories that have been suggested as the core elements of teachers' moral competence by reflecting on and analysing their own perceptions. They learn to identify theoretical concepts in real-life contexts, and apply theories in collaborating and teaching in international and intercultural teams. For example, in 2017 the module had 25 international students representing 14 different countries. In the course of the module, the students constantly put into practice the theories they were studying. They also practised scientific thinking and knowledge construction. The module offers tools for analytical thinking and experience in using research methods. After completing the module, students will have:

- Knowledge of teachers' moral competence and students' holistic growth in a school context
- Skills to apply their learning to different practices in the teaching profession
- Skills in critical thinking and drawing conclusions
- Knowledge of the interactional relationship between theory and practice
- Understanding of peer-group support in teachers' work
- And, hopefully, an attitude that shows how important these skills are in themselves and a desire to use these skills to contribute to a democratic intercultural society.

4　Description of the Module

4.1　*Schedule, Instructions, and Evaluation*
The module 'Teachers' Moral Competence in Pedagogical Encounters' is designed to be taught during one month's time: two weeks are devoted to

intensive study and two weeks are used to finalise the course tasks (Table 5.1). The module consists of a commentary, a course diary, lectures, and group work on one of the module topics (Table 5.2). Each student will write a commentary and an individual course diary. The commentary is to be written during the first week of the module. Each student writes a commentary on an article related to one of the group's topics. The commentary is presented and discussed in the four groups, based on the topic in self-directed meetings. The aim is that all group members become familiar with the articles related to the topic of their group work.

In the course diaries, students reflect on the contents of the module in light of the research literature and from each of their own perspectives, while also explicating their personal learning process. In the diary students are expected to apply theoretical concepts, compare articles, and express their opinions, i.e. evaluate and use what they have heard and read during the module.

In the group work, students carry out a mini-study on one of the theoretical perspectives of teachers' moral competence. The data for the mini-studies are gathered during lectures. During guided group work, the students analyse and write their mini-study and also prepare power point slides, which are presented on the last day of the module in a mini-conference.

Based on the individual learning diaries and the groups' mini-studies, students are evaluated on a scale of 0 to 5 (0 = fail, 1=lowest grade, 5=highest grade). The evaluation criteria are given in Table 5.3. Students earn 5 ECTs in this module. In addition, they have the opportunity to write an optional essay (2.5 ECT) based on the following instructions:

> Choose one of the course topics which was not the topic of your mini-study (ethical sensitivity, moral dilemma, mindset, purpose). Read a minimum of three articles and make reference to these articles as you answer the following question: Why is [this theory/theoretical framework] important from the perspective of teachers' moral competence in pedagogical encounters? Write an essay 5–10 pages in length. Use APA style in references and in the list of references.

4.2 Examples of Students' Mini-Studies

In this section we present examples of mini-studies from a module that was arranged in November 2017 at the University of Helsinki, Finland. Participants included 25 students (Female n = 20, Male n = 5, Age M = 22.25, SD = 2.801) from 14 different countries. All students were studying educational sciences. The mini-studies addressed four topics: ethical sensitivity, moral dilemmas, mindsets about learning, and purpose in life. Each group was given a theory along

TABLE 5.1   Schedule of the module

Week	Day	Time	Content	Deadline for tasks to be uploaded to Moodle-platform
1	Monday	4x45 min	*Introduction* – Introduction to the course and to EDIC – Lecture: Finnish educational system and teacher education – Questionnaire: results will be presented at the mini-conference	
	Tuesday-Friday	4h per each day	*Commentary* – Students read articles and write their commentaries – Group meets to share all commentaries	Commentaries Friday at 6 pm
2	Monday	4x45 min	*Ethical Sensitivity* – Lecture: Ethical sensitivity – Lecture: Moral dilemmas in schools	Reflective tasks Monday at 6 pm
	Tuesday	4x45 min	*Mindset and Purpose* – Lecture: Mindsets in learning – Lecture: Purpose in life	Reflective tasks Tuesday at 6 pm
	Wednesday	4x45 min	*Data Analysis* – Lecture: Qualitative content analysis – Guided group work: Data analysis	
	Thursday	4x45 min	*Writing* – Guided group work: Writing the mini-study and preparing power point slides	
	Friday	4x45 min	*Mini-Conference* – Each group presents results of their mini-study, 15 min per presentation + 15 min discussion – Feedback and wrapping up the course	
3			*Time to finalise tasks*	
4			*Time to finalise tasks*	Learning diary, mini-study, slides, Friday at 6 pm

TEACHERS' MORAL COMPETENCE IN PEDAGOGICAL ENCOUNTERS 91

TABLE 5.2   Instructions for the course tasks

Commentary (individual and group tasks)
The commentary task is given on the first Monday. Students have one week to complete the task. Each student writes a commentary on an article related to one of the group's topics. Group topics: Moral dilemma, Ethical sensitivity, Mindset, Purpose. At the end of the first week each student presents the commentary to the group members.

Commentary and question: a question is open, an argument is closed. An argument demands reacting, which enhances interaction. It reveals gaps in your knowledge and skills. It leads to searching, justification and sharing information. It precedes finding the answer. It transfers the viewpoint from the present situation to the examination of new possibilities.

When you read, try to determine: What is the author's aim? What is his/her main idea? What does the author mean by the 'big picture' (of the article) or by a specific detail? What does the author argue for/ask about/criticise/summarise? How does the author justify his/her arguments?

After careful and thorough reading, write down at least two comments or questions about the article. Your aim is to have one of the comments or questions deal with the article's main idea and the other deal with a more specific point or detail in the article. Commentaries are thorough arguments; they consist of a short background to the topic followed by a question or comment. The length of the commentary is between 15 lines to half a page. Each participant shares their commentary in the group meeting and each article is discussed so that every member of the group has a good understanding of the message of every article.

Learning diary (individual task)
Write a learning diary at the end of each of the 6 days (max one page):
a. What did you learn today about teachers' moral competence in educational encounters?
b. What would you like to know/ask more about?
c. How is the knowledge you learned today related to your professional and personal life?

Mini-study (group task)
Title page (Title, authors' names)
1 Introduction (Why this study is important, theory, context, research question)
2 Data and methods
  2.1 Participants
  2.2 Data gathering
  2.3 Data analysis (Deductive or inductive content analysis)
3 Results
4 Discussion (What were the research questions? What were the answers? What do the results mean in light of the theory? What were the limitations of the study, future studies?)

(cont.)

TABLE 5.2   Instructions for the course tasks (*cont.*)

Upload to Moodle as one document in Doc, docx or pdf-format Font size 12, double-spaced Include your name, Student ID, Date APA style: references and list of references http://www.apastyle.org/	References Length: 5–10 pages, font size 12, double-spaced lines APA style: references and list of references http://www.apastyle.org/ Writing style 'This study investigates ...', 'The data were categorised by utilizing deductive content analysis ..."
Data gathering for the mini-studies (individual tasks) Data are gathered during lectures on Mondays and Tuesdays Reflective tasks related to each topic will constitute the research data. Students upload the texts to Moodle at the end of the day. Name will not be included to the data, but it is important so that each group does not analyse its own answers. In addition, at the end of the text write your gender, age, and nationality.	*Power point presentation (group task)* Based on the group's mini-study 5–10 slides including text, figures, tables, pictures 10–15 min/presentation During presentations, other groups make notes in their course diaries and create 1–3 questions related to each presentation.

TABLE 5.3   Evaluation criteria for the learning diary and the mini-study

Grade	Course diary and mini-study
5 excellent	– is in accordance with task specifications – in a coherent way shows personal thinking, reflection, analysis, and independent view on topics related to teachers' moral competence – connects theoretical knowledge (course literature and theories presented during lectures) with practical applications in an outstanding way – APA style is applied correctly in references and list of references

(*cont.*)

TABLE 5.2   Evaluation criteria for the learning diary and the mini-study (*cont.*)

4 very good	
3 good	– is in accordance with task specifications
	– shows personal thinking and reflection and independent view on topics related to teachers' moral competence without special merit
	– attempts to connect theoretical knowledge (course literature and theories presented during lectures) with practical applications
	– APA style is applied mostly correctly in references and list of references
2 satisfactory	
1 adequate	– follows the task specifications poorly
	– shows inadequate personal reflection and knowledge of topics related to teachers' moral competence
	– theoretical knowledge poorly connected with practical applications
	– APA style is applied mostly correctly in references and list of references
0 fail	– one or more of the components of the criteria do not meet the requirements

with articles for reference, a basic research question to be further modified, and data collected during the lectures. The data included answers from every student who participated in the course. However, the small groups did not analyse their own data, but rather analysed the students' answers from other groups. The aim was to teach and apply the rules of scientific research. The students were also taught to conduct qualitative content analysis deductively and inductively in line with Elo and Kyngäs's (2008) article. Table 5.4 shows the topics, research questions, theoretical articles, data-gathering instruments, analytical methods and questions for discussion used by the groups in November 2017. The next section presents the results of the students' mini-studies, tables introducing categories, frequencies of the sentences coded into each category, and examples from the data.

4.2.1   Results of the Ethical Sensitivity Group

The ethical sensitivity group found that 'Caring by connecting to others' appeared in most of the stories ($n = 18$), while the other dimensions occurred fewer than 5 times (Table 5.5). Ethical sensitivity was shown with 'oral support', which was mentioned 11 times, with 'Practical support' found 16 times,

TABLE 5.4　Topics of the mini-studies, research questions, related articles, instruments, data analysis, and discussion

Topic for the group	Research question(s)	Articles presenting theory	Data-gathering instrument	Data analysis following Elo and Kyngäs's (2008) instructions	Discussion
Ethical sensitivity	How is ethical sensitivity actualized in schools?	– Bebeau, Rest, & Narvaez, 1999 – Narvaez & Endicott, 2007 – Gholami, Kuusisto, & Tirri, 2015.	Write a short story about a situation in which a teacher was caring for students. (designed for this module).	– Deductive content analysis: Detecting Narvaez's (Narvaez & Endicott, 2007) seven dimensions in the stories. – Inductive content analysis: The group created three new categories related to how ethical sensitivity was shown by the teacher: Oral support, Practical support, Emotional support.	How can your topic and results contribute to a more democratic and intercultural society?

(*cont.*)

TABLE 5.4   Topics of the mini-studies, research questions, related articles, instruments, data analysis, and discussion (*cont.*)

Topic for the group	Research question(s)	Articles presenting theory	Data-gathering instrument	Data analysis following Elo and Kyngäs's (2008) instructions	Discussion
Moral dilemma	What kinds of moral dilemmas did student teachers experience in a school context?	– Tirri, 1999, 2003 – Hedayati, Kuusisto, Gholami, & Tirri, 2017a, 2019.	Write the most challenging moral dilemma you have ever experienced in a school context by answering the following questions: What was the moral dilemma you experienced? Where and when did this happen? Who were the other people involved? How did you resolve the dilemma? (Tirri, 1999).	Deductive content analysis by utilizing Tirri's categories: – categories for teachers' moral dilemma (Tirri, 1999) – categories for students' moral dilemmas (Tirri, 2003).	How can your topic and results contribute to a more democratic and intercultural society?

(*cont.*)

TABLE 5.4   Topics of the mini-studies, research questions, related articles, instruments, data analysis, and discussion *(cont.)*

Topic for the group	Research question(s)	Articles presenting theory	Data-gathering instrument	Data analysis following Elo and Kyngäs's (2008) instructions	Discussion
Mindset	How do student teachers' expressions reflect growth and a fixed mindset?	– Kuusisto, Laine, & Tirri, 2017 – Laine, Kuusisto, & Tirri, 2016 – Mueller & Dweck, 1998 – Rissanen, Kuusisto, Hanhimäki, & Tirri, 2018a, 2018b – Rissanen, Kuusisto, Tuominen, & Tirri, 2019.	Data were gathered after a mindset-lecture in order for students to practice growth-mindset messages: Imagine a pupil from an impoverished community who is struggling with his studies. Write a letter to this pupil and give encouragement and convince her/him of the expandable nature of intelligence. (Aronson, Fried, & Good, 2002) Another option would be that data are also gathered *before* the mindset lecture: Imagine a pupil from an impoverished community who is struggling with his studies. Write a letter to this pupil and give encouragement.	Deductive content analysis by using Dweck's (2000; as cited in Rissanen et al., 2018a) categories of growth and fixed mindset. Statements that did not indicate either the growth or the fixed mindset were coded as "mixed mindset" (Laine et al., 2017).	How can your topic and results contribute to a more democratic and intercultural society?

(cont.)

TABLE 5.4   Topics of the mini-studies, research questions, related articles, instruments, data analysis, and discussion (*cont.*)

Topic for the group	Research question(s)	Articles presenting theory	Data-gathering instrument	Data analysis following Elo and Kyngäs's (2008) instructions	Discussion
Purpose	– What are the purposes of student teachers' lives? – Do the students justify their goals by focusing on themselves or also on others?	– Damon, Menon, & Bronk, 2003 – Hedayti, Kuusisto, Gholami, & Tirri, 2017b – Manninen, Kuusisto, & Tirri, 2018 – Roberts & Robins, 2000.	– What do you think is your life purpose, or the closest thing you have to a life purpose? – Why do you want to accomplish this life purpose? (Magen, 1998).	Contents of the purposes were analysed deductively by utilizing Robert and Robins's (2000, Hedayati et al., 2017b; Manninen et al., 2018) categories and inductively by creating subcategories based on the data.	How can your topic and results contribute to a more democratic and intercultural society?

TABLE 5.5   Ethical sensitivity group: Dimensions of ethical sensitivity

Dimensions of ethical sensitivity	F	Examples from the data
Reading and expressing emotions	3	– The teacher saw that she was crying.
Taking the perspective of others	2	– My teacher arranged rides to visit our sick colleague so he is not so bored.
Caring by connecting with others	18	– She took time to talk to this friend who was very upset.
Working with interpersonal and group differences	1	– The teacher invited us to her home to prepare the presentation.
Generating interpretations and options	5	– That's when the teacher introduced me to a programme in our school for only the best students.
Identifying consequences of actions and options	1	– The teacher also negotiated with the other school teachers so that when the student returns to school the teachers don't put too much pressure on her [...].
Preventing social bias	0	

whereas 'Emotional support' appeared only 3 times (Table 5.6). The group also combined their analyses on ethical sensitivity and teachers' support and found that caring was shown both orally and practically (Figure 5.1). Emotional support appeared only when a student was reading and/or expressing emotions.

4.2.2   Results of the Moral Dilemma Group

The moral dilemmas identified by the students were written from the perspective of teachers and students (Table 5.7). Teachers' dilemmas ($n = 8$) were related to the teachers' work, the students' work, and general school rules. Students' dilemmas ($n = 13$) were related to teacher behaviour, peer relations, general school rules, and harassment.

4.2.3   Results of the Mindset Group

In all, the group found 61 growth-mindset statements, 7 fixed-mindset statements, and 6 mixed-mindset statements in letters to an impoverished pupil. The results indicate that most of the students showed that they had understood the idea of a growth mindset and were able to use it in their letters. The results might have been different had the letters been written before the lesson

TABLE 5.6 Ethical sensitivity group: Teachers' ways of showing support

Ways of showing support	F	Examples from the data
Oral support	11	– Every week the teacher would ask if I was ok and how my mum was doing.
Practical support	16	– The teacher heard [that the student's father could not participate] and decided to accompany the student to the [school] ceremony as her "father" or representing one of her family members.
Emotional support	3	– The teacher always noticed when we had a problem between us or at home.

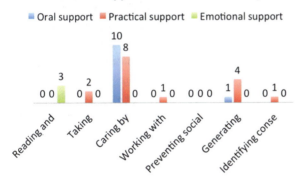

FIGURE 5.1 Teachers' support in ethical sensitivity

on mindsets. Categories, sub-categories, and examples from the data are presented in Table 5.8.

4.2.4 Results of the Purpose Group

The purpose group found a total of 36 different life goals which students desired to achieve (Table 5.9). The first main category was called 'Meaningful for the self', which included two subcategories: 'Family and relationships', referred to as *family and stable relationships* and *self-acceptance*, and 'Economic and hedonistic', which meant that students pursued a *successful and secure job*, a *good place to live* and *happiness*.

TABLE 5.7   Moral dilemma group: Teachers' and students' perceptions of moral dilemmas in schools

Main categories	Subcategories	F	F	Examples from the data
Teachers' moral dilemmas			8	
	Teachers' work	5		– I could be creating a conflict that could ruin the positive teaching environment [...] and the consequences [...] were not necessary as he didn't usually behave like that.
	Morality of the students	2		– Last semester when I did my internship in a secondary school [...] there was a little girl who usually got really good marks [...] who came to me and told me that she could not study the day before [...] after a while I saw her cheating looking at her neighbour's paper. I decided not to say anything.
	General school rules	1		– Sexual relations were forbidden in the summer programme. We found signals of sexual relations in one of the rooms, but we did not have evidence of who was involved. We reported the issue to the head of the company [sponsoring the summer school] and informed the families.
Students' moral dilemmas			13	
	Teacher behaviour	2		– Consequently, we were punished severely but we could win the games.
	Peer relations	6		– The dilemma was whether to turn my friend in to be the only one punished for that action.

(*cont.*)

TEACHERS' MORAL COMPETENCE IN PEDAGOGICAL ENCOUNTERS 101

TABLE 5.7 Moral dilemma group: Teachers' and students' perceptions of moral dilemmas in schools (*cont.*)

Main categories	Subcategories	F	F	Examples from the data
	General school rules	3		– The father of one of my friends had been sick the day before the exam and she did not have time to study. I know she is a good student, and it was not about being lazy. I did not know whether to tell him the answers or not.
	Harassment	2		– One of my friends was being bullied. I was in 8th grade and I did not know if I should tell the teacher or not. '[...] I was picked on a little bit [by the bullies], about my background because I was half Chinese and half Japanese [...] I was told if I wanted to join their group, I had to stop saying that. And I did'.

The second main category was 'Beyond the self'. Students aspired to 'Act in public life', meaning that the students wanted to *contribute to the well-being of society* by *teaching* and *become (good) teachers.* They also desired to be 'social' by *helping others* and *connecting with people from different cultures.* The third main category was called 'No sense of purpose', indicating that students did not acknowledge a purpose or did not want to express their deep-seated aspirations.

5 Process and Conclusions

This chapter presented the EDIC (Education for Democratic Intercultural Citizenship) module called 'Teachers' moral competence in pedagogical encounters', which was intended to provide student teachers with theoretical and practical tools with which to foster democratic and intercultural citizenship in their future pupils. This chapter presented the idea that ethical sensitivity, a growth mindset about learning, and purpose in life are possible core elements

TABLE 5.8 Mindset group: Categories, subcategories, and examples from the data

Main category	Sub-category	F	Examples from the data
Growth mindset f=61	Perseverance and learning as a process	14	– Don't be afraid to make mistakes.
	Learning as a goal	4	– The process of trying to learn is far more important than the product of your learning.
	Context-based interpretation of behaviour	2	– You are struggling with learning now, but it is important to remember that everyone has times when they feel like this.
	Encouragement and safe learning environment	24	– Ask me for help.
Fixed mindset f=7	Performance goals	3	– Your parents and I know that it's so important that you achieve good results on exams.
	Fixed personal traits	4	– You are a very smart boy.
Mixed mindset f=6			– Failure is something that doesn't exist. – Nobody knows everything.

of teachers' moral competence, aspects that teachers need in order to carry out the ethical responsibilities of their profession.

The module's pedagogical idea was to teach the above core elements by combining lectures, personal reflections, and group work. The goal was for students to learn to apply theories in intercultural real-world contexts and learn to identify, acknowledge, and apply the theoretical issues on both personal and professional levels. The idea was also to teach students collaborative skills and make sure they understood components of the research process and how scientific knowledge is constructed.

Student teachers who participated in the module at the University of Helsinki in the autumn of 2017 felt that the topics and the course were educative. It provided important tools and practices for their future work as teachers. Theories, practical applications, and self-reflection were seen as important for the learning process. The course was an intensive one. The students' main

TEACHERS' MORAL COMPETENCE IN PEDAGOGICAL ENCOUNTERS   103

TABLE 5.9   Purpose group: Categories, subcategories, and examples from the data

Categories			f	Examples from the data
Meaningful for the self f= 17	Family and relationship	Family	5	– I want to have a family.
		Self-acceptance	1	– I'm trying to achieve self acceptance.
	Economic and hedonistic	Successful and secure job	2	– I want to have a safe job.
		Good place to live	1	– I want to have a good place to live.
		Happiness	8	– I want to be happy.
Beyond the self f = 17	Active in public life	Contribute to the well-being of society by teaching	7	– [I want to] be remembered as a positive contributor within society".
		Becoming a (good) teacher	3	– I want to be a good teacher and share this described ability with them.
	Social	Help others	5	– [I want to]reach a point where I'm also able to help others with their own growth and well-being.
		Connecting with people from different cultures	2	– By travelling, you learn a lot about prejudice and stereotypes as well as different world views.
No purpose f = 2				– I would not say that right now I have a life purpose.

criticism was that the schedule was too tight. For this reason, the module was modified to last for one month, as presented in this chapter. The module now includes more time for students to process the research literature and finalise their learning diary and group tasks. The course could be developed further by including school visits or excursions to non-governmental organizations that promote the human rights of students in school. During the first week of the module, participating students could also interview teachers and thereby learn more about the real-world aspects of intercultural realities in schools today as well as how teachers' moral competence and society's moral and democratic values are constructed and challenged in classrooms.

Teaching ethical professionals how to promote democratic and intercultural education in schools is the main task of Finnish teacher education (Tirri, 2014). Teachers are expected to become holistic educators who help students become good democratic citizens and active agents who can encounter diversities in their society in a constructive manner. For this task teachers need moral competence, or in other words, ethical sensitivity, a growth mindset about learning, and purpose in life.

References

Aronson, J., Fried, C. B., & Good, C. (2002). Reducing the effects of stereotype threat on African American College Students by shaping theories of intelligence. *Journal of Experimental Social Psychology, 38*, 113–25.

Bebeau, M., Rest, J., & Narvaez, D. (1999). Beyond the promise: A perspective on research in moral education. *Educational Researcher, 28*(4), 18–26.

Blackwell, L. S., Trzesniewski, K. H., & Dweck, C. S. (2007). Implicit theories of intelligence predict achievement across an adolescent transition: A longitudinal study and an intervention. *Child Development, 78*(1), 246–263.

Bundick, M., & Tirri, K. (2014). Teacher support and competencies for fostering youth purpose and psychological well-being: Perspectives from two countries. *Applied Developmental Science, 18*, 148–162.

Damon, W. (2008). *The path to purpose.* New York, NY: Free Press.

Damon, W., Menon, J., & Bronk, K. C. (2003). The development of purpose during adolescence. *Applied Developmental Science, 7*(3), 119–128.

Dweck, C. S. (2000). *Self-theories. Their role in motivation, personality, and development.* New York, NY & London: Psychology Press, Taylor & Francis Group.

Dweck, C. S. (2006). *Mindset: The new psychology of success.* New York, NY: Ballantine Books.

Elo, S., & Kyngäs, H. (2008). The qualitative content analysis process. *Journal of Advanced Nursing, 62*, 107–115.

Finnish National Board of Education. (2014). *National core curriculum for basic education.* Helsinki: Finnish National Board of Education.

Frankl, V. E. (1988). *Man's search for meaning.* New York, NY: Pocket Books.

Gholami, K., Kuusisto, E., & Tirri, K. (2015). Is ethical sensitivity in teaching culturally bound? Comparing Finnish and Iranian teachers' ethical sensitivity. *Compare: A Journal of Comparative and International Education, 45*, 886–907.

Gunderson, E. A., Gripshover, S. J., Romero, C., Dweck, C. S., Goldin-Meadow, S., & Levine, S. C. (2013). Parent praise to 1–3-year-olds predicts children's motivational frameworks 5 years later. *Child Development, 84*, 1526–1541.

Hanhimäki, E., & Tirri, K. (2009). Education for ethically sensitive teaching in critical incidents at school. *Journal of Education for Teaching, 35*, 107–121.

Hedayati, N., Kuusisto, E., Gholami, K., & Tirri, K. (2017a). Gender-specific religious moral dilemmas in Iranian schools. In R. Elmesky, C. Yeakey, & O. Marcucci (Eds.), *The power of resistance: Culture, ideology and social reproduction in global contexts* (pp. 365–381). London: Emerald Group Publishing Limited.

Hedayati, N., Kuusisto, E., Gholami, K., & Tirri, K. (2017b). Life purposes of Iranian secondary school students. *Journal of Moral Education, 46*(3), 283–294.

Hedayati, N., Kuusisto, E., Gholami, K., & Tirri, K. (2019). Moral conflicts in Iranian secondary schools. *Journal of Beliefs & Values*. doi:10.1080/13617672.2019.1618151

Kamins, M., & Dweck, C. S. (1999). Person vs. process praise and criticism: Implications for contingent self-worth and coping. *Developmental Psychology, 35*, 835–847.

Kuusisto, E., Laine, S., & Tirri, K. (2017). How do school children and adolescents perceive the nature of talent development? A case study from Finland. *Education Research International, 2017*. doi:10.1155/2017/4162957

Kuusisto, E., & Tirri, K. (2013). Kasvun ajattelutapa opettajilla ja vanhemmilla: Tapaustutkimus suomalaisista kouluista [Growth mindset of teachers and parents: A case study of Finnish schools]. In *Uusi oppiminen* [New learning]. Publication of The Committee for the Future. The Parliament of Finland.

Kuusisto, E., Tirri, K., & Rissanen, I. (2012). Finnish teachers' ethical sensitivity. *Education Research International, 2012*. doi:10.1155/2012/351879

Laine, S., Kuusisto, E., & Tirri, K. (2016). Finnish teachers' conceptions of giftedness. *Journal for the Education of the Gifted, 39*, 151–167.

Magen, Z. (1998). *Exploring adolescent happiness: Commitment, purpose, and fulfilment.* Thousand Oaks, CA: Sage Publications.

Manninen, N., Kuusisto, E., & Tirri, K. (2018). Life goals of Finnish social services students. *Journal of Moral Education, 47*, 175–185.

Mueller, C. M., & Dweck, C. S. (1998). Praise for intelligence can undermine children's motivation and performance. *Journal of Personality and Social Psychology, 75*, 33–52.

Narvaez, D., & Endicott, L. G. (2007). *Ethical sensitivity, nurturing character in the classroom.* Notre Dame: Alliance for Catholic Education Press.

Rattan, A., Good, C., & Dweck, C. S. (2012). "It's ok – Not everyone can be good at math": Instructions with an entity theory comfort (and demotivate) students. *Journal of Experimental Social Psychology, 48*, 731–737.

Rissanen, I., Kuusisto, E., Hanhimäki, E., & Tirri, K. (2018a). Teachers' implicit meaning systems and their implications for pedagogical thinking and practice: A case study from Finland. *Scandinavian Journal of Educational Research, 62*, 487–500.

Rissanen, I., Kuusisto, E., Hanhimäki, E., & Tirri, K. (2018b). The implications of teachers' implicit theories for moral education: A case study from Finland. *Journal of Moral Education, 47*, 63–77.

Rissanen, I., Kuusisto, E., Tuominen, M., & Tirri, K. (2019). In search of a growth mindset pedagogy: A case study of one teacher's classroom practices in a Finnish elementary school. *Teaching and Teacher Education, 77*, 204–213.

Roberts, B. W., & Robins, R. W. (2000). Broad dispositions, broad aspirations: The intersection of personality traits and major life purposes. *Personality and Social Psychology Bulletin, 26*, 1284–1296.

Ronkainen, R. (2018). *Kasvun ajattelutavan ilmeneminen opetuksen toteutuksessa ja reflektoinnissa* [Growth mindset in teaching and reflection] (Unpublished master's thesis). University of Helsinki, Helsinki, Finland.

Schmidt, J. A., Shumow, L., & Kackar-Cam, H. (2013). Exploring teacher effects for mindset intervention outcomes in seventh-grade science classes. *Middle Grades Research Journal, 10*, 17–32.

Tirri, K. (1999). Teachers' perceptions of moral dilemmas at school. *Journal of Moral Education, 28*, 31–47.

Tirri, K. (2003). The moral concerns and orientations of sixth- and ninth grade students. *Educational Research and Evaluation, 9*, 93–108.

Tirri, K. (2011). Holistic school pedagogy and values: Finnish teachers' and students' perspectives. *International Journal of Educational Research, 50*, 159–165.

Tirri, K. (2014). The last 40 years in Finnish teacher education. *Journal of Education for Teaching, 40*, 1–10.

Tirri, K. (2017). Finland – Promoting ethics and equality. In W. Veugelers, I. de Groot, & V. Stolk (Eds.), *Research for CULT committee – Teaching common values in Europe* (pp. 83–90). Brussels: European Parliament, Policy Department for Structural and Cohesion Policies.

Tirri, K., & Nokelainen, P. (2007). Comparison of academically average and gifted students' self-rated ethical sensitivity. *Educational Research and Evaluation, 13*, 587–601.

Tirri, K., & Ubani, M. (2013). Education of Finnish student teachers for purposeful teaching. *Journal of Education for Teaching, 39*, 21–29.

Veugelers, W., De Groot, I., & Stolk, V. (2017). *Research for Cult Committee – Teaching common values in Europe.* Brussels: European Parliament, Policy Department for Structural and Cohesion Policy. Retrieved from http://bit.ly/2pm5Yh9

CHAPTER 6

Educational Activities in Civil Society

Dana Moree and Terezie Vávrová

1 Introduction

According to annual studies conducted by the Czech NGO People in Need many Czech high schools' students are not interested in public issues and don't want to engage in their future civic life (JSNŠ, 2017). In addition, most students don't feel equipped with any kind of civic skills, neither they believe they can change anything in the society of which they live. Such disbelief and low self-efficacy (Bandura, 1997) proves that the Czech educational system doesn't offer enough opportunities to learn civic skills and train those in a safe space of school.

Even though citizenship education is a separate subject prescribed by the Czech National Curriculum, this subject and the way it is actually taught and doesn't meet current educational demands of its students and society in general. The formal approaches are still quite common or rather of a classical standard. The slackening results of Czech students in national and international studies (ICCS, 2009; JSNŠ, 2017) have shown that the current practice is not enough to produce the desired outcomes. Citizenship education despite its importance has a rather low status in Czech schools. Compared to the natural sciences, learning civic skills is perceived as less worthy by students. Also apparently, teachers in the Czech Republic fail to mediate the importance of citizenship education for the world and society outside of school as the *Teaching Common Values* study showed (Veugelers, De Groot, & Stolk, 2017).

A big contribution to overcoming this educational challenge is the civil society. Many teachers value the fruitful cooperation with NGOs which represent a popular source for new approaches and activities offered to schools for free. These NGOs manage to choose methods related to real-life situations that played out in the school, community or the wider world. Linking subject matter with real life can create greater interest and motivation amongst students to engage in discussions about these specific issues. So NGOs arrange mock elections and discussions with witnesses of certain period (e.g. holocaust survivors), offer ready-to-use tools, such as, short documentary films, or adopt international know-how to the Czech context (e.g. in storytelling, philosophy for children, or Theatre of the Oppressed).

© KONINKLIJKE BRILL NV, LEIDEN, 2019 | DOI: 10.1163/9789004411944_006
This is an open access chapter distributed under the terms of the CC-BY-NC 4.0 License.

In the following, we explain the theoretical and empirical background of the module and the programme of the module itself. First however, we briefly introduce the Czech education system, and the impact of existing policies on the ability of academic staff and students to advance citizenship education in the country. We link this to the needs of university education and how the Theatre of the Oppressed approach can respond to those needs. Finally, we describe the Czech EDIC module, its development, current schedule and perception of students.

2 Czech Education System and Becoming a Young Citizen

The development of the educational system in the Czech Republic mostly followed as a consequence of the reaction to political changes in 1989. After this breaking point, we see increasing openness in Czech society, but also a certain amount of inertia. For example, the school act from 1984 was valid up until 2004, when the first significant change took place. The main feature of the education system during communism was that all its parts were subordinated towards political goals. First, the state had control over the types of schools (Kozakiewicz, 1992). It was impossible to found a private or church-led school because the state was the only authority which could take this legal step. Consequently, the state had strong control over the content of education, including textbooks and teachers (Tomusk, 2001). Moreover, students of the pedagogical faculties were very carefully chosen based on their "personal background" and loyalty towards the regime.

After 1989, the main change came with the educational reform in 2004 that brought significant changes through several levels of the system. The educational system was decentralised, and it began to propose broader educational contents (rather than exactly prescribing specific topics for each class) and introduced the idea of key competences. The schools themselves were given increasing freedom but also responsibility for preparing the so-called School Educational Programme based on national guidelines. Its implementation process, however, was insufficiently funded and teachers' salaries still remain very low today.

On the curriculum level, the reform brought two essential changes compared to the previous school system. First, the results of the teaching and learning process are no longer assessed only by the amount of cognitive information gained by students (which was very much the case in previous curricular documents), but also by the broader competences developed. The curriculum for attaining these competences is divided into two levels. Level one covers educational areas (e.g. language and communication, mathematics and its application, the human being and society), while level two covers the so-called cross-curricular educational topics, implying social skills education, awareness of the European and global context, multicultural education, environmental education and media education (Research Institute of Education in Prague, 2007). Cross-curricular topics penetrate all subjects and areas. This is what is known as the 'infusion model' (Anderson, MacPhee, & Govan, 2000).

The vast majority of primary schools and high schools in Czech Republic are state institutions, although quite a big number of private and church-led schools have been established since 1989. While the 9 years of primary schooling are compulsory, the secondary level of education is voluntary. The main types/tracks of secondary education are grammar schools, and pre-vocational schools or 'expert schools', oriented towards trade, agriculture, etc. Decentralisation of the educational system in 2004 thus brought more freedom to schools and teachers, but at the same time also plenty of confusion and practical problems maintaining schools 'above the standard level'. Citizenship was amongst the areas most affected by these issues.

The Czech schooling tradition emphasises teaching citizenship as a separate compulsory subject (more in Veugelers, de Groot, & Stolk, 2017). Next to it, schools can use the opportunity to implement citizenship issues in all subjects as cross-curricular topics. However, more precise criteria for evaluating and assessing these learning outcomes are still missing. The state has not shown interest in creating criteria and collecting data on the effectiveness of citizenship education in Czech schools, only participating in the ICCS study in 2009. Since than it remains to the civil society to find out about the current state of citizenship in Czech schools and the results are alarming.

Recent studies indicate that schools have significant problems educating and training young citizens (JSNŠ, 2017; ICCS, 2009). Why so? Teachers typically manage to pass on knowledge, but don't know how to deal with values and skills. Also to teach those two areas can't be evaluated easily and needs more time. So, the productive step is to cooperate with NGOs which have specific educational know-how and offer students experience-based, skill-oriented learning.

Therefore, the cooperation of NGOs and schools in educating and training young citizens is the main topic of the presented module that aims to provide students with in-depth insight into the work of NGO's, by visiting and analysing concrete projects in light of relevant literature. This aim is attained via two approaches. First, experts from NGOs will be invited into the EDIC course and students will be able to observe and experience some concrete activities of NGOs during field trips. Second, a significant part of the course will be based on theatre of the oppressed methodology, where students will work together with "people outside of university" – NGO workers and their clients in our case. With the module, the students will take away not only a deeper knowledge about NGOs – what kind of citizens those intend to educate in schools and how they do this – but they will also experience the direct outreach to the community.

2.1 Theoretical Background

The above mentioned situation is especially relevant for primary and secondary schools. However, universities deal with their own issues. Universities and high schools face new situation given by reform articulated in Act 137/2016 in the Czech Republic. One of the results of this reform is that the universities would be divided into those, which are more practically oriented and those, which are more academically oriented.

Universities perceived, as so called academic oriented, produce rather practically oriented graduates, e.g. disciplines like pedagogy, social work, special pedagogy and others. At the same, time we can see these universities face an increasing tendency to be reduced to producers of high achieving academic publications, where international competition is seen as more and more important than anything else. Academic achievement is highly followed and rated in the university, pedagogical interaction with students, teaching and learning culture, school culture and other soft aspects of education are rated insufficiently or not at all. This manifests a dilemma for the teaching staff as they are pushed to focus on academic achievement.

When we look at the same issue from the perspective of students, we can see their pressing needs. Those university students are prepared, amongst others, to also work with a wide range of disadvantaged children and adults. E.g. Charles University provides possibilities to study pedagogy, special pedagogy, social work, psychology or civil society, which are disciplines that go hand in hand with social justice, equality and inequality in the society. Skills necessary for working in these professions are not only transmitted by studying theory, but by also working with people directly, by analyzing issues related to social injustice, intercultural issues, democratic citizenship and others. When we look at the composition of students in university environment, we can see that universities world-wide often reproduce power differences in societies (Mann, 2008). Students with different social or ethnic background are still underrepresented (Ghofa, 2017; Mann, 2008). This is also the case in the Czech Republic where minority students are underrepresented and the majority of university students have very limited experiences with minority groups.

EDUCATIONAL ACTIVITIES IN CIVIL SOCIETY

This situation has several consequences. Students in Pedagogy and social work, who will typically work with a disadvantaged population after graduation, have limited possibilities to engage with such people in their daily lives. This is given by students' community composition. The same students study at least at part of universities theoretically oriented disciplines, which do not provide sufficient practical training or other kind of activities, which would help to address this lack of experience. Moreover, students come to a situation, where they are perceived as passive absorbers of curricula, which are given by difficult system of accreditations (Mann, 2008). And they do not experience many possibilities to change their own educational environment and the means in which they learn.

We know how the learning process should look if we want to prepare professionals who are not only experts equipped with theoretical knowledge but also skilled people able to reflect, make decisions and react properly in difficult situations. Scholars like Dewey (1938), Freire (1974), Oser and Veugelers (2008), and others brought enough evidence regarding the necessity to create nurturing learning environment, as well, as ideas how to develop such environment. We can see that many scholars around the world try to react to this situation, to bring and test new methods, which would help to cross this gap between the privileged and competitive university world and parts of the society with a higher amount of disadvantaged population.

Theatre of the Oppressed is perceived as one of the methods, which might serve to these goals (Christensen, 2014; Desai, 2017; Giesler, 2017; Stahl, 2018). Charles University of Prague started to implement this method several years ago. Experiences have so far indicated that Theatre of the Oppressed (TotO) is a valuable source for fostering intercultural competences in students, it was included into the module for EDIC. In the next section, we introduce the method: we first explain the path which led our university to use TotO as one of the teaching methods, and introduce TotO with practical and ethical issues that need to be taken into account. We then discuss some advantages and limits regarding TotO implementation at the universities, and its potential for research. Then, we will describe more concretely how Theatre of the Oppressed is implemented in Charles University of Prague.

2.2   *Path to the Theatre of the Oppressed*
Theatre of the Oppressed has been inherently linked to university environment for about ten years in the Czech Republic. The so-called Cabinet for Theatre of the Oppressed [Kabinet divadla utlačovaných] was founded at Masaryk University in Brno. It took however several years for the method to spread across Czech Republic. The Department of Civil Society at Faculty of Humanities,

Charles University began promoting the method in 2014 when the *Training for Trainers* was organized in cooperation with British Council. This event put the faculty in an 'expert role' for the Theatre of the Oppressed method.

When new topics, e. g. multicultural education, citizenship education and environmental education were introduced as a part of the school reform of 2004, teachers were not prepared for this, due to these disciplines being quite new in the Czech context (Moree, 2008) while concurrently embodying a sense of resistance. Teaching, which would be oriented towards changes of attitudes, reminded teachers too much of the ideological utilization of the education system prior to 1989 (Moree, 2013).

Faculty of Humanities tried to support school reform utilizing several activities. One activity being the development of Czech Kid, a teaching tool for multicultural education based on stories of children. (www.czechkid.cz). This tool offers an introduction to more than 60 topics linked to multicultural education, more than 400 pages of theoretical material written in a way which is acceptable for teachers and roughly 60 suggestions for concrete teaching lessons. Czech Kid was introduced in 2007 as a low-threshold internet tool that can be used by teachers without formal training.

Next to these supportive materials, it was clear that working with concrete groups would encourage people to discuss topics which are taboo in society, such as, discrimination, racism or sexual abuse. Theatre of the Oppressed was introduced through training led by Terry O'Learry of Cardboard Citizens in London, since noone in Czech Republic was qualified train the trainers in this method. Twenty participants were trained, opening the door to also implement the method at the university.

2.3 Theatre of the Oppressed at Universities

Theatre of the Oppressed is a method to start a dialogue about possible social change. It was created by Augusto Boal in Brazil almost fifty years ago and spread all over the world. Its main aim was to provoke societal change and empower the disadvantaged (Conrad, 2004; Christensen, 2014; Saeed, 2015; Desai, 2017; Giesler, 2017; Stahl, 2018). As such, the method is inherently linked to critical pedagogical approaches. Practically, it works as follows:

A group of people having an experience of un-just, troubles, difficulties or oppression work together utilizing a wide range of methods promoting the ability to re-call their experiences, to express them through their body and incarnate previous experiences into a new story, which is translated into theatrical language. This specific methodology is described by Augusto Boal and his followers in many books (Boal, 1979, 1992).

EDUCATIONAL ACTIVITIES IN CIVIL SOCIETY

When the theatre piece is ready, it is performed in front of the audience, which is not allowed to be a passive absorber of the given story. The audience is asked to change it. Audience members are invited the stage to solve the protagonist's issue. This stage of group work is called 'forum theatre'.

TotO was originally targeted to work with disadvantaged groups in slums, prisons, ghettos etc. (Boal 1979, 1992), thought Augusto Boal later adapted this methodology to work with more fortunate people, who do not experience external oppression (like being beaten on the street), but who experience internal oppression derived from possible societal, family or institutional pressure. Shortly thereafter, he developed methods to cope with any form social pressure. This method was called Rainbow of Desire and is perceived as therapeutic method (Boal, 1995).

Theatre of the Oppressed is implemented in different countries by a wide range of institutions and for various target groups. In some countries, there are NGOs working for a long time with one target group by means of this method (e.g. Cardboard Citizens in the UK has worked for more than 25 years with homeless people or Kurunga center in Berlin working with gender issues). There are centers of Theatre of the Oppressed in many countries in the world with NGOs or independent groups of trainers using TotO only as one of their daily activities.

By implementing TotO, the teaching staff may help students bridge the gap between theory and practice, and between privileged students and underprivileged members of society. However, TotO come with ethical and practical issues. As we mentioned above, the university environment is in fact a privileged environment. It does not mean that students cannot experience oppression. The opposite is true – we know e.g. that a significant volume of students experience some kind of sexual harassment (Christensen, 2014). Do note, this form of oppression is different than oppression seen in disadvantaged societal areas.

Moreover, university environment is hierarchical. Teachers are owners of credits, set the conditions of classes, and there is not much space for negotiation with the students. Methods like Theatre of the Oppressed requires the opposite – an abundance of safe space for negotiation and a nurturing environment (Stahl, 2018), which might be contradictory to requirements of university studies.

Sensitive issue can be treated carefully when they emerge by asking several questions: who is going to participate, how is the participation defined and what is the result of the Theatre of the Oppressed implementation. We can look at these questions step by step:

- Who is going to participate – in many of published studies, only university students became participants of the Theatre of the Oppressed groups (Desai, 2017; Stahl, 2018), which definitely has many advantages – students know each other and it is easier to create a safe space in well-known environment. However, at the same time, disadvantaged groups are still underrepresented.
- How is participation defined – if the Theatre of the Oppressed is offered as a course, students have to fulfill the prescribed requirements (e. g. participation) of the course. The ethical issue is how to react in situation when the topic is too sensitive (Stahl, 2018) and when working on these sensitive issues can harm the students.
- What is the result of implementing the Theatre of the Oppressed – the original method leads to public performance, which is called forum theatre. Audiences can visit the performance and react, try to change the destiny of the main protagonist and provoke social change. Is participation in a performance an obligatory part of Theatre of the Oppressed group at the university?

Being aware of these questions, we started to implement Theatre of the Oppressed at Charles university since 2015 (Moree, Vavrova & Felcmanová, 2017). A group of university students work together with clients or members of some NGO or any other disadvantaged group (like minority groups, people with refugee's experiences etc.). The basic course leads to formulating the problem of the group and creating the basic line of a new story. Then, students as well as other participants, may decide if they want to perform publicly or not.

2.4 *Theatre of the Oppressed as a Research Method*

Theatre of the Oppressed was not originally created as a research method. It is a method, aimed at social change, transformation of the experience of the oppressed individuals and groups, and empowerment. However, working by means of this method is highly intensive and the work generates deep insight into a problem, which the group solves. Then it is logical that it attracts researchers to make a use of available data. Research on, and of, Theatre of the Oppressed performances is generally defined as action research (Lewin, 1946). The group process is described in detail and results and reflection of its participants are shared (Call-Cummings & James, 2015).

At the Charles University of Prague, we also applied this strategy for several years, but due to the fact that we worked with a mixed group, it appeared to be insufficient. Reasoning being, we often faced situations in which tiny reinterpretation of concepts happened as a side product of the group process. And the same theory created by the group was tested and redefined during the interaction with the audience. We often saw data from our mixed groups that they went further than we were able to capture by action research. It was

EDUCATIONAL ACTIVITIES IN CIVIL SOCIETY

more similar to research analyzing these tiny reinterpretations like those by Yanov & van der Hart (2013), but we were not able to catch the subtle moments by action research methodology.

It led us to look for new research designs, which would be useful for this kind of groups. In the end we used a mixed methodology divided into two stages:

> Stage 1 – preparation of the theatre performance. This stage started to be perceived as a process of formulating research question, where the group of participants formulates the question. We started to use ethnography based on field notes in this stage.

> Stage 2 – performing with the audience. This stage began to be perceived as collecting data, which should answer research question formulated in stage 1. We taped the performances and coded audience created combined with field notes of the teachers.

Theatre of the Oppressed is now used within our faculty in a myriad ways:
- University offers a course on Theatre of the Oppressed where students work together with representatives of target groups outside the university. By those means ca. two theatre performances are made every academic year. Students cooperated with a broad demographic of people outside university like Roma, Vietnamese immigrants and representatives of other minority groups. Topics chosen were e.g. sexual abuse at school, discrimination, racism and sexism.
- Performances are available online – every performance is advertised on theatre web pages and outside institutions can order these performances. We have co-operated with several institutions like schools, NGOs, festivals and conferences.
- In collaboration with NGO's performances are used in some trainings and seminars – in the last two years the performances became regular part of trainings for teachers organized by NGOs, trainings for teachers in kindergartens or for American students coming for a term to the Czech Republic.
Combination of these approaches is used also in EDIC module.

3 Czech EDIC Module

3.1 *Aims of the Module*
The EDIC module is implemented at the department of Civil Society, Faculty of Humanities, Charles University. Before the production and implementation

of the module started, there were several preparation activities in last years. The department has a close link to NGOs from the very beginning. Guests from various NGOs participated in teaching while providing their own expertise. The department perceives the lack of practical training at the university level of education and therefore, it strives for a difference. Practical learning is an inherent part of the studying program and students must choice how they will spent 107 hours of practical training. The Department of Civil Society is not a place for pre-service teacher preparation and in such, the topic of education was not been explicitly threaded into the program from its inception. However, when the School reform act was introduced in 2004, NGOs started to play a service role for schools (Moree, 2010). Teachers were not experts at implementing so called cross-curricula themes and NGOs were very often quickly able to offer programs for schools. However, the quality of their programs varied (Moree, 2010).

Differences in quality was a leading reason to implement a new course on Education and civil society in 2015. The course composed of faculty teachers, as well as, external teachers and trainers, and provided students with theoretical background with concrete strategies, promoting democratic citizenship education in schools. This course became a source of inspiration while preparing the EDIC module with Theatre of the Oppressed activities of the same department. In the EDIC module, we combined these two approaches and build upon previous experience.

3.2 Description of the Module

When we look at the module concretely, we can see that it further develops activities started by the Faculty of Humanities (at Charles University), placing them in an international context to bring them closer to citizenship education in schools. We make use of the concept of the 'Theatre of the Oppressed' (Boalo, 1992), additionally drawing from previous research from the field of education and transformation of society after the fall of communism (Moree, 2008, 2013). We further elaborated in the directions mentioned below.

In particular, the course reflects on citizenship education in the light of societal changes over the last twenty years, specifically focusing on the following topics:

1. We analyse the extent to which education and civil society is linked to the societal context with a special focus on the transformation from communism to a more open system. An important aspect the module is the cooperation between civil society and schools (Kymlicka, 2001; Parker, 2007).

2. In the course, we analyse particular cases where civil society and NGOs help schools with citizenship education. We work and research via

EDUCATIONAL ACTIVITIES IN CIVIL SOCIETY

concrete examples of several projects or disciplines such as multicultural education, history and citizenship education, school parliaments, etc. This part of the course is based on an interdisciplinary approach (Banks, 2004; Moree, 2008; Osler & Starkey, 2010; Anthias, 2011).

3. Finally, we analyse empowerment and oppression as part of citizenship education. We believe through this method, we can create a more critical and engaged democratic citizenship. The 'Theatre of the Oppressed' is the main method of this part of the module.

The module combines several teaching and learning methods: literature analyses and presentations are combined with interactive learning, dialogical learning, field visits and personal reflections. Dividing the module into two parts, the first being dedicated to citizenship education in Czech Republic and what role do the NGOs play in it. We organize field trips and observe concrete activities and approaches the NGOs do in, for and with schools. Students apply literature and theoretical concepts discussed in the class to their experience in NGOs and critically discuss their ideas together. The second part is a bloc seminar of Theatre of the Oppressed methodology where a story based on observed pressing issues is prepared. Afterwards, the students decide whether they want to perform the story or not. Usually they do, so the module is crowned with this performance of participatory forum theatre and discussion of the topic with the audience.

3.3   *NGOs as Key Agents for Citizenship Education in Schools*

Cooperation with NGOs is an inevitable part of the course and it is realised by several means. First, there are planned excursions to NGOs with long-term links to the Department of Civil Society who operate directly with schools. Therefore, these NGOs are educational agents, bringing citizenship education topics to school environments.

- *Pragulic* is an NGO working with homeless people who guide tours around Prague. Routes or particular tours are linked to the life story of the guide. This NGO was founded by students and graduates of the Department of Civil Society. Its activities show how marginalized people can experience empowerment through storytelling while concurrently creating work opportunities. Tours are offered to schools as well.

  Students learn how to work with marginalized groups on topics of social (in)justice and citizens empowerment, including how to address difficult topics with pupils and school audiences.

- *CEDU – Centre for democratic learning* works with school parliaments. It is another NGO linked to the Department of Civil Society as two PhD students of the NGO were involved in the module and its predecessors from the very beginning.

CEDU operates directly in schools, therefore students of the EDIC course observe activities of this NGO, experience school council meeting and how this tool foster active citizenship between involved pupils.

– Other NGOs linked to minority issues include *Slovo 21*, *Ara Art* and *InBáze*. All are integrated in the module, all organize seminars focused on multicultural education, and opening dialogue in controversial issues in schools. Students observe direct work of the groups of pupils and lead some activities themselves.

Adding, the Theatre of the Oppressed is always organised in cooperation between module students and people linked to NGOs. One limitation is the language barrier, due to the module's offering in English. This issue is solved by working together with NGOs whose staff members or clients are able to speak at a minimum, an elementary level of English. Basic English is a necessary condition for basic communication between all participants of the theatre. Therefore, we perceive the EDIC module as an opportunity and the international group of students have an advantage as English is more natural for these groups.

Cooperation with NGOs is reflected in the final paper which links theory to practice. By the end of the course, students produce a final paper where they choose to elaborate and reflect on one of their experiences from the field (excursion or Theatre of the Oppressed) in the light of theories which they studied in the first (theoretical) part of the module.

4 Syllabus

4.1 Aims of the Module
After completing the module, students have:
– Knowledge of the education system and civil society in the Czech Republic, an overview of current standing of citizenship education in Czech schools.
– Knowledge of educational activities in various Czech NGOs in schools.
– Skills and methods to perform and analyse field observation from the perspective of introduced theoretical concepts.
– Skills to apply theoretical concepts to different practices.
– Skills to engage with Theatre of the Oppressed – empathy, team-work, critical thinking and presenting.

4.2 Sessions Schedule
1. *Education system and civil society in the Czech Republic*
    – Transformation of Czech society and educational reforms
    – Cross-curricula themes and NGOs

EDUCATIONAL ACTIVITIES IN CIVIL SOCIETY

119

2. *Citizenship Education*
   - History, recent developments and practices
   - Human rights and education in post-totalitarian society
   - Human rights and education in regions with open conflicts

3. *History and its reflection*
   - Narratives of unjust and modern history in schools
   - Activities of NGOs in the field

4. *Oppression and empowerment – bloc seminar with students-refugees, who came to the Czech Republic without parents*
   - Theatre of the Oppressed – students preparing theatre performance together with representatives of marginalized groups.
   - Research among and with marginalized groups

5. *Citizenship Education, inclusion and moral*
   - Citizenship and special education
   - Citizenship education in inclusive school context
   - Being citizen with special educational needs or similar topics

6. *Active citizenship and activities initiated in schools by NGOs*
   - Participation in schools
   - School Parliaments
   - One World festival at schools

7. *Oppression and empowerment – bloc seminar with students-refugees, who came to the Czech Republic without parents*

8. *NGO activities in the field of education*
   - Different NGO projects (Pragulic, Antikomplex, Slovo 21, Centre for Citizenship Education and ARA ART)
   - Field trips
   - Field observations
   - Presentations

9. *Theatre of the oppressed performance*

4.3 Assessment 7 ECTS
- Active participation in the contact teaching activities and Theatre of the Oppressed.

- Final paper – reflection of one activity of the course from the perspective of theoretical concepts, which were introduced (minimum 5 references).

5 Conclusions

The aim of the module is to focus on the role of NGOs in citizenship education in the formal environment of schools, fulfilled by three steps. First, students talk to NGOs operating in the field of their motivation, vision and best practices. That step brings deeper knowledge and understanding of what is going on in schools, what are the needs of the Czech educational system concerning citizenship.

> Meetings with representatives of NGOs opened my eyes. I did not know what the current school situation looks like and I have never experienced a similar lesson on citizenship. So much can be done! The course helped me clarify the role of the civic sector in the education system and how we – future NGO staff – can participate in the education of future citizens. (Student of the course)

While observing the NGO's educational activities students think through the topics and reflect on the educational moments they witnessed, and learn research methods to describe, analyse and evaluate what they saw during the field trips.

> I learned to look more critically and take field notes. This I have found very helpful for my future studies. (Student of the course)

Finally, students have the opportunity to participate in the process based on Theatre of the Oppressed methodology and together with NGOs'representatives (employees as well as clients), they create a story which addresses their pressing issues connected to education and previous experience.

> I got a lot of emotions out of myself. After the weekend, when I played the aggressors, I noticed I was much calmer. I always exploded at the theatre, but afterwards, I was never angry. It's psychohygienic. The theatre meetings provide us with a nice space where we can be entrusted, even if we know each other only for a moment. It is a powerful experience when you step on stage to perform in front of the audience and hear all of their suggestions. This is how social change can be achieved! (Student and actor of the theatre)

EDUCATIONAL ACTIVITIES IN CIVIL SOCIETY

There are several reasons why we work by means of combining the above mentioned methods and goals. Universities play an inevitable role in preparing professionals to work with disadvantaged groups. Their graduates need theoretical knowledge and a deep understanding of the topics they will support. At the same time, they need not only experience with disadvantaged people, but also relationships uninfluenced by power differences. These are main reasons leading us to combine academic means of working and thinking with tools to create space for new equal relations.

The goals we want to achieve are two-folded. We would like to create an open environment for student reflection so they are able to attain deep insight into what they do and why they do it. At the same time, we try to enlarge tools leading to empowerment, which students can not only use in the module, but also in their future professional work. Theatre of the Oppressed is a strong tool, which creates new memories, new type of experiences and new skills to cope with difficult situations. Performing together with those labeled as disadvantaged may become a moment in which people open themselves for new ways of thinking and even living.

Acknowledgement

This publication was supported by the Ministry of Education, Youth and Sports – Institutional Support for Longterm Development of Research Organizations – Charles University, Faculty of Humanities (2018).

References

Anderson, S., MacPhee, D., & Govan, D. (2000). Infusion of multicultural issues in curricula: A student perspective. *Innovative Higher Education, 25,* 37–57.

Anthias, F. (2011). Intersections and translocations: New paradigms for thinking about cultural diversity and social identities. *European Educational Research Journal, 10,* 204–216.

Bandura, A. (1997). *Self-efficacy: The exercise of control.* New York, NY: Freeman.

Banks, J. (Ed.). (2004). *Diversity and citizenship education; Global perspectives.* San Francisco, CA: Jossey-Bass.

Boal, A. (1979). *The theatre of the oppressed.* New York, NY: Urizen Books.

Boal, A. (1992). *Games for actors and non-actors.* New York, NY: Routledge Press.

Boal, A. (1995). *The rainbow of desire.* London: Routledge.

Call-Cummings, M., & Christine, J. (2015). Empowerment for whom? Empowerment for what? Lessons from a participatory action research project. *Networks: An Online Journal for Teacher Research, 17*(2).

Christensen, M. (2014). Engaging theatre for social change to address sexual violence on a college campus. *British Journal of Social Work, 44*, 1454–1471.

Conrad, D. (2004). Exploring risky youth xxperiences: Popular theatre as a participatory, performative research method. *International Journal of Qualitative Methods.* Retrieved from http://ejournals.library.ualberta.ca/index.php/IJQM/article/viewFile/4482/3787

Desai Shiv, R. (2017). Utilizing theatre of the oppressed within teacher education to create emancipatory teachers. *Multicultural Perspectives, 19*(4), 229–233.

Dewey, J. (1938). *Experience and education.* New York, NY: KappaDelta PI.

Freire, P. (1974). *Education: The practice of freedom.* Santiago: Institute for Agricultural Reform.

Giesler, M. (2017). Teaching note – Theatre of the oppressed and social work education: Radicalizing the practice classroom. *Journal of Social Work Education, 53*(2), 347–353.

Gkofa, P. (2017). Promoting social justice and enhancing educational success: Suggestions from twenty educationally successful Roma in Greece. *Urban Review, 49*, 498–509.

ICCS. (2009). In P. Soukup (Ed.), *Národní zpráva z Mezinárodní studie občanské výchovy* [National report on international study of civics]. Praha: Ústav pro informace ve vzdělávání.

JSNŠ. (2017). *Jeden svět na školách: Zpráva o dotazníkovém šetření na středních školách z roku 2017 včetně porovnání s rokem 2014, 2012 a 2009* [One world at schools: Report on survey in secondary Schools from 2017]. Praha.

Kozakiewicz, M. (1994). The difficult road to educational pluralism in Central and Eastern Europe. *European Education, Fall, 1994.*

Kymlicka, W. (2001). *Politics in vernacular: Nationalism, multiculturalism and citizenship.* Oxford University Press.

Mann, S. (2008). *Study, power and the university: The institution and its effects on learning.* New York, NY: McGraw-Hill Education.

Moree, D. (2008). *How Teachers Cope with Social and Educational Transformation; Struggling with multicultural education in the Czech classroom.* Utrecht: University of Humanistic Studies.

Moree, D. (2013). *Učitelé na vlnách transformace; kultura školy před rokem 1989 a po něm* [Teachers on the waves of transformation: School culture before and after 1989]. Praha: Karolinum.

Moree, D. (2016). Leaving a trail: Sense of life and women's activism. *Communio Viatorum, LVIII, 1,* 94–116.

Moree, D., Vávrová, T., & Felcmanová, A. (2017). Blue or red, why do categories attract? *Urban Review.*

Moree, D. (2010). Organizace občanské společnosti a multikulturní výchova v České republice. (NGOs and multicultural education in the Czech Republic)

In M. Skovajsa (Ed.), *Občanský sektor; organizovaná občanská společnost v České republice* [Civil society sector; Organised civil society in the Czech Republic].

Oser, F., & Veugelers, W. (Eds.). (2008). *Getting Involved; Global citizenship development and sources of moral values*. Rotterdam, The Netherlands: Sense Publishers.

Osler, A., & Starkey, H. (2010) *Teachers and human rights education*. London: Trentam Books.

Parker, W. (2007). *Imagining a cosmopolitan curriculum. A working paper developed for the Washington State Council for the Social Studies*. Seattle, WA: University of Washington.

Saeed, H. (2015). Empowering unheard voices through theatre of the oppressed: Reflections on the legislative theatre project for women in Afghanistan. *Journal of Human Rights Practice, 7*(2), 299–326.

Skovajsa, M. (2010) *Občanský sektor: Organizovaná občanská společnost v České republice* [Civil society sector; Organised civil society in the Czech Republic]. Praha: Portál.

Stahl, S. (2018). Acting out to call in: Practicing theatre of the oppressed with high school students. *The Educational Forum, 82*, 369–373.

Tomusk, V. (2001). Enlightenment and minority cultures: Central and East European higher education reform ten years later. *Higher Education Policy, 14*, 61–73.

Veugelers, W., De Groot, I., & Stolk, V. (2017). *Research for cult committee – Teaching common values in Europe*. Brussels: European Parliament, Policy Department for Structural and Cohesion Policy. Retrieved from http://bit.ly/2pm5Yh9

Yanov, D., & van der Hart, M. (2013). People out of place: allochthony and autochthony in the Netherlands' identity discourse – Metaphors and categories in action. *Journal of International Relations and Development, 16*, 227–261.

CHAPTER 7

Educational Policy and Leadership to Improve Democratic Citizenship Education

Eve Eisenschmidt, Triin Lauri and Reet Sillavee

1 Introduction

In the debates on educational policy, rather than actually understanding what is the intention behind the policy, the participants usually focus on how well a set of regulations is implemented. Instead of understanding how schools are coping with often contradictory policy demands, immediate results and following orders is expected (Ball, Maguire, & Braun, 2012). To educate proactive and responsible democratic citizens, educational leaders and teachers should first understand how a policy is developed. Teachers and leaders should be aware what are the possibilities to actively participate in policy development, who are the most relevant stakeholders, and what is the connection between international trends and local needs. What is needed is the understanding that school, next to families, is a very important development environment for educating active citizens – educators have the responsibility to lead the students in understanding their opportunities and obligations as citizens.

Europe and its member states need a strong democracy, an inclusive society, and active citizens (Veugelers, de Groot, & Stolk, 2017). Citizenship education in teacher education and educational studies, particularly with a focus on democracy and intercultural dialogue, has not received much attention (Veugelers, 2011). Teaching Common Values (TCV) is fairly important in half of the EU member states, but compared to other topics and subject areas, attention given to TCV is still lacking (Veugelers et al., 2017, p. 9). Therefore, every member state should consider how to integrate citizenship education more thoroughly into school curriculum.

In Estonian context, some important milestones should be considered in the education of future teachers and leaders regarding citizenship education. Since 1996, schools are encouraged to develop their own curricula within the national core curriculum framework (i.e. school-based curriculum development) (Estonian Government, 1996). This is considered as a way of increasing school autonomy and democracy in education. Like many reforms in transitional countries, including Estonia, school-based curriculum development

© KONINKLIJKE BRILL NV, LEIDEN, 2019 | DOI: 10.1163/9789004411944_007
This is an open access chapter distributed under the terms of the CC-BY-NC 4.0 License.

was adopted before schools acquired the necessary competence and before teachers were ready to take a proactive approach to curriculum development and use their autonomy. This means also that educational system was decentralised and principles of shared leadership and engagement of all teachers in school development were introduced, but not implemented. Furthermore, policy guidelines for professional school leaders emphasise team building and delegation of responsibilities and duties (Innove, 2015, p. 8), but how to do that, was unclear to teachers and leaders. Although we state that transition phase is over, teachers and school leaders still need to develop proactive attitude and knowledge of how to develop school curriculum, how to work with local community and involve parents into discussions, so that the teachers and school leaders will become policy developers on both local and school level. For that they should also have a wider perspective and understanding of global trends.

Content-wise, it seems that developments are several steps ahead. The national curriculum for basic schools and upper-secondary schools from 2011 declares that schools shall create conditions for the balanced development of pupils with a variety of abilities, for self-actualization, and for shaping a knowledge-based worldview. Every student should have a strong basic education, be capable of integrating into society, and be able to contribute to sustainable social, cultural, economic and ecological development of Estonian society. The Estonian Lifelong Learning Strategy 2020 (Estonian Ministry of Education and Research, Estoninan Cooperation Assembly, & Estonian Education Forum, 2014a, p. 5) lists under the success factors of current Estonian education alternative approaches to education as a way of making the formal education system more flexible, innovative and diverse for all learners. The strategy emphasises that values like democracy and tolerance are strongly needed to develop an inclusive education system and focus on the development of every learner's capabilities.

Master's level course *Educational Policy and School Leadership* sets off in the above- mentioned conditions. The course is designed so that learning about the changes and developments in education go in parallel with the changes in governance of education, including the effects on labour market, and trends in citizenship development as well as in social inclusion and tolerance. The main outcome is on the one hand, a broader understanding of wider paradigmatic shift in educational governance and educational policy making, and on the other hand, an understanding of what are the responsibilities and opportunities of each individual to contribute to policy making.

Three main topics form the course outline: (1) European context and comparative perspective on national educational policy; (2) educational governance and policy making, (3) influence of social change and globalization on policy development. Each of the themes are covered by both theoretical lectures with teachers' key notes or reversed classroom method, and a seminar with practical assignments and self-analyses that help to reinforce new knowledge and beliefs. The balance between theory and practice help to shape a proactive attitude in students towards development and change. A proactive student becomes a proactive teacher or school leader who helps students to become active citizens. The following gives an overview of main concepts which are the basis for topics of the course.

2 Theoretical Background

2.1 *Comparative Perspective on National Educational Policy*

Comparative perspective helps to learn from other educational systems, at the same time avoiding borrowing from other systems. Researchers have cautioned against the direct transplant of educational "solutions" from one context to another (Crossley & Watson, 2003). There are very big differences between countries, systems and contexts, and the context matters often much more than policy makers realize, and de-contextualized policy borrowing is not without its risks (Harris & Jones, 2015). It could be a simple solution to get familiar with the best performing countries based on some international surveys (e.g. PISA, TIMSS, ICCS, etc.) and adapt policies and curricula from these systems. The experts working in comparative education warn that policies and practices should not be readily transferred from one context to another and they advise against transnational policy borrowing (Steiner-Khamsi, 2014). Harris and Jones (2015) point to the fact that there is a substantial international literature that outlines a positive relationship between school leadership and organizational performance and improving the quality of leadership has been a priority for educational policy makers in many countries for many years. Still, every country or system should find their solutions which suit the best in their particular context. The field of comparative education has demonstrated again and again that context plays an essential role in interpreting educational outcomes and effects (ibid., p. 316).

Steiner-Khamsi (2014, p. 154) compares two types of questions in policy borrowing research – normative versus analytical questions. Normative questions are such as "Which are the 'best practices' that should be adopted?"; "How can 'best practices' be effectively disseminated?"; "What has been improved as a result of policy borrowing?". Analytical questions are such as "Why and whose practices are considered as 'best practices'?"; "Under which conditions is dissemination of a practice likely to occur?"; "Who benefits, who loses in

EDUCATIONAL POLICY AND LEADERSHIP

the act of lesson drawing?". When studying different educational systems and practices, both types of questions should be included. Seeking for just "best practices" is very common for practitioners without being aware of broader context and external factors. During the teacher education or leadership programmes, the participants should develop an understanding about how national educational systems work and why one or the other system is built the way it is built. Even more so, teachers and school leaders should understand that the same practices may yield different results, even for organisations that are part of the same national education system, if the contextual factors are different.

2.2   *Educational Governance and Policy-Making*

According to Lipsky's (2010) well-known argument, a policy is made in the daily encounters between street-level bureaucracy and citizens. The same holds in case of education policy, where school leaders and teachers (i.e. street-level bureaucrats) are important stakeholders in educational governance. Therefore, it is important that they understand the main changes in educational governance. This part of the course explains the underlying logic of the changes in educational governance, the changing meaning of public education, the importance and modes of citizenship education, and the relationship between welfare state and educational inequality.

The paradigm shift from government to governance is widely analyzed phenomenon in political science. It refers to different stakeholders participating in governing to cope with the ever-increasing complexities of governing tasks. According to Rhodes (1997), governance is self-organizing, inter-organizational network characterized by interdependence, resource-exchange, rules of the game, and significant autonomy from the state. In focusing on the paradigmatic shift from government to governance in educational policy and consequent reforms, we aim to emphasize, first, the changing role of government in (educational) governing; second, the increasing challenge to cope with more active stakeholders (such as parents – for instance, by giving them more freedom in choosing the school for their child, i.e. school choice) and third, diversity in educational supply on the one side and educational equity on the other side. In public policy, the doctrine of "new governance" is emerging. Far from being unanimous, the main challenge of the doctrines under this heading is the search for a new governing mode adequate for increasing social and cultural diversity, and acknowledging the social embeddedness of individuals' choices (Bevir, 2010). The main characteristics of these ideal-typical governing modes in educational policy and school choice policy in particular are explained (see Table 7.1).

TABLE 7.1   The main characteristics of ideal-typical governing modes in educational policy
and school choice (Source: Lauri, 2013)

		SCHOOL CHOICE MODELS		
		classical (government)	NPM	New Governance
C R I T I	allocation mechanism	central catchment area based assignment and self-financed choice of private schools	parents' choices	central criteria vs the preferences of parents
C A L A	the meaning of education	the source of loyal and culturally homogeneous citizenship	instrumental meaning	how to live together differently, i.e. the integrative choice
S P E C	argument	higher investments = better results	market ensures optimal allocation and efficiency (incentives)	holistic, balanced, multi-actor governanace
T S	"good" choice	the closest school	excellent academic results	cohesivity-enhancing
	problems	anachronistic; residential choice	segregating, socially inefficient; publicness diffuses	how to coordinate different actors

According to New Public Management (NPM), the solution to the inefficiency of classical governing is hoped to be found in the market solutions and/or privatization (Hood, 1991). In cases where handing service delivery over to the market is not possible, the creation of a market within the public service is preferred. The main slogan of NPM – "choice, diversity, market and competition" – presumes that the market enables all parties to take part in a transaction to satisfy their needs, as the market empowers people to be aware of the "market situation" and to take responsibility for their choices. The ever-more flexible options from the demand side (school choice instead of catchment-based assignments, for instance) are believed to allow suppliers to react to diverse social needs (Lauri, 2013). Paradoxically, the hoped ability of NPM to

EDUCATIONAL POLICY AND LEADERSHIP

respond to the diverse needs fails, and the drive towards efficiency leads to a narrower approach to public service and stratified service delivery (Bevir, 2010; Lauri, 2013). While there are countries where NPM-led initiatives have been a clear political choice, in many countries, the principles of NPM emerge to the political agenda and/or pubic services more covertly (Lauri & Põder, 2013). In Estonia, the competitive entrance of some schools in Tallinn with entrance tests and prep-schooling is one of the examples of this hidden and covert route of NPM-led policies. While this phenomenon is highly criticized by scientists and its detrimental social effects have been revealed, this problem of educational inequality has been rather neglected by policy-makers.

The New Governance developments are hoped to be a more adequate reaction than NPM to hierarchies and market-based inequalities, and better able to respond to contemporary heterogeneity. However, while NPM is a rather coherent doctrine, the concept of governance or New Governance is much more ambivalent and there are several interpretations and variety of initiatives (whole-up and joined-up governance, post-NPM to name some). Still, these varieties of policy initiatives tend to emphasize collaboration, partnership, networks and empowerment instead of competition. As stressed by Bevir (2010), public service has to reflect collaboration and trust, even while being market-based.

The discussion about the potential harm competition-oriented and market-based solutions in education might cause has motivated scholars (Schütz, Ursprung, & Wößmann, 2008) to show that equality in educational opportunities is strongly influenced by the institutional set-up of countries education system. Following this literature, Lauri and Põder (2013) and many others have shown that educational efficiency and equity can be complementary (see Figure 7.1). However, this complementarity is very much dependent on the design of educational policy. In other words, the question of how to govern and what are the key characteristics of educational policy is fundamental in terms of educational equity. As shown by Lauri and Põder (2013), there are more or less school choice prone countries that do well in terms of showing good results in both dimensions, educational efficiency and equity. However, there are important criteria which have to be met in order to mitigate the choice-caused harm to equity. The restrictions on schools to "skim the cream" is the most important one among these criteria.

With focusing on the changing meaning and importance of public education, and the essence and quality of civic and citizenship education, our aim is to emphasize that contemporary society is especially demanding in terms of both, education in general and education for social and political participation in particular. Therefore, it becomes crucial to ensure that education is

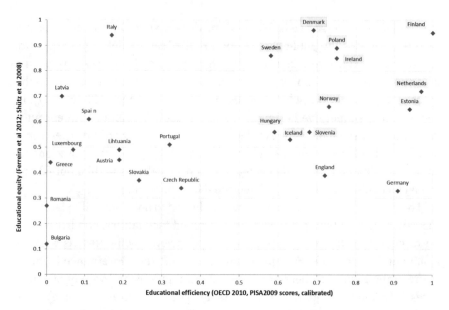

FIGURE 7.1   Efficiency and equity in education (Source: Lauri & Põder, 2013)

capable of equipping young citizens with knowledge needed to take up new and expanded participation possibilities (Hedtke & Zimenkova, 2013). However, ideally, a public school should be defined and evaluated by its unique goal – to renew the public by providing the young with the skills, dispositions, and perspectives required to engage with others about their shared interests and common fate (Feinberg, 2012). Yet, just what does it mean to renew the public and to engage with one another? According to Feinberg (2012), general goals of education that is public in the strict sense of the term is to encourage students to act as if everyone had the requisite knowledge and was willing to comply, with the understanding that their act has a communicative value and serves to encourage compliance. This requires a pedagogical strategy and a curriculum where students are treated with respect, and where they learn to air their different views while respecting the views of others. The aim of this module of the course is to introduce educational practices and challenges in providing this publicness by schools. Publicness is defined as a way of talking about the combinations of things, ideas, issues, people, relationships, practices and sites, that have been made public (Newman & Clarke, 2009). The main challenge for Estonia and stakeholders responsible for civic and citizenship education is the ethnic gap in the educational outcome. More specifically, there are remarkable differences between the educational outcome of students studying in Russian and Estonian language schools and this gap is prevalent across all subjects studied, including civic and citizenship

EDUCATIONAL POLICY AND LEADERSHIP

(Lauri, Põder, & Rahnu, 2017). As an inheritance of Soviet era, Estonia have bilingual schools system where Russian speakers and Estonian speakers study in parallel. While there have been many policy initiatives to integrate these two, the distinctive character of school system has remained unchanged and the gap in educational outcomes, political activism and preferences, and even in media usage is reinforced.

Besides the most relevant topics for Estonia, the more general trends and evidence about civic and citizenship education are examined during the course. The main topics covered are, first, salient issues in terms of citizenship enhancement (such as classroom climate, contextual notion of citizenship, socio-economic embeddedness of civic knowledge). This saliency is mostly identified (Knowles, Torney-Purta, & Barber, 2018) based on international large-scale assessments, such as the International Civics and Citizenship Education Studies (ICCS) arranged by International Association for the Evaluation of Educational Achievement (IEA). These surveys are designed to provide insights to teachers, researchers and educational policy experts, and they are important sources for future policy-making. The second issue covered in this subtopic is devoted to institutional and contextual factors of quality in civic and citizenship education (Toots & Lauri, 2015). With elaborating on the quality assurance in civic and citizenship education, we show that the quality is affected by the so-called remote social factors, such as level of economic and social human development, public investment in education and type of civic culture, as well as more proximate factors, such as national approaches to civic and citizenship curriculum and teaching, civic activation initiatives at schools and assessment practices. Furthermore, different contexts require different approaches to quality assurance (ibid., 2015), which means policy learning instead of policy borrowing in order to gain from best practices worldwide.

In the subtopic of relationship between welfare regimes and educational inequality, the main concerns are social inequality and educational systems' role in this. There is a long debate in comparative political science literature on the role of educational policy as a social policy (Di Stasio & Solga, 2017), stemming from the contradicting views on education policies' ability to tackle social inequality. For a quite a long time, educational policy has been neglected in comparative studies on welfare state (Busemeyer & Nikolai, 2010; Iversen & Stephens, 2008). The recent paradigmatic turn to socially investing welfare states has contributed to bringing education policy at the forefront of the conceptualization of welfare states. This turn emphasizes the importance of creation, mobilization and preservation of human skills (Garritzmann, Häusermann, Palier, & Zollinger, 2017) throughout the entire life course in order to address new social risks not met by the so-called old welfare state approach. Education has a major role in providing these goals of socially investing policies. However, while the importance of education has indeed become prevalent, the ability of social investment policies to mitigate social inequalities tend to be sometimes overestimated (Solga, 2014), or the frameworks too narrow to capture how to achieve the enhancement of human capital should or how to generate the expected private and social returns to education (Di Stasio & Solga, 2017). This is not to say that educational inequalities and their reinforcement mechanisms should not be analyzed based on social investment approach, but rather that future research should clarify the relationships between educational investment, educational institutions, and the distribution of life chances in different welfare state and education regimes (ibid., p. 315). Education policies themselves may generate social problems, i.e. instead of being the solution they might be part of the problem.

2.3 *Citizenship and Curriculum Development*

There is always a dilemma to what extent education should respond to labour market needs and needs of society and personal needs of the citizens. OECD is arguing not only for excellence in knowledge, but also for skills, values and attitudes, for new solutions in a rapidly changing world, and for learners' agency enabling them to navigate through a complex and uncertain world (OECD, 2016a). World Economic Forum is demanding better social skills (2016). Social-emotional competences, multiculturalism and values like tolerance, democracy, open-mindedness are getting more and more attention and thus, it is problematic that most schools still focus solely on academic skills (Veugelers et al., 2017). Non-academic and social-emotional skills – such as self-regulation, problem-solving, social awareness, and growth mindset – have a strong impact on academic outcomes and success in the workforce and in society (Stafford-Brizard, 2016).

The Estonian Lifelong Learning Strategy 2020 (Estonian Ministry of Education and Research et al., 2014a) and the strategy document "Wise and active people" (Estonian Ministry of Education and Research, 2014b) both emphasise the so-called "changed" or "new" learning and teaching paradigm as one of the most important presumptions of educational change. It is defined as "learning and teaching paradigm which supports the individual and social development of each learner, including the learning-to-learn skills, creativity and entrepreneurship" (Estonian Ministry of Education and Research et al., 2014a, p. 4). Despite the promotion of student-centred social constructivist instruction by existing policies since 1996, research indicates that these practices are not sufficiently used by Estonian teachers (ibid.).

The last curriculum reform was initiated with the 2011 national curriculum (revised in 2014) for basic and upper-secondary schools. Both curricula emphasised cross-curricular themes and integration of subjects, and put more stress on key competences. National curriculum includes eight general competences and one of these is social and citizen competence – the ability to become self-actualized; to function as an active, well-informed, helpful and responsible citizen and to support the democratic development of society; to know and follow values and standards in society; to respect the societal diversity, rules of various environments,, and particularities of religions and nations; to engage in cooperation with other people in different situations; to accept differences in people and their values and to take them into account in interaction with people (Estonian Government, 2011a).

In addition to supporting students' self-actualization and self-directedness, changes in the assessment system of students included the introduction of formative assessment in addition to summative assessment. Moreover, to support the development of cooperation competences, the basic school curriculum includes the so-called "creative project" as a way of developing and assessing student's creativity and entrepreneurship while promoting cross-curricular integration (Estonian Government, 2011a). In upper secondary school, it is mandatory for each student to conduct a personal practical or research project. The curriculum for upper secondary school required the development of distinctive school profiles with different study directions (Estonian Government, 2011b). Since the last curriculum reform, many schools offer elective courses or extracurricular activities. The aim of these electives is to support the development of individual interests of the students, but also to integrate learning with everyday life surrounding the school, in order to develop responsiveness towards needs of the society.

The Estonian school system was decentralised in the early 1990s, and responsibility for the local school system was devolved on the municipalities (Estonian Parlament, 1992). Estonian school principals have very high levels of autonomy, including the authority to hire and fire staff, negotiate working conditions and job contracts, make decisions about school finances, educational priorities and development plans for the school (Kitsing & Peterson, 2011). But the most important task is to develop school-based curriculum as a core of education. As every school compiles its own school-based curriculum, then teachers and leaders of schools and kindergartens should have a broad understanding of the national curriculum development, expectations of the society and labour market, and also about different forms of democracy and related intercultural aspects.

3 Module of Educational Policy and Leadership in Tallinn University

The 6 ECTS module of Education Policy and Leadership is an open course for students in the field of education. The module is recommended for Educational Leadership students who will take a leading role in school curriculum development and create conditions for teachers' professional development.

3.1 *Aims and Outcomes*

The general aim of the module is to create opportunities for analysing how interculturalism and three components of democracy, that is,participation, democratic politics, and democratic society, are displayed in national educational policy and school curriculum. Students will analyse their own values and opportunities as leaders for shaping and implementing educational policy at different levels of educational system to reinforce three components of tolerance: interpersonal relations, tolerance towards different social and cultural groups, and an inclusive society.

3.2 *Objectives of This Module*

Objectives of this module are to create possibilities for:
- understanding different national educational systems, global context (e.g. European Union) and trends of educational policy development;
- evaluating the influence of educational policy on a specific educational institution;
- understanding how global trends and the needs of the society actualise in school curriculum, reinforcing democratic intercultural citizenship education;
- understanding the responsibilities and opportunities of teachers and leaders to participate proactively in policy making process.

This module provides the broader context of education policy and creates a basis for proactive citizenship (see Figure 7.2). The module will address the following questions: what is education policy, how it is formulated at global, international and national levels, and how it affects democratic intercultural citizenship education, especially equality in education. The module also covers key perspectives and concepts in the analysis of education policy at global, European and national levels. Further, the role of global, transnational, and international trends will be also discussed. The case of Estonia will be used as a particular example of national transition.

The students who pass the course should be able to:
- analyse critically EU and global education policy trends and understand their impact on their national educational system from the perspective of democratic intercultural citizenship education;

FIGURE 7.2   The process of raising proactive citizens

- understand education policy trends and their connections with the local socio-cultural environment;
- assess the impact and implementation of education policy at a particular level of an educational institution;
- understand their own role and possibilities for proactively participating in implementing education policy;
- continuously monitor education policy initiatives and participate in debates in a proactive manner.

3.3   *Description of the Module and Study Process*

Based on the objectives, the module has three main topics: (1) European context and comparative perspective on national educational policies; (2) educational governance and policy-making; (3) influence of societal changes and globalization in policy development. Learners' attitudes and values, fundamental to build the desired competencies (see Figure 7.3), provide a basis for achieving the learning outcomes.

In the area of European context and comparative perspective on national educational policy, the focus is on: (1) understanding the main characteristics of national educational system; (2) the importance of international organisations in educational policy-making and the Europeanization of education. Students compare national educational systems using Eurydice database, OECD annual reports "Education at the Glance" and other comparative reports such as ICCS. Main challenges are described and students are guided to propose possible policy improvement areas. In this area, the students take a careful look at current trends in education policy at the European as well as global level. Different stakeholders' possible input to policy making is compared, while special attention is given to inclusion through civil society organisations. Managing educational systems, co-operation and competition under different leadership models as well as shaping educational policy, educational reforms and their outcomes is covered.

The area of educational governance and policy-making has three main focal points: (1) the paradigm shift from government to governance in education policy and consequent reforms; (2) the changing meaning and importance of public education and citizenship education; (3) the relationship between welfare regimes and educational inequality. When tackling this topic, the students

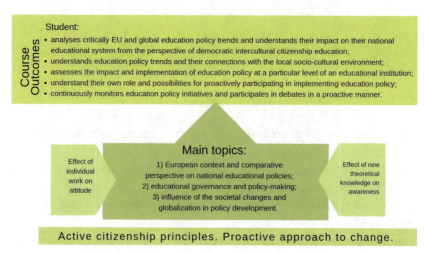

FIGURE 7.3   Concept of the module

are empowered to critically examine the main challenges related to educational governance in a contemporary, pluralistic frame, and to develop the awareness of related problems and the opportunities to mitigate these problems. The linkages between wider institutional settings of education systems and educational outcomes are emphasized and the changing role of different stakeholders (school leaders, teachers, parents) in them conceptualized.

In the area of the societal change and globalization in policy development, the students are encouraged to analyse national strategies and how strategies influence educational policy and school curriculum. Students will have the opportunity to apply their knowledge in comparative case studies during study-visits to educational institutions and organisations.

Throughout the module, the students analyze international comparative reports and current educational policy topics, and evaluate the impact of policy issues on educational institutions. Special focus is on the analysis of policy design process and how interest groups are involved in them. Important part of the independent work is an interview with an active shaper of educational policy outside of the formal educational system (NGOs, public authorities, politicians, etc.). To support proactivity of the future leaders, short videos are created by the students. Current problems in education, with the focus on democratic intercultural citizenship education are highlighted and possible solutions are proposed. Students should prepare for topics discussed in the class by reading literature and fulfilling individual tasks (see Table 7.2).

Course is organised as a two-month intensive course. Every week, there is one 6–8-hour day where lectures and seminars are tightly integrated. For every class, the students have independent reading and individual or group works to

TABLE 7.2   Outline of the module

Topics	Literature to read for the class	Classwork to develop students' proactivity	Homework for this class
Topic 1: Educational systems of EU member states and comparison with the Estonian system, EU educational policy as "soft policy"	OECD (2017), Veugelers et al. (2017)	Analysis of OECD and European Commission policy documents	Getting familiar with Eurydice database
Topic 2: Main characteristics of describing education systems, educational reforms and educational governance (competition, collaboration, participation)	Lauri (2013)	Group work: designing a framework for analysis of educational reforms	Analysing the main characteristics and main educational reforms in one particular country: (1) What are the main characteristics of the chosen reforms and why? (2) What have been the underlying logic of these reforms (NPM, governance)?
Topic 3: National educational systems, their main characteristics and challenges; comparing the systems of different countries	Webpages of national educational agencies	Presentation of national educational systems (group work for teams of 2–3 students)	Introduction of the educational system of students' home country: structure, strengths, weaknesses, main trends in educational policy (group work for teams of 3–4 students); comparing educational systems of the three different countries based on Eurydice database

(*cont.*)

TABLE 7.2   Outline of the module (*cont.*)

Topics	Literature to read for the class	Classwork to develop students' proactivity	Homework for this class
Topic 4: Teachers as moral professionals, value education	Rissanen, Kuusisto, Hanhimäki, and Tirri (2018)	Group work: analysing different national contextual factors of teachers' work	Analysis of student's own pedagogical values and their actualisation in teaching process
Topic 5: Global trends in educational policy – EU and OECD trends	OECD (2016). Trends Shaping Education	Pair work: analysing some recent policy recommendations by EC or OECD	Recommendations to national educational systems while considering international trends
Topic 6: Policy-making in education – new arenas; from government to governance – the challenge of mitigating educational inequality in case of a more diverse system	Ball et al. (2012), Lauri (2013)	Group work: analysing possibilities to participate in policy development	Describing the main changes recently implemented in one particular school and the logic underlying these changes in the light of paradigmatic shift of governance
Topic 7: Participation in debates on the formulation of educational policy	Web-pages for civil participation in the decision-making process	Mapping possible stakeholders in school-based curriculum development	Finding one TED Talk that describes how a socially sensitive problem is solved by an initiative from citizens and preparing to introduce the talk in class

TABLE 7.2   Outline of the module (*cont.*)

Topics	Literature to read for the class	Classwork to develop students' proactivity	Homework for this class
Topic 8: The meaning of public education, the importance and determinants of civic and citizenship education	Toots (2013)	Mapping possibilities to support active citizenship in a particular school	Description of the main challenges for civic and citizenship education in contemporary societies
Topic 9: Governing by numbers	Grek (2009), Knodel, Martens, and Niemann (2013)	Analysing messages of public debates (e.g media news) about PISA survey	Analysis of the reactions to PISA and its importance in policy-making process and debates in a particular country
Topic 10: Changes in society and labour market and their impact on educational policy; future skills, balance between cognitive, socio-emotional and professional skills	Estonian Lifelong Learning Strategy 2020	Comparing national curricula and societal needs, mapping possible implications	Recommendations to change learning process in one particular school based on future skills
Topic 11: How "policy of competences" and future skills influence educational institutions, their leadership, procedures and culture?	Future trends of work	Analysis of the leaders' behaviour from the perspective of distributed leadership	Case analysis of how educational institution (school, kindergarten, etc.) develops future skills and how developing future skills is integrated into school curriculum

(*cont.*)

TABLE 7.2   Outline of the module (*cont.*)

Topics	Literature to read for the class	Classwork to develop students' proactivity	Homework for this class
Topic 12: Educational policy in practice, national curricula as an agreement; impact of educational policy on leadership of an educational institution	National curricula and Estonian educational act	Discussion on how to create school-based curriculum and vision of the school to strengthen democracy and tolerance in education	Analysis of the leaders' activities for involving teachers into curriculum development
Topic 13: Education and welfare state; education and social inequality	Busemeyer and Nikolai (2010)	Group work: how to support equity in education at schools	Analysing national policy examples regarding equity and democracy in education
Topic 14: Youth organisations and citizenship education	European Youth Forum: youth organisations' contribution to citizenship education	Analysis of videos and mapping good examples of how youth organisations can be involved in school governance	Preparation of short videos about policy recommendations (group-work for teams of 3–4 students)

(*cont.*)

TABLE 7.2   Outline of the module (*cont.*)

Topics	Literature to read for the class	Classwork to develop students' proactivity	Homework for this class
Topic 15: Content of education and implementation of educational policy on institutional level	National curriculum for basic schools, Education Act	A study visit to an educational institution and an interview with leader(s) about participation in policy development	Short analysis of national curriculum from the perspective of personal interest; suggesting changes to the way a particular educational institution can be led to improve citizen education
Topic 16: Diverse educational systems – opportunities and challenges	Nikolai and West (2013)	Discussions on how everyone can be proactive in improving equity in their own educational institution	Recommendations to improve national policy in order to increase equity in educational system

prepare for the class, including site visits, interviews with stakeholders, following related media, etc.

For the final examination, the students write the analysis of one relevant topic of educational policy in their national context, (1) evaluating the impact of this policy to concrete educational institution or learner or to the system in general, (2) describing how different stakeholders/interest groups could be involved in policy development and implementation, and (3) evaluating their personal possibilities to participate in policy debates as active citizens.

In the first try-out year, around 60 students participated, out of whom 5 were international students. Vast majority of Estonian students studied either Educational Management or Early Childhood Education, it was a compulsory course for them. There were also few students from the Subject Teacher MA programme. In the second year, around 70 students participated. Ten students were from Educational Innovation and Leadership programme, which is an international MA programme with international students from Taiwan, Nigeria, Cameron, Russia, Georgia, Bangladesh and Afghanistan.

The second try-out with the bigger group of international students added a whole other dimension – many Estonian students were not aware of the educational situations in the countries some of the foreign students came from. Sharing such knowledge and experience enriched the whole course. It showed in particular when the students presented the works they had to do in a small international group: several groups gave examples of problems or solutions from the perspective of different countries.

4 Reflection and Future Implications for Improving the Course

After the completion, students gave feedback on the course. They considered the course to be interesting and challenging. The students also found that generally, the course met their expectations and they acquired the learning outcomes of the module; however, some suggestions for improvement were also offered.

Furthermore, critical friends, in the first try-out year Ghazala Bhatti from Bath Spa University and in the second year Elina Kuusisto from the University of Helsinki participated in the course during one day, gave a lecture and also made suggestions. The following reflection and possible improvements to the module are based on students' and critical friend's feedback.

4.1 Content of the Module
First, the students are made to think more globally. With reference to global aspects and how they relate to the future educational opportunities for children

world-wide, it is useful for students to look at the current education systems in different parts of the world, not just in Europe. It means that students will not only be thinking of their own country, but also about the role this country may play in the rest of the world in the future. Today's students must be prepared to take risks and find solutions that present generation has not even begun to imagine. For example, the students learn about a country in Africa or in Asia and to look at the history of the country and the context of their educational challenges. In this way, the students will get familiar with a much broader context and analyse the educational systems from historical and socio-economic perspectives. This means looking at the population, what percentage of boys and girls go to school, what percentage of the population is literate, what are the needs of the society, how many people from that country have migrated to other countries, which social groups these emigrants were from and why did they emigrate. Moreover, taking this wider perspective includes also the analysis the economic side of education, e.g. what percentage of GDP is spent on education – primary, secondary, higher education, etc. – and what is the rate of unemployment and how healthy is the nation (% of live births in 100). In addition, the work of international organisations like World Health Organisation, United Nations and international agreements like The Dakar Agreement, Salamanca Agreement and the United Nations Charter on the Rights of the Child are be analysed from the perspective of democracy and equality in society.

Secondly, although the module aims to address the three components of democracy – participation, democratic politics, and democratic society (see Veugelers et al., 2017) – these components were not equally covered during the course. There should be several individual works that require the students to analyse their possibilities for participating in debates and policy development, involving different partners and creating open discussion about new educational policy initiatives. Distinction between national and international policy developments is already made in the course, but some more tasks could be added to help the students understand how politics can support creation of democracy and tolerance in society.

Thirdly, this module should develop students' understanding of how to teach values. As mentioned by Veugelers and colleagues (2017, p. 9), there are four ways for teaching values: a specific value-oriented subject; integration of value education into related subjects; cross-curricular activities establishing links with the community; a democratic school culture involving more dialogical methodologies of teaching and learning; and inclusive education bringing together different groups of students and teachers. In addition, although the course elaborated on diversity in school community and shared leadership, these areas could be analysed more deeply on the example of students' personal experiences.

4.2 Students' Learning Process

As it is an intensive course (two months), the students have several individual works in a short time range. As one of the fundamental aims of the programme is to support students' proactive behaviour and willingness to take responsibility, the individual works should be more linked with case studies of everyday problems where students can propose concrete solutions (e.g. how to implement a certain change in their own institutions).

Students mentioned that the course should also allow to improve their everyday practices as teachers or leaders, for example, in developing democracy and opening dialogue at schools. As most of the students are already working in various educational institutions, one task could be to carry out a small-scale action research on how to teach values, e.g. by integrating different subjects or carrying out cross-curricular activities. Another possibility is to observe and collect data about school culture – how inclusion is supported, or how the links with community are established.

The course is also opened for international exchange students. With this, we create an opportunity for the students to enrich their learning and start a dialogue over first-hand experiences of different educational contexts. Although students are encouraged to learn from each other, the process still needs facilitating and support in bridging practical encounterings with theoretical reasons behind them.

As course development is a continuous process, all of the above-mentioned areas of improvement will be considered during the preparation for the next year's course.

References

Ball, S. J., Maguire, M., & Braun, A. (2012). *How schools do policy: Policy enactments in secondary schools*. New York, NY: Routledge.

Bevir, M. (2010). *Democratic governance*. Princeton, NJ: Princeton University Press.

Busemeyer, M. R., & Nikolai, R. (2010). Education. In F. G. Castles, S. Leibfried, J. Lewis, H. Obinger, & C. Pierson (Eds.), *The Oxford handbook of the welfare state* (pp. 494–508). Oxford: Oxford University Press.

Crossley, M., & Watson, K. (2003). *Comparative and international research in education: Globalisation, context and difference*. London & New York, NY: RoutledgeFalmer.

Di Stasio, V., & Solga, H. (2017). Education as social policy: An introduction. *Journal of European Social Policy, 27*(4), 313–319.

Estonian Government. (1996). *Eesti põhi-ja keskhariduse riiklik õppekava* [Estonian National Curriculum for basic and secondary education]. Retrieved from https://www.riigiteataja.ee/akt/29725

EDUCATIONAL POLICY AND LEADERSHIP 145

Estonian Government. (2011a). *Põhikooli riiklik õppekava* [National Curriculum for basic schools]. Retrieved from https://www.riigiteataja.ee/akt/114012011001

Estonian Government. (2011b). *Gümnaasiumi riiklik õppekava* [National Curriculum for Gymnasia]. Retrieved from https://www.riigiteataja.ee/akt/114012011002

Estonian Parliament. (1992). *Republic of Estonia Education Act*. Retrieved from https://www.riigiteataja.ee/en/eli/524042014002/consolide

Feinberg, W. (2012). The idea of a public education. *Review of Research in Education, 36*(1), 1–22.

Garritzmann, J. L., Häusermann, S., Palier, B., & Zollinger, C. (2017). *WoPSI-the world politics of social investment: An international research project to explain variance in social investment agendas and social investment reforms across countries and world regions* (LIEPP Working Paper No. 64).

Grek, S. (2009). Governing by numbers: The PISA 'effect' in Europe. *Journal of Education Policy, 24*(1), 23–37.

Harris, A., & Jones, M. (2015). Transforming education systems: comparative and critical perspectives on school leadership. *Asia Pacific Journal of Education, 35*(3), 311–318.

Hedtke, R., & Zimenkova, T. (Eds.). (2013). *Education for civic and political participation: A critical approach* (Vol. 92). New York, NY & London: Routledge.

Hood, C. (1991). A public management for all seasons? *Public Administration, 69*(1), 3–19.

Estonian Ministry of Education and Research, Estonian Cooperation Assembly & Estonian Education Forum. (2014a). *Eesti elukestva õppe strateegia 2020* [Estonian Lifelong Learning Strategy 2020]. Retrieved from https://www.hm.ee/sites/default/files/strateegia2020.pdf

Estonian Ministry of Education and Research. (2014b). *Haridus-ja teadusministeeriumi arengukava "Tark ja tegus rahvas" 2015–2018* [The development strategy of the Ministry of Education and Research "Wise and active people" 2015–2018]. Tartu. Retrieved from https://www.hm.ee/sites/default/files/tark_ja_tegus_rahvas_2015_2018_final.pdf

Innove. (2015). *Õppijakeskse kooli juhtimine*. Juhendmaterjal üldhariduskoolide juhtidele. SA Innove juhitava ESF programm "Üldhariduse pedagoogide kvalifikatsiooni tõstmine 2008–2014" [Leading a student-centred school. Guideline for leaders of general education schools. The Programme of ESF, led by Foundation Innove: "Raising the Qualification of General Education Educators 2008–2014"]. Retrieved from http://www.innove.ee/UserFiles/%C3%9Cldharidus/ESF%20programmid/Juhendmaterjal_2015.pdf

Iversen, T., & Stephens, J. D. (2008). Partisan politics, the welfare state, and three worlds of human capital formation. *Comparative Political Studies, 41*(4–5), 600–637.

Kitsing, M., & Peterson, K. (2011). Estonian report. In J. Bolhöfer (Ed.), *European synopsis. The making of: Leadership in education* (pp. 77–85). Hildesheim: NLQ. Retrieved from http://www.leadership-in-education.eu/index.php?id=27

Knodel, P., Martens, K., & Niemann, D. (2013). PISA as an ideational roadmap for policy change: Exploring Germany and England in a comparative perspective. *Globalisation, Societies and Education, 11*(3), 421–441.

Knowles, R. T., Torney-Purta, J., & Barber, C. (2018). Enhancing citizenship learning with international comparative research: Analyses of IEA civic education datasets. *Citizenship Teaching & Learning, 13*(1), 7–30.

Lauri, T. (2013). School choice as the problem of educational governance in a pluralistic frame. *Italian Journal of Sociology of Education, 5*(2), 160–188.

Lauri, T., & Põder, K. (2013). School choice policy: Seeking to balance educational efficiency and equity. A comparative analysis of 20 European Countries. *European Educational Research Journal, 12*(4), 534–552.

Lauri, T., Põder, K., & Rahnu, L. (2017). Challenges facing the Estonian school system: The achievement gap between language-stream schools and school choice of immigrants. In Estonia in the Migration Era. In T. Tammaru, R. Eamets, & K. Kallas (Eds.), *Human development report 2016/2017* (pp. 155–162). Retrieved from https://inimareng.ee/en/immigration-and-integration/challenges-facing-the-estonian-school-system/

Lipsky, M. (2010). *Street-level bureaucracy, 30th ann. Ed.: dilemmas of the individual in public service.* New York, NY: Russell Sage Foundation.

Newman, J., & Clarke, J. (2009). *Publics, politics and power: Remaking the public in public services.* London: Sage Publications.

Nikolai, R., & West, A. (2013). School type and inequality. In R. Brooks, K. Bhopal, & M. McCormack (Eds.), *Contemporary debates in the sociology of education* (pp. 57–75). Basingstoke: Palgrave Macmillan.

OECD. (2016a). *Global competency for an inclusive world.* Retrieved from https://www.oecd.org/education/Global-competency-for-an-inclusive-world.pdf

OECD. (2016b). *Trends Shaping Education 2016.* Paris: OECD Publishing. Retrieved from http://dx.doi.org/10.1787/trends_edu2016-en

OECD. (2017). *Education at a Glance 2017* (OECD Indicators). Paris. OECD Publishing. Retrieved from http://dx.doi.org/10.1787/eag-2017-en

Rhodes, R. A. (1997). *Understanding governance: Policy networks, governance, reflexivity and accountability.* Philadephia, PA: Open University Press.

Rissanen, I., Kuusisto, E., Hanhimäki, E., & Tirri, K. (2018). The implications of teachers' implicit theories for moral education: A case study from Finland. *Journal of Moral Education, 47*(1), 63–77.

Schütz, G., Ursprung, H. W., & Wößmann, L. (2008). Education policy and equality of opportunity. *Kyklos, 61*(2), 279–308.

Solga, H. (2014). Education, economic inequality and the promises of the social investment state. *Socio-Economic Review, 12*(2), 269–297.

Stafford-Brizard, K. B. (2016). Nonacademic skills are the necessary foundation for learning. *Education Week*. Retrieved from http://www.edweek.org/ew/articles/2016/07/21/nonacademic-skills-are-the-necessary-foundation-for.html?r=491400431&cmp=eml-enl-eu-news1-RM&preview=1&user_acl=0&intc=es

Steiner-Khamsi, G. (2014). Cross-national policy borrowing: Understanding reception and translation. *Asia Pacific Journal of Education, 34*(2), 153–167.

Toots, A. (2013). Motivated by education or encouraged by opportunities? A comparative perspective on knowledge and participation nexus. In A. Toots (Ed.), *Education for civic and political participation* (pp. 107–124). New York, NY: Routledge.

Toots, A., & Lauri, T. (2015). Institutional and contextual factors of quality in civic and citizenship education: Exploring possibilities of qualitative comparative analysis. *Comparative Education, 51*(2), 247–275.

Veugelers, W. (2011). Theory and practice of citizenship education: The case of policy, science, and education in the Netherlands. *Revista de Educacion,* 209–224.

Veugelers, W., De Groot, I., & Stolk, V. (2017). *Research for cult committee – Teaching common values in Europe*. Brussels: European Parliament, Policy Department for Structural and Cohesion Policy. Retrieved from http://bit.ly/2pm5Yh9

World Economic Forum. (2016). *The future of jobs. Employment, skills and workforce strategy for the fourth industrial revolution*. Retrieved from http://reports.weforum.org/future-of-jobs-2016/

CHAPTER 8

Preparing Educators and Researchers for Multicultural/Intercultural Education: A Greek Perspective

Anastasia Kesidou

1 The Challenges

Immigration is not a recent development in European societies, and the same applies to cultural diversity. Cultural pluralism and immigration are reinforced nowadays by globalization and internationalization; therefore, young people in Europe will be called upon in their adult lives to live in conditions of cultural pluralism, irrespective of population movements caused by immigration. Immigration continues to gain more attention, since it is indeed a growing phenomenon in the European arena: at least 10% of the school population at age 15 within the EU countries was either born abroad or both his/her parents were born in another country. In some countries, such as Ireland, Italy and Spain the percentage of school students born in another country has multiplied three or four times since 2000.

A further crucial challenge for the European continent is currently set by the recent refugee crisis and, at the same time, the education of refugee children constitutes a major global demand. However, according to the UN High Commissioner for Refugees, more than 3.5 million refugee children aged 5 to 17 were not able to attend school in 2016. In particular, about 1.5 million refugees did not go to elementary school, while 2 million adolescents did not attend secondary education (UNHCR, 2017). In other words, this clearly has a dramatic impact on their right to education, which would help them to lead fulfilling and useful lives.

In this context, imperative orientations for the European education systems include key objectives, such as the development of a young generation, which respects human rights and is well-placed to live in open, democratic and pluralistic societies. This issue is of major importance, if the challenges posed by the arrival of a large number of immigrants and refugees, along with the alarming strengthening of nationalism, intolerance and racism in recent years, are taken into consideration. Recognizing this necessity, the European Parliament recently initiated the study "Teaching Common Values in Europe",

© KONINKLIJKE BRILL NV, LEIDEN, 2019 | DOI: 10.1163/9789004411944_008
This is an open access chapter distributed under the terms of the CC-BY-NC 4.0 License.

which focuses on the policy and practice of teaching democracy and tolerance in secondary schools of all 28 European Union Member States (Veugelers, De Groot, & Stolk, 2017). In addition, equal access to school is a legitimate act of respecting children and young people's fundamental human right to education. It is the most democratic and fair approach, but also a choice with only positive results for both children and the wider society. Otherwise, there is the danger of widening social differences, which can be transmitted from one generation to the other, exclusion on personal or community level, as well as conflicts among the ethnic groups within the wider society.

1.1 The Concept 'Multicultural/Intercultural Education'

The human communication, which takes place when people of different cultural capitals meet, is based on certain conditions, such as the acceptance of being different, tolerance, the ability of identification and empathy with others, the ability of comparison and adoption of "different" cultural elements. However, since it is not always easy to understand multiculturalism, the acquisition and the exercise of certain competences through an education oriented towards intercultural principles appears to be of crucial importance. In this framework, intercultural education is defined as a new conception about education, which requires differentiated practice in educational institutions. This is based on the acceptance that the narrow nationally oriented education is historically outdated and does not correspond to the reality of the 21st century (Dietrich, 1997). In the following, the main aims of intercultural education, as presented in the international bibliography, are discussed further.

According to Helmut Essinger (1991) the main principles of intercultural education are as follows: (a) *Education for empathy*. This is about learning to understand others, to put ourselves in their shoes and to regard their beliefs and problems from their own point of view. If this is to become possible, education should encourage the young to show interest in the "difference" or the problems of the "others", whether they are immigrants living next to us as neighbors or other people who live outside our borders. (b) *Education for solidarity*: this is about the students developing a collective conscience, which exceeds the boundaries of groups, countries and races, on the basis of which all people have the same value and could potentially acquire the same problems. Under these circumstances it is a reasonable expectation to support one another. (c) *Education for intercultural respect*. This respect can be achieved through us "opening up" to foreign cultures and at the same time through inviting others to participate in our own culture. (d) *Education against the nationalistic way of thinking*, which aims at the openness toward other peoples, mutual communication as well as the elimination of national stereotypes and prejudice.

Georg Auernheimer (1995) discusses a range of aspects, which intercultural education emphasizes. According to the first point, intercultural education is seen as *social learning*, whereby a person acquires social competences such as empathy, tolerance, solidarity and the ability to overcome tensions. The second aspect refers to intercultural education as the one that provides a person with the *ability for dialogue between the cultures*. A condition for the latter is the acceptance of cultural difference and the ability to deal with it. The third aspect concerns a general education, which provides *multiperspectivity*. In the case of Greece, this would mean that the knowledge provided in schools does not only refer to the world of the Greeks but also to that of the immigrant students represented in the Greek classrooms (Hodolidou, 2018). This can be applied in all subjects of the curriculum. In this way, it is possible to acknowledge the cultural similarities that unite people. This is desirable and the desideratum, if we are to establish and enforce the spirit of peaceful cooperation and multilevel understanding and interaction. Another aspect suggested by Auernheimer is intercultural education as *citizenship education* and as *antiracist education*. It is not difficult to trace the relation between intercultural and citizenship education. This would mean education against nationalistic way of thinking, and also an education aimed at intercultural respect. This would, for example, include discussion in class of phenomena such as xenophobia and the attacks against the immigrants. These are clearly important elements of civic education. The connection of intercultural and antiracist education is also apparent, since the former aims at the elimination of stereotypes, prejudice and potentially racist attitudes and behavior. The difference between the two is that antiracist education focuses mainly on the institutions and the structures in society, in the sense that the change of the attitudes of people in general and of teachers and students in particular is not enough. It is also important to try and change the educational and social structures, which are not always free of racist elements. Finally, intercultural education is directly connected with *bilingual education*. The latter is very important for the normal development of the identity of students from linguistic minorities. Therefore, it is stressed that the mother tongue/first language of all students should be represented in the educational system, both as the medium of teaching and for teaching the language. The aim is the good acquisition of the second language as well as of the mother tongue (Cummins, 2001). The emphasis on bilingual education as an aim of intercultural education does not only involve immigrant children but also linguistic minorities.

From the above it should be obvious that intercultural education is not only intended for the minority students and their education, perceiving them as an educational problem, but also involves the majority, which means the students

MULTICULTURAL/INTERCULTURAL EDUCATION: A GREEK PERSPECTIVE   151

who come from the dominant culture (Dietrich, 1998). Another important issue is that intercultural education refers both to a "state" and an "interstate" level. The former refers to immigrants, repatriates, refugees and to other minorities living within the boundaries of a specific state, whereas the latter involves the cultural communication and interaction of people living in different states. In addition, intercultural education ultimately concerns all schools, even those without a single culturally diverse student in their school population.

From principles, which have been presented above, one can derive certain practices of intercultural education: (a) The main practice consists in the *coeducation* of children with different languages and cultural backgrounds, which means that the children from the dominant culture and the ones from minorities are educated within the same schools. In this way, the marginalizing of minority students, which can happen if the latter are educated in separate schools, can be avoided. (b) *Opening up of the school curricula towards the minority cultures* (Marburger, 1991). The above mentioned coeducation does not make sense or can even lead to cultural assimilation, if the curricula do not include the "view of the other". The intercultural perspective can be included in all the subjects of the curriculum. Today this happens to a very limited extent. (c) The *removal of prejudice, stereotypes and images of enemies from the curricula and textbooks.* This means showing not only the cultural differences but also the similarities among peoples. This practice also applies very well to the case of the Balkan countries and is supported by the international textbook research, the results of which with regard to the Balkans are especially revealing (Xochellis & Toloudi, 2001). (d) Organization of *common projects* of students of different cultural origin using history, literature, music, etc., which allows the contact between cultures, as well as the realization among students of existent cultural similarities. This practice is particularly important, as it does not only involve the cognitive but also the affective domain of the student's personality. This is very significant if we consider that knowing and accepting certain things on the cognitive level is quite far from turning them into attitudes and actions. (e) Introduction of intercultural education principles in *teacher education and in-service training.* This is a very important need, since teachers have a special role in this procedure. The introduction of intercultural education in teacher education should aim firstly to provide teachers with particular abilities and skills (acceptance of the multicultural society, openness, acceptance of the difference, elimination of prejudice and racist views) and secondly to provide suitable educational and didactic know-how. For, it is one thing being willing to do something and another to know how to actually put it into action. In this framework the training of teachers about the aims and practices of intercultural education is currently regarded as an indispensable part of teachers' preparation for the accomplishment/ realization of their professional role.[1]

2 Developing and Implementing the EDIC Course Multicultural/ Intercultural Education[2]

Intercultural education has been an issue of importance in Greek education since the 1990s, when Greece became a receiving country for immigrants, and when educational policy and research started focusing more on minority education as a whole. After the onset of the economic crisis in 2009, as well as the dynamic appearance of an extreme-right extremist group on the political scene, it became evident that the idea of intercultural education had to be reconsidered and linked to Education for Democratic Intercultural Citizenship (Kesidou, 2017). This is in order to help fight xenophobia, racism, chauvinism and Euro-skepticism. The challenges presented to Greece and Europe by the recent refugee crisis, along with the necessity to uphold education viewed as a basic human right, to provide refugee children with equal educational opportunities and to develop inclusive schools and societies, also highlight the importance of linking Intercultural Education to Human Rights and Citizenship Education.

Intercultural education has been a part of teacher education (both at BA and MA level) in Greece during the last two decades, even though programmes offered by different universities vary in the extent to which they deal with the issue. Furthermore, relevant research has shown that the programmes are usually restricted to the provision of knowledge and do not necessarily enable student teachers to have first-hand experiences of practice-oriented work.

The issue "Multicultural/Intercultural Education" has been offered in the context of the MA Programme of the Department of Education of the School of Philosophy and Education/Aristotle University of Thessaloniki for over a decade in the Greek language and has led to extensive research. The main challenge in developing a new MA course on the same topic in the context of EDIC was to avoid having merely a similar version of the existing course in English, but to create a totally new course perspective. Indeed, the challenge of linking the main topic with democracy, citizenship and human rights and the refugee issue called for a strong *interdisciplinary* perspective. The linkage itself broadens the range of the academic field of Intercultural Education, which constitutes a novelty, as well as an innovative feature of the module. Delving into the refugee crisis in Europe involves introducing a more holistic approach, as well as a comparative perspective. In this context, the main features of the EDIC course

Multicultural/Intercultural Education are interdisciplinarity, linkage of intercultural education to the issues of democracy/citizenship and human rights, a strong consideration of the current refugee crisis in Greece and in Europe and a comparative approach to the challenges of multicultural European societies, as well as to the relevant respond of European education systems.

2.1 Aim of the Course

The aim of the course is for MA students to locate the challenges of "otherness" in the society, to understand in depth the philosophy of the intercultural approach in educational policy and practice and to apply the intercultural theory in basic fields of minority education in Greece and at an international level. In particular, MA students will understand the importance of the inclusion of the values of democracy, human rights and intercultural understanding in the educational policy and practice, identify main challenges and problems besetting the education of children with an immigrant or minority backgrounds, and they will familiarize themselves with effective interventions and policies that enable minority students to enjoy equal opportunities and to benefit from positive educational outcomes. The course is set to create a platform for young educators and researchers from different European countries, who will be able to gain international academic experience, work together and learn from each other in a joint effort to take full cognizance of the essentials of a positive educational change, so that the aim of an "education for all" can be realized.

2.2 Learning Outcomes

2.2.1 Knowledge

Students will

– understand, compare and evaluate the principles of "universalism" and "cultural relativism" of values;
– identify the main challenges and main problems that the research highlights as related to the education of children with immigrant background in Greece, Europe and internationally;
– understand the process of "negotiation of identity" for culturally diverse students in national education systems and how this is linked to their school success/failure;
– understand that the inclusion of intercultural education in educational practice is related to the adaptation of school work on multiple levels (communication in school, teaching and learning, curricula and textbooks, teacher education and training, bilingualism/multilingualism);
– understand the link between educational policy and education for democracy and human rights;

- be enabled to identify the main challenges of the education of immigrant/ refugee children in a comparative perspective according to the relevant research in their countries;
- understand the challenges of the refugee crisis and the education of refugee children in Greece and in other European countries;
- realize the interdisciplinary (philosophical, sociological, legal, linguistic, etc.) character of the topic Multicultural/Intercultural education.

2.2.2 Competences

Students will
- be able to develop coherent and logical argumentation in the context of academic oral and written discourse;
- be able to formulate a research question and develop a research design in order to reach a response;
- conduct scientific research individually or in group using the international literature, official research and policy documents/reports of International Organizations and other research centers, databases, etc.;
- be able to submit a proposal for the education of different cultural/minority groups in terms of educational policy and educational practice;
- be sensitized to the challenges of Multicultural/Intercultural Education (interculturalism, democracy, citizenship, human rights, peace).

2.3 *Course Content*

The course puts special emphasis on the relationship between multicultural-ism and democracy, different concepts and practices of citizenship education, the rights of immigrants and refugees, human rights and education, the status and the education of minorities in Greece, the current refugee crisis and its impact upon children, the main aims and practices in Intercultural Education, as well as Intercultural Education in Greece. Special emphasis is also placed on research and fieldwork in the area of Multicultural/Intercultural education. Specifically, apart from the lectures, students also have the opportunity to takepart in field visits and activities: for example, in spring semester 2018, in the context of the first try-out of the course, they had the opportunity to visit the Jewish Museum of Thessaloniki as well as to go on the "Jewish walk" in the city and also to visit a Refugee Day Care Centre in Thessaloniki. Field visits provide first-hand experiences of the issues in the context of the local community and also to create links with the work of civil society organizations. In this way, the gap between academic knowledge/scientific research and practice-oriented work in teacher education, which was highlighted above, can be bridged.

The course also draws, among others, on the expertise and the resources of the Research Centre for Intercultural Education (KEDE) of the School of Philosophy and Education, the UNESCO Chair on Education for Human Rights, Democracy and Peace of the Aristotle University of Thessaloniki (the national coordinator of the "European Master's Degree in Human Rights and Democratisation" of the European Inter-University Center for Human Rights and Democratization/Global Campus of Human Rights) and the Hellenic Observatory for Intercultural Education (a growing community of academics, researchers, school advisers and teachers, aiming to implement intercultural education). This is an effort to combine several academic resources and initiatives of the Aristotle University of Thessaloniki for the benefit of the developing EDIC course. Creating these horizontal linkages could be regarded at the same time also as a desideratum for the university; in this sense, the EDIC project and course also offer a relevant benefit to the university itself.

In detail, the course schedule for spring semester 2018 included the following content:

Aristotle University of Thessaloniki
School of Philosophy and Education
'Education for Democratic Intercultural Citizenship' (EDIC)
(Erasmus+ – KA2 Strategic Partnerships)

Course: Multicultural/Intercultural Education
Spring Semester 2018 – 7.5/10 ECTS

Mondays 18:00–20:00, Room 111 (Old building of the Faculty of Philosophy)

5.3.2018   Multicultural/Intercultural Education
Anastasia Kesidou
Assistant Professor, School of Philosophy and Education, AUTh

12.3.2018   Liberal Democracy: the Bare Essentials
Filimon Peonidis
Professor, School of Philosophy and Education, AUTh

19.3.2018   Different Concepts and Practices of Citizenship Education: a Plea for a Critical-Democratic Intercultural Citizenship Education
Wiel Veugelers
Professor, University of Humanistic Studies, Utrecht
EDIC coordinator

26.3.2018	The Rights of Immigrants and Refugees
	Konstantinos Tsitselikis
	Professor, School of Balkan, Slavic and Oriental Studies,
	University of Macedonia
	Hellenic League for Human Rights
16.4.2018	The Current Refugee Crisis and its Impact upon Children
	Eleni Hodolidou
	Associate Professor, School of Philosophy and Education,
	AUTh
30.4.2018	Human Rights and Education
	Christos Tsironis
	Assistant Professor, School of Theology, AUTh
7.5.2018	The Status and Education of Minorities in Greece
	Konstantinos Tsitselikis
	Professor, School of Balkan, Slavic and Oriental Studies,
	University of Macedonia
	Hellenic League for Human Rights
4.6.2018	Intercultural Education in Greece
	Eleni Hodolidou
18:00–21:00	Associate Professor, School of Philosophy and Education, AUTh
	Anastasia Kesidou
	Assistant Professor, School of Philosophy and Education, AUTh
	Course Evaluation

Visits during the Semester

Wednesday 21.3.2018 10:00	Visit to the Jewish Museum of Thessaloniki/'Jewish walk' in the city http://www.jmth.gr/
Tuesday 8.5.2018 11:30	Visit to the Refugee Day Center Alkyone Orfanidou 5, 54626 Thessaloniki https://el-gr.facebook.com/alkyonedaycenter/
May 2018	Visit to Diavata Open Centre of Temporary Reception for Refugees

---

Additional Lecture

Thursday 3.5.2018 14:00–16:00	A Disturbing View of Intercultural Communication: Findings of a Study into Hate Speech in Polish *Anna Szczepaniak-Kozak* Assistant Professor, Institute of Applied Linguistics, Adam Mickiewicz University Poznań
	Offered by the UNESCO Chair on Education for Human Rights, Democracy and Peace, AUTh to the MA students of the Faculty of Philosophy

The course try-out was held throughout spring semester (March to June) 2018. In particular, *eight sessions* were offered in the form of seminars, which were taught by members of the faculty of the Aristotle University of Thessaloniki and the University of Macedonia. The effort was made to ensure participation of experts in the particular topics taught within the wider areas of Education, Philosophy, Social Science, Law, etc. Lessons were taught by Filimon Peonidis (also course co-organizer), Eleni Hodolidou,[3] Christos Tsironis, Konstantinos Tsitselikis and Anastasia Kesidou (course organizer and leading teacher). Wiel Veugelers, EDIC coordinator and critical friend for the particular module, visited Aristotle University during the semester and was also one of the course teachers. In addition, *one workshop* was offered to the students in cooperation with the UNESCO Chair on Education for Human Rights, Democracy and Peace under the title "A Disturbing View of Intercultural Communication: findings of a Study into Hate Speech in Polish". The workshop was led by Anna Szczepaniak-Kozak, Institute of Applied Linguistics/Adam Mickiewicz University Poznań, and focused on the research material and the results of the European project "Regulating AntiDiscrimination and AntiRacism (RADAR)". It brought the students of the EDIC course together with MA students of Social Psychology of the Aristotle University and MA students of the European Master's Programme in Human Rights and Democratisation (E.MA) of the UNESCO Chair, which created a stimulating interdisciplinary academic environment.

As mentioned above, field visits included the Jewish Museum of Thessaloniki and important Jewish sites in the city center (with the valuable contribution of an expert guide), as well as the Refugee Day Center Alkyone. Even though permission had been secured to visit Diavata Open Centre of

Temporary Reception for Refugees, unexpected events, which affected existing conditions in the Centre, finally made the visit impossible.

At the end of the semester, there was *one last session,* which involved the *evaluation* of the course, as well as an *extensive discussion* on the final paper that the students were asked to prepare (a 2500/5000 word essay on a specific topic/research question, in which they had to take into account the relevant bibliography). Some examples of the topics of the papers were as follows:

(a) "Ronald Dworkin's Theory of Rights as 'Trumps'", (b) "Using G.F.Z. Bereday's comparative method, compare the way that two European countries deal with the education of refugee children. Focus on one level of the provided education/training. e.g. vocational education, inclusive education, primary, secondary", (c) "The human rights universality Vs cultural relativism debate based on the argumentation of Jack Donnelly and M. Goodhart", (d) "Social integration for immigrants and refugees in Greece", (e) "Bilingual minority schools of Thrace: major challenges", (f) "The participation of the Hellenic Armed Forces in resolving the refugee influx in Greece 2016 – Diavata Temporary Open Reception Center", etc.

Students were expected to actively participate in the teaching activities and field visits throughout the semester. The bibliography and educational material of the course was uploaded on the e-platform "E-learning" of the Aristotle University, which was accessible to all participating students.

Eight Greek and five foreign students participated in the course. Six out of eight Greek students were MA and two were PhD students, either in Education or Philosophy. One of them attended the MA Programme of the School of Primary Education of the Aristotle University, which indicated that the EDIC course can attract interest also among other Schools of the University. The five foreign students were Erasmus students of Humanistic or Social Sciences (one of Geography), either from Germany (Humboldt University Berlin, University of Hamburg) or Italy (University of Padova). For students the study load was 7,5 ECTS, while in two cases it was 10 ECTS (corresponding to a 5000 word essay).

Three of the course participants also participated in the EDIC Intensive Programme (IP), which took place at the University of Tallinn and the University of Helsinki in May 2018 (two were MA students in Educational Science/ International Education and one was a PhD student in Philosophy). Since the emphasis of the specific IP was on *teaching practices* in Education for Democratic Intercultural Citizenship, the research of both teachers and students, of the Aristotle University, which was presented in the IP, focused on teaching and learning in the framework of intercultural education (an expertise of Aristotle University and also the topic of the university's EDIC course). The lectures provided by the teachers were "Teaching and Learning in Culturally

Diverse Schools and Societies", and "Speaking about Conspiracy Theories to Students", while the students presented their own research based on the posters that they had prepared and received useful feedback on it from the other EDIC teachers and students. The topics of their presentations were: (a) "The gender identities' construction in the Greek language school textbooks currently used in the 6th grade of Primary Education in Greece", (b) "Why, what and how should we teach about the Holocaust in Secondary Education" and (c) "Managing cultural diversity in compulsory education in Greece and Finland: a comparative approach". At the same time, their group research, which they designed and conducted from February until May 2018 especially for the IP, dealt with "Teaching Practices in EDIC: the Case of Greece".

The group presentation first focused on the analysis of the educational policy and the school curricula with regard to EDIC in Greece, then it referred to the quantitative and qualitative analysis of primary research data gathered by the students based on a questionnaire concerning the actual teaching practices used by Greek teachers. Finally, it referred to the preparation of prospective teachers in EDIC teaching practices in Greece, again on the basis of primary research on the Programmes of Studies offered by Greek universities in teacher education. The successful participation of the Greek students in IP Tallinn/Helsinki was followed by the completion of their post- IP task "How can teaching practices taught during this EDIC course, promote Education for Democratic Intercultural Citizenship in your country?" and the finalization of their learning diaries that they kept during the IP. Their detailed diaries provided a valuable contribution to the overall evaluation of the IP and the better organization of the EDIC IP to be organized in Thessaloniki in March 2019.

It should also be noted that during the academic years 2016–2017 and 2017–2018 the Aristotle University finalized bilateral Erasmus agreements with all EDIC partner universities. In winter semester 2018–2019 one of the MA students who had participated in the EDIC course on "Multicultural/Intercultural Education" spent a semester at the University of Helsinki, where she was able to also successfully participate in the respective EDIC module on "Teachers' Moral Competence in Pedagogical Encounters". After having completed *two* modules of the Programme, she was entitled to an "EDIC Certificate". An additional contribution of the student's EDIC stay at the University of Helsinki was that she was able to finalize a part of the research conducted for her MA thesis at the Aristotle University of Thessaloniki, under the title "Managing Cultural Diversity in Compulsory Education in Greece and in Finland: a Comparative Approach". Thus, the EDIC Programme was able to provide the student with extended educational benefits and opportunities. In addition, at the same time several exchanges with the EDIC universities were initiated on BA level

(UvH, Bath Spa, Charles University Prague and Tallinn), which is also to be considered as a positive contribution of the Programme as a whole.

Finally, it should be noted that the EDIC course is seen positively by the School of Philosophy and Education and the Aristotle University of Thessaloniki, among others, due to its European and international character, which can further support and promote student exchange. The course will be offered again to MA students in spring semester 2019, taking the evaluation of the previous academic year, along with the comments of the critical friend, into consideration. Also in this new try-out, the module will be supported again by an EDIC critical friend, Maria Rosa Buxarrais, University of Barcelona. The sustainability of the EDIC course has been secured by the fact that it will constitute an integral part of the new Master's Programme of the Department of Education, School of Philosophy and Education, on "Educational Science", which is to be launched in the academic year 2019–2020.

3 Student Evaluation

As mentioned above, the evaluation of the course was conducted in June 2018. Specifically, it had the form of a focus group discussion led by one of the course organizers. The discussion followed four main questions, considering the practice followed in the evaluation of the EDIC Intensive Programmes. Four questions/statements were set to the students, which they were asked to answer/comment on:

1. One useful thing I learnt in the EDIC course this semester.
2. One thing I would change in the course.
3. Relevance of the EDIC course to my studies in my own university.
4. Any messages for teachers?

Students were encouraged to freely express their assessment and thoughts, as these were considered crucial for the improvement of the course try-out. The focus group discussion resulted in a large amount of qualitative data, the most important of which are presented as follows:

1. *One useful thing I learnt in the EDIC course this year*
   The students seemed to have strongly appreciated the clarification of *academic terminology*, such as 'intercultural education', 'liberal democracy', 'hate speech', as well as the *legal aspect* of the course, especially the rights of immigrants and refugees and mostly the legal definitions discussed during the lectures, which they found very enlightening. The three types of citizenship, discussed in "Different Concepts and Practices of Citizenship Education", was found very interesting and an incentive

MULTICULTURAL/INTERCULTURAL EDUCATION: A GREEK PERSPECTIVE 161

for more profound research and understanding, especially in terms of their application in schools. Most students stressed that the most crucial course benefit was the link created between academic knowledge and real life/issues and problems: "we were able to overcome the academic 'bubble' and see the importance of academic knowledge for the real world". In this context, they stressed the importance of the study visits and the created links to civil society institutions. They also said that they appreciated very much the interdisciplinary character of the module, as well as the originality of the research-oriented workshop on hate speech.

2. *One thing I would change in the course*
The students asked for a more active role for themselves during the lectures, more sessions in the form of seminars/workshops, as well as strengthening the comparative dimension of the course. Concerning the latter, they stated that they would like to learn more about the issues in terms of their relevance with the different countries of students represented in the course (especially in the form of short individual or group presentations). Another interesting proposal was to initiate a *reflection* upon completion of the first half of the course. A visit to a Greek school would clarify even more "Intercultural Education in Greece". Finally, the students noted that it would be helpful to have access to the educational material of the lectures at the very start of the semester.

3. *Relevance of the* EDIC *course to my studies in my own university*
The Greek students noted that the EDIC course was highly relevant to their studies, considering that the focus in their work was on "International Education", including Intercultural Education, Critical Peace Education and Comparative approaches in education. A very positive feedback was that at the end of the semester they were indeed able to find links of intercultural education with citizenship education and education for human rights, which they considered as definitely one step forward in their studies. The Erasmus students also responded positively to the same question; one of them emphasized that he was going to proceed with this topic in the framework of his studies, probably even choosing to write his MA thesis on one of the aspects discussed within the EDIC course.

4. *Any messages for teachers?*
Perhaps the most important message for teachers was to add a more practical aspect to their lecture (discussion, activity, reflection or even a small workshop). This could, for example, be the case in "Human Rights and Education", where important educational material could be used, such as "Compass" by the Council of Europe, etc. In general, students stressed

how much they appreciated the high expertise of their professors, which could be even more exploited in terms of including practical links. One student highlighted the important aspect of trying to consciously 'find the thread' of lectures through the semester, as well as the possible contribution of the individual teachers to it. Finally, some of them asked for a more research-oriented literature list, which would, among others, include the absolute "core research references".[4]

In conclusion, the students were very appreciative of the opportunity to attend the EDIC course on Multicultural/Intercultural Education, which they evaluated very positively. They also appreciated the study visits and the linkages made to the course content and highlighted the positive impact of the interdisciplinarity of the course. At the same time, they also provided useful ideas for the fine-tuning of the course during the following academic year. In addition, both Greek and Erasmus students also stressed the European environment and the opportunity to take the course in the English language. Especially for Erasmus students, the existence of such a course additionally filled a need, in terms of enriching the relatively small selection of MA courses in English, currently offered at the Aristotle University of Thessaloniki.

4   Course Literature

Adamczak-Krysztofowicz, S., & Szczepaniak-Kozak, A. (2017). A disturbing view of intercultural communication: Findings of a study into hate speech in Polish. *Linguistica Silesiana, 38*, 285–310.

ARSIS/Association for the Social Support of Youth. (2019). *Stories of people from the "Other Shore"*. Thessaloniki: ARSIS.

Banks, J. A., Cookson, P., Gay, G., Hawley, W. D., Irvine, J. J., Nieto, S., Schofield, J. W., & Stephan, W. G. (2001). Diversity within unity: Essential principles for teaching and learning in a multicultural society. *Phi Delta Kappan, 83*(3), 196–203.

Banks, J. A., & Mc Gee Banks, C. A. M. (Eds.). (2007). *Multicultural education: Issues and perspectives*. Hoboken, NJ: John Wiley & Sons.

CBC Radio. (2015). *No one puts their children in a boat unless ...* Retrieved from http://www.cbc.ca/radio/thesundayedition/let-them-in-where-s-the-poetry-in-politics-what-is-the-middle-class-trump-and-the-know-nothings-1.3223214/no-one-puts-their-children-in-a-boat-unless-1.3224831

Delpit, L. (1995). *Other people's children: Cultural conflict in the classroom*. New York, NY: The New Press.

DOME Network of Ambassadors Report. (2017). *Refugee-led initiatives across Euromena: aspects of representation, ownership and empowerment, The DOME Project*. Retrieved from https://goo.gl/PyHmPz

MULTICULTURAL/INTERCULTURAL EDUCATION: A GREEK PERSPECTIVE   163

Dossou, K., Klein, G., Strani, K., Caniglia, E., & Ravenda, A. (2016). *RADAR trainees' handbook: Anti-hate communication tools in an intercultural perspective*. Perugia: Key & Key Communications. Retrieved from https://pureapps2.hw.ac.uk/ws/portalfiles/portal/15961643/RADAR_Trainees_Handbook_EN.pdf

European Commission. (2008). *Migration and mobility: Challenges and opportunities for EU education systems* (Green Paper). Brussels: European Commission.

Eurydice. (2012). *Citizenship education in Europe*. Brussels: Education, Audiovisual and Culture Executive Agency.

Coulby, D., Gundara, J., & Crispin, J. (Eds.). (1997). *Intercultural education*. London: Kogan Page.

Heckmann, F. (2008). *Education and migration. Strategies for integrating migrant children in European schools and societies: A synthesis of research findings for policymakers*. Report submitted to the European Commission by the NESSE network of experts. Retrieved from http://www.nesse.fr/nesse/activities/reports/activities/reports/education-and-migration-pdf

Lenhart, V., & Savolainen, K. (2002). Human Rights Education as a field of practice and of theoretical reflection. *International Review of Education, 48*(3–4), 145–158.

McAllister, G. & Irvine, J. J. (2002). The role of empathy in teaching culturally diverse students: A qualitative study of teachers' beliefs. *Journal of Teacher Education, 53*(5), 433–443.

Morfidis, G. (2018). *Could CIMIC foster the civil-military interaction in national response to refugee influxes? Case Study: the participation of the Hellenic Armed Forces in resolving the refugee influx in Greece 2016. Diavata Open Temporary-Accommodation Center* (Unpublished master thesis). Aristotle University of Thessaloniki. Retrieved from https://ikee.lib.auth.gr/record/295981/files/GRI-2018-21010.pdf

Peonidis, F. (2013). *Democracy as popular sovereignty*. Lanham, MD: Lexington Books.

Peonidis, F. (2014). Citizenship. In H. ten Have (Ed.), *Encyclopedia of Global Bioethics*. Cham: Springer.

Tibbits, F. (2002). Understanding what we do: Emerging models for Human Rights Education. *International Review of Education, 48*(3–4), 159–171.

Tsitselikis, K. (2012). *Old and new Islam in Greece: From traditional minorities to immigrant newcomers*. Leiden & Boston, MA: Martinus Nijhoff.

Tsitselikis, K. (2018). Refugees in Greece: Facing a multifaceted labyrinth. *International Migration*. doi:10.1111/imig.12473

UNESCO. (2011). *Contemporary issues in human rights education*. Paris: United Nations Educational Scientific and Cultural Organization. Retrieved from http://unesdoc.unesco.org/images/0021/002108/210895e.pdf

Veugelers, W. (2017). Education for critical-democratic citizenship: Autonomy and social justice in a multicultural society. In N. Aloni & L. Weintrob (Eds.), *Beyond bystanders* (pp. 47–60). Rotterdam, The Netherlands: Sense Publishers.

Viviani, A. (Ed.). (2018). *Global citizenship education, multiculturalism and social inclusion in Europe: The findings of the project "I have rights"*. Coimbra. Retrieved from https://ihaverights.pixel-online.org/files/book/Final%20Publication.pdf

Notes

1 For a detailed discussion of the main aim and practices of Intercultural Education, see also Kesidou (2004).
2 Special thanks are due to Filimon Peonidis, Professor of Moral and Political Philosophy at the School of Philosophy and Education/Aristotle University of Thessaloniki and EDIC course co-organizer, for his important contribution to the curriculum development and implementation, and also for providing his academic expertise in important aspects of the course, such as democratic theory, citizenship, tolerance and the philosophical foundations of human rights. Our joint effort in the context of this course also acted as a bridge between Education and Philosophy, which are the two academic disciplines represented at our School.
3 Many thanks are due to colleague Eleni Hodolidou, Associate Professor at the School of Philosophy and Education, who enriched the EDIC Course with her academic expertise in Cultural Studies and identity and also with her important work in the field of refugee education in Greece, which is a crucial aspect of the course. She also provided valuable ideas and opened doors with regard to the field visits organized and undertaken in the context of the course try-out.
4 The study by Veugelers et al. (2017) was mentioned here as an example of a core research reference, with regard to the topic of Citizenship Education. The students requested more references of this kind on the other topics, as well.

References

Auernheimer, G. (1995). *Einführung in die interkulturelle Erziehung* [*Introduction to Intercultural Education*]. Darmstadt: Wissenschaftliche Buchgesellschaft.
Cummins, J. (2001). *Negotiating identities: Education for empowerment in a diverse society*. Ontario: California Association for Bilingual Education.
Dietrich, I. (1997). Die Bedeutung der interkulturellen Erziehung im Schulalltag [The importance of intercultural education in everyday school life]. *Lernen in Deutschland. Zeitschrift für Interkulturelle Erziehung, 2,* 106–117.
Dietrich, I. (1998). Das Ende der monokulturellen Erziehung [The end of monocultural education]. In V. Strittmatter-Haubold & T. Häcker (Eds.), *Das Ende der Erziehung. Lehren und Lernen für das nächste Jahrtausend* [*The end of education: teaching and learning for the next century*] (pp. 75–88). Weinheim: Deutscher Studien Verlag.

MULTICULTURAL/INTERCULTURAL EDUCATION: A GREEK PERSPECTIVE 165

Essinger, H. (1991). Interkulturelle Erziehung in multiethnischen Gesellschaften [Intercultural education in multi-ethnic societies]. In H. Marburger (Ed.), *Schule in der multikulturellen Gesellschaft. Ziele, Aufgaben und Wege interkultureller Erziehung* [*School in the multicultural society: goals, tasks and paths of intercultural education*] (pp. 3–18). Frankfurt a. M.: Verlag für Interkulturelle Kommunikation.

Hodolidou, E. (2018). Identity and differences. In A. Viviani (Ed.). *Global citizenship education, multiculturalism and social inclusion in Europe: The findings of the project "I have rights"* (pp. 149–167). Coimbra. Retrieved from https://ihaverights.pixel-online.org/files/book/Final%20Publication.pdf

Kesidou, A. (2004). Aims and practices in intercultural education. In N. Terzis (Ed.), *Intercultural education in the Balkan countries* (pp. 97–105). Thessaloniki: Kyriakidis.

Kesidou, A. (2017). Citizenship and tolerance in the cradle of democracy. In W. Veugelers, I. de Groot, & V. Stolk (Eds.), *Research for cult committee – Teaching common values in Europe* (pp. 107–114). Brussels: European Parliament, Policy Department for Structural and Cohesion Policy.

Marburger, H. (1991). Von der Ausländerpädagogik zur Interkulturellen Erziehung (From Foreigner Pedagogy to Intercultural Education). In H. Marburger (Ed.), *Schule in der multikulturellen Gesellschaft. Ziele, Aufgaben und Wege interkultureller Erziehung* [*School in the multicultural society: goals, tasks and paths of intercultural education*] (pp. 19–34). Frankfurt a. M.: Verlag für Interkulturelle Kommunikation.

UNHCR. (2017). *Left behind: Refugee education in crisis*. Report. Retrieved from https://www.unhcr.org/59b696f44.pdf

Veugelers, W., De Groot, I., & Stolk, V. (2017). *Research for cult committee – Teaching common values in Europe*. Brussels: European Parliament, Policy Department for Structural and Cohesion Policy. Retrieved from http://bit.ly/2pm5Yh9

Xochellis, P., & Toloudi, F. (Eds.). (2001). *The image of the 'other'/neighbour in the school textbooks of the Balkan Countries*. Proceedings of the International Conference, Thessaloniki, 16–18 October 1998. Athens: Typothito, George Dardanos.

CHAPTER 9

Experiencing Democratic Intercultural Citizenship: EDIC Intensive Programmes

Elina Kuusisto, Dana Moree and Reet Sillavee

1 Introduction

This chapter is based on two Education for Democratic Intercultural Citizenship (EDIC) Intensive Programmes held in Prague in 2017 and in Tallinn-Helsinki in 2018.[1] In introducing the themes and methods used during these Intensive Programmes, this chapter focuses particularly on local flavour. It also addresses the participating students' most important learning experiences.

EDIC Intensive Programmes were created to test, share and calibrate elements of each of the seven modules (see other chapters in the present volume) into a joint EDIC curriculum. Seven EDIC universities each sent two teachers and three students who came together for a ten-day-long Intensive Programme. Intensive Programmes created opportunities to learn democratic intercultural citizenship by literally practising social inclusion and civic competence.

The Intensive Programmes (IP) consisted of lectures, roundtable discussions, field visits, and interactions with the civic society. The lectures given by the teachers from the seven EDIC universities presented parts of each module. In roundtable discussions, students had brief group time with each of the EDIC teachers and were able to learn more about the topics of each module. These activities, as well as teachers' meetings (Table 9.1), formed an integral part of the development of the EDIC curriculum.

Field trips and interactions with civic society addressed the interdisciplinary nature of academic cooperation by including a broad range of partners representing social sciences, humanities, and teacher education. By offering holistic education for democratic intercultural citizenship, the EDIC Intensive Programmes aimed to support the education of future teachers and educational professionals, and to train them in how to promote European values (Veugelers, de Groot, & Stolk, 2017) such as preventing violent radicalisation, fostering social integration, and enhancing intercultural understanding. The teaching and learning activities envisaged in IPs were intended to help participants build a sense of belonging to a European community and a social capital by empowering them to participate actively in European societies.

© KONINKLIJKE BRILL NV, LEIDEN, 2019 | DOI: 10.1163/9789004411944_009

This is an open access chapter distributed under the terms of the CC-BY-NC 4.0 License.

EXPERIENCING DEMOCRATIC INTERCULTURAL CITIZENSHIP 167

The values of democracy and tolerance were strongly supported in Intensive Programmes by enhancing the common values of freedom, tolerance and non-discrimination through education and allowing the participants to experience intercultural dialogue and cultural diversity. The participants of the Intensive Programmes represented not only the seven EDIC countries, but also included students from all over Europe as well as students from Africa, Latin America, North America, the Middle East and Asia. These international students were registered for degrees at different EDIC universities and had opted to participate in this enrichment programme offered by EDIC. Thus, the Intensive Programmes were internationally oriented educational activities in themselves, in addition to which they served as inspiration for the development of the modules in each country. In the Intensive Programmes, parts of the modules were tried out and critically reflected on by fellow teachers and students.

2 Themes of Intensive Programmes: European Inclusiveness, with a Focus on National, Regional and Local Differences

The EDIC programme was created to be research-oriented, comparative, and linked with civil society. This transnational nature of the project was highlighted during the Intensive Programmes: teachers and students were given opportunity to experience and express European inclusiveness, with attention for national, regional and local differences and academic traditions. The themes of the Intensive Programmes were chosen to highlight the academic and cultural traditions of intercultural and civic education in the country and university organising the Intensive Programme.

2.1 Educational Activities in Civic Society: Charles University in Prague

In Prague, the theme was *Educational Activities in Civic Society* in order to highlight the role of civic society in building and developing the Czech Republic after the end of the Soviet regime in 1991. Because of the relatively short history of the Czech Republic's civic society, the Intensive Programme was able to provide opportunities to meet both founding and current activists, and to experience the educational activities that Charles University is advocating and developing with a wide range of partners across the country.

Since the Velvet revolution in 1989, civic education has had to go through a turbulent development. During the Cold War, this field of education was used to pass on ideology to all the students with the intention to create obedient citizens of the totalitarian state. Citizenship education went through rapid development after 1989, and is still in progress. The Intensive Programme in Prague offered a condensed experience of sharing and re-building a topic like citizenship education from the perspective of the agents of change from past and present generations, who still play an active role in its definition and practice.

During the Intensive Programme, participants experienced educational activities of Czech civic society in four ways: (1) a discussion with one of the co-founders of Czech civic society; (2) a field trip guided by NGO Antikomplex to an abandoned village and a prison camp in Sudetenland, the northern border area of the Czech Republic; (3) a play by the Theatre of the Oppressed; and (4) a guided tour in Prague led by homeless people (see Table 9.1).

2.1.1 Meeting a Co-Founder of Czech Civic Society

During the first evening in Prague, IP participants were introduced to and conversed with Mr Igor Blaževič, who is regarded as one of the co-founders of civic society in the Czech Republic. Born in Bosnia and Herzegovina, Igor Blaževič graduated from the Faculty of Philosophy in Zagreb, Croatia, and has lived and worked in Prague since 1991. At the time of the IP, he was working at the Prague Civil Society Centre, where he has fulfilled the position of head of the Transitions Programme since 2016. Mr Blaževič has been engaged with People in Need (PIN) since 1992, first as the head of PIN's communications department and later as director of all of PIN's democracy assistance and human rights programmes. With PIN, Igor was involved in the support of dissidents and political activists across the globe. In 1997, Igor was reporting from Hong Kong and South East Asia for several media organisations in the Czech Republic. Together with his wife, he has co-authored ten TV documentary films for Czech Television. Igor Blaževič was also the founder and the executive director (1998–2010) of the One World Film Festival in Prague, which is regarded as Europe's biggest human rights documentary international film festival. From 2011 to early 2016, he worked in Burma/Myanmar as the Lead Lecturer for Educational Initiatives, providing Comparative Political Science courses to local civil society and political activists. With his extensive experience as an activist in the Czech Republic and various parts of the globe, Igor Blaževič was able to share his knowledge and offer critical perspectives. Although Igor shared his passion and purpose in life with the IP participants, he really wanted to continue to address the challenges and difficult issues relating to the democracy and human rights in today's world. In doing so, he hoped to offer a realistic view to challenge unrealistic or over-optimistic and over-idealistic approaches that might not succeed and might be easily dismissed as pipe dreams, and thus make a difference in the world.

EXPERIENCING DEMOCRATIC INTERCULTURAL CITIZENSHIP 169

2.1.2 *Field Trip to Sudetenland*

Sudetenland in North Bohemia is a special area near the German border in the northern Czech Republic. Before the Second World War this area was populated by three million German speaking citizens who were deported after the war, in 1945–1946. At the same time, two million settlers from the inner parts of the country were transported to the area. It should be noted that at that time, the territory that today constitutes the Czech Republic (Matějka, n.d.) had a population of approximately nine million. The settling of these new people was not successful and eventually, in the early 1960s, many villages were abandoned and even disappeared. During the Soviet regime (from 1948 to 1989), a large prison camp was established in a Sudetenland town called Jáchymov. During the field trip under the guidance of the volunteers of an NGO called Antikomplex, Jáchymov and one of these abandoned villages were visited.

Antikomplex (2019) was founded to discuss the tragic and widely unacknowledged and forgotten history of Sudetenland. It aims to educate and critically reflect on the past of Sudetenland by raising awareness and promoting people's "ability to openly reflect on one's own history", which is considered to be "one of the basic skills of any free society since World War II". Antikomplex also highlights that "there are no age-old traumas from the past before us that could scare anyone. Liberation in this case means to recognise all questions that our past has left open and to face them" (Antikomplex, 2019). All EDIC participants were able to walk in the footsteps of the prisoners and experience what are now the ruined homes of the fleeing German families.

The field trip started with a visit to the prison camp in Jáchymov. The prisoners were opponents of the Soviet regime, and they were forced to mine uranium under very tough conditions. The ruins of the large camp are located on a mountain. To illustrate the harshness of the life of prisoners, the IP participants climbed the same stairs that chained-together prisoners used to climb up and down every day. The mining industry in Jáchymov was closed in 1961. Many of those who worked in the mines were seriously ill later (Wikipedia, 2019).

Antikomplex also took the group to visit one of the abandoned, originally German villages, Königsmühle. Before entering the ruins, the volunteers of the Antikomplex explained the history of the village. After that, the students and academics had time to explore the remains, and were all instructed to write a poem describing their feelings and thoughts about this abandoned village, located in a beautiful valley with small brooks running through. Finally, the whole group gathered in one of the buildings, where some of the poems were read aloud and discussed. A number of poems were also discussed next day during classes held in Charles University.

2.1.3 Theatre of the Oppressed

The IP participants were given an opportunity to see a play performed in English by the Theatre of the Oppressed, titled Havlonáda (see chapter XX in this volume). The performance was created by students and young activists of Charles University, Prague, co-operating with people from various NGOs, including Ara Art, the first NGO in Czech Republic aimed at supporting LGBT and Roma minorities. The main character of the play, Klara, returns to the Czech Republic after a long stay in the USA and wants to organise an event where people from ethnic majorities and minorities can come together as a protest against racism and the growing violence in Czech society. She seems to get some support from her friends, who are PR and marketing professionals. However, the clash of values and ideas about what such an event means, seems to make it be impossible.

The play addresses problems that young people experience in the Czech Republic of today; in fact, these issues concerned universal topics such as feeling of loneliness, exclusion, and human rights. The Theatre of the Oppressed engages its audience, inviting them to actively participate in working through the issues and dilemmas and process the topics on stage, and the Intensive Programme participants actively offered input during the scenes. Two students and an academic took part on the stage. This type of learning was memorable and powerful. It made everyone present become immersed in the issues presented on stage, leading them to process and develop their democratic intercultural citizenship at the level of emotions and attitudes.

2.1.4 Guided Tour by Homeless Persons

The fourth experiential learning experience related to the guided tour in Prague from the perspective of a homeless man. The tour was organised by Pragulic (2019), an organisation founded by students and graduates of the Department of Civil Society Studies of Charles University. The basic idea is that trained homeless people prepare guided tours around Prague that are linked to their life experience. Students of the Intensive Programme could spend two hours of their time walking around together with a homeless man. The strong aspect of such an experience is that it is the homeless person who brings his or her experience and expertise and educates the audience. Power positions are subverted and power inequalities are transformed into a new teaching and learning experience.

2.2 *Educational Practices in Schools: Universities of Tallinn and Helsinki*

The second Intensive Programme was arranged in two countries, Estonia and Finland. Both countries have been highly successful in Programme for

Day	Prague: Educational activities in civil society	Tallinn-Helsinki: Educational practices in schools
1	*Introduction to EDIC* – Poster session: Students present their posters – Lecture: Sentenced to freedom, comparison of two schools, Dana Moree (CZ) – Tour: Walk around the city guided by students from Charles University – Guest speaker Igor Blazevic, co-founder of civic society in Czech R. after the communist regime	*Introduction to EDIC* – Poster session: Students present their posters – Lecture: Social Inclusion, Chloe Yeh (UK) – Tour 1: Around the Tallinn University: Introduction to Estonian education, by the Estonian participants – Tour 2: Tallinn guided tour by students from Tallinn 21. upper secondary school – Guest speakers: Ivor Goodson and Marko Rillo: School of future – a workplace, a club or a hospital?
2	*Citizenship education* – Lectures: Mock elections in citizenship education, Isolde de Groot (NL), How can purpose be taught?, Elina Kuusisto (FI), School performance of immigrant children and immigrant policy, Anastasia Kesidou (GR), Becoming a teacher, Fransisco Esteban (ES)	*Citizenship education* – Reflection: Students write learning diary – Lectures: Democratic citizenship, Terezie Vávrová (CZ), Cultural diversity, Anastasia Kesidou (GR), Ethical competences, Elena Noguera (EE) – Roundtables – Special: Learning Estonian national dances

(cont.)

TABLE 9.1   Schedule of the EDIC Intensive Programmes in Prague and Tallinn-Helsinki *(cont.)*

Day	Prague: Educational activities in civil society	Tallinn-Helsinki: Educational practices in schools
3	*Civic society healing the wounds –* *Field trip to North Bohemia of Czech Repub.* – Visit to a work camp established after the II World War – Visit to abandoned German village and writing a poem about the experience	*Educational practices in Estonian schools –* *Field trip to Peetri Kindergarten-Primary School* – Lectures: Innovative practices, Eve Eisenschmidt (EE), Science curricula, Kristi Mets-Alunurm (EE), Classroom research, Kreet Piiriselg (EE) – Classroom observations – Talk with the school representatives – Roundtables
4	*Democratic education* – EDIC lectures: Non-formal citizenship education, Reet Sillavee (EE), Social and educational inclusion, Ghazala Bhatti (UK) – Roundtables: students discuss with the lectures in small groups	*Democratic education* – Reflection: Students write learning diary – Lectures: Mock elections, Isolde de Groot (NL), Social and educational inclusion, Ghazala Bhatti (UK) – Students' presentations on teacher work – Roundtables – Guest speaker: Young Estonian Russian activist speaking about his personal experience

(cont.)

Day	Prague: Educational activities in civil society	Tallinn-Helsinki: Educational practices in schools
5	*Theatre of the Oppressed* – Group work: Students reflected on the topics of the seven EDIC+ modules – Teachers' meeting – Visit: Theatre of the oppressed performance "Havlonáda"	*Closing of the Estonian part of IP* – Reflection: Students write learning diary – Lecture: Teachers on the waves of transformation, Dana Moree (CZ) – Group work: Photo hunt – Teachers' meeting – Closing reception
6	*Free day*	*Free day for students/Teachers' meeting*
7	*Tour*: Prague guided by homeless people	*Free day*
8	*Intercultural education* – Group work: Students' presentations – Lectures: Teachers' implicit meaning systems, Kirsi Tirri (FI), Educational policy, Eve Eisenschmidt (EE)	*Ferry to Helsinki – History of Finnish educational practices* – Lectures: History of Finnish educational system, Mikko Niemelä (FI), Moral Education at School, Maria Rosa Burrarrais (ES) – Field trip to Helsinki City Museum: Experiencing Finnish teaching practices at 1930s

(*cont.*)

TABLE 9.1   Schedule of the EDIC Intensive Programmes in Prague and Tallinn-Helsinki (*cont.*)

Day	Prague: Educational activities in civil society	Tallinn-Helsinki: Educational practices in schools
9	*Moral education* – Lectures: Understanding human rights, historical perspective, Filimon Peonidis (GR), Family and moral education, Maria Rosa Buxarrais (ES) – Roundtables	*Current educational practices in Finnish schools - Field trip to Normal Lyceum School* – Lectures: Ethical sensitivity, Kirsi Tirri (FI), Speaking about conspiracy theories to students, Filimon Peonidis (GR) – Roundtables – Classroom observations – Talk with the principal Tapio Lahtero
10	*Future perspectives* – Lecture: Future of EDIC, Wiel Veugelers (NL) – Evaluation: Feedback from students – Closing reception	*Future perspectives* – Lectures: Life purpose, Elina Kuusisto (FI), Future of EDIC, Wiel Veugelers (NL) – Evaluation: Feedback from students – Closing reception

CZ = Charles University, Prague, Czech Republic; EE = University of Tallinn, Tallinn, Estonia; FI = University of Helsinki, Helsinki, Finland; GR = Aristotle University, Thessaloniki, Greece; NL = University of Humanistic Studies, Utrecht, the Netherlands; ES = University of Barcelona, Barcelona, Spain; UK = University of Bath Spa, Bath, United Kingdom

International Student Assessment (PISA) studies, and their educational systems have many similarities (see Tirri, 2014; Sarv, 2014). The countries are located on the opposite sides of the Gulf of Finland – it takes about two and a half hours by ferry to travel from Tallinn to Helsinki. The second Intensive Programme offered participants an opportunity to become familiarised with two globally acknowledged educational systems, with a focus on the education of democratic intercultural citizenship. Thus, the topic of the Tallinn-Helsinki Intensive Programme was *Educational Practices in Schools*. Participants of the Intensive Programme were introduced to Estonian and Finnish educational practices from three perspectives, namely past, present and future: (1) How have the Estonian and Finnish educational systems developed throughout history? (2) What kind of educational practices are used in today's schools? (3) What is the future of the school in general?

2.2.1 Educational Practices in the Past

Lectures were held to introduce the history of the educational systems of Estonia and Finland, teaching the participants about the paths that have led to the current situation. Both countries have been subject to Swedish rule, which influenced the development of schooling and the establishment of the first universities. Around 1686, the Swedish king Charles IX ordered that peasants be taught to read, as it was a principle of the Lutheran church that everybody should able to read the Bible by themselves. In Estonia, a teacher training seminary was established in 1684–1688 by Bength Gottfried Forselius (Sarv, 2014); in Finland, the first teacher training college was founded in 1863 by Uno Cygnaeus (Tirri, 2014).

Finland was part of Sweden until 1809, when it became an Autonomous Grand Duchy of the Russian Empire. In Estonia, Swedish rule lasted from 1629 to 1710, followed by periods under Russian rule, independence, German rule and again Russia. Both Estonia and Finland became independent from Russia in 1917. A six-year primary education became compulsory and free for everybody in Estonia in 1920 and in Finland in 1921. Further, parallel school systems offered secondary education in both countries. In Finland, the parallel system was replaced in the 1970s when Finnish educational policy started to emphasise educational equality, resulting in a nine-year basic education that is the same for all children (Tirri & Kuusisto, 2013).

After the Second World War, Finland and Estonia followed different educational paths. Finland kept its independence, but Estonia was occupied by the Soviet Union until 1991, when it regained independence. During the Soviet era, all Estonian schools were centralised. The courses, teachers and content of studies were controlled by the Soviet government. However, Estonia was one of very few countries in the few Soviet Union that managed to keep its native Estonian language as the main language of instruction. Estonian language and culture was also kept alive by the communities in exile (Rannap, 2002).

In addition to learning about the historical developments of these educational systems, students of the Intensive Programme visited the Tallinn University Pedagogical Museum and the historical classroom. In Helsinki, they participated in a typical Finnish lesson from the 1930s at the Helsinki City Museum. This museum includes a typical classroom from that era, and special guided tours are available in which the guide acts as a 1930s teacher (Helsinki City Museum, 2019). At the beginning of the class, the museum guide asked the women to dress in aprons and the men in shirts. The "teacher" herself was also dressed in 1930s fashion. The lesson experience included, for instance, the singing of a religious hymn at the beginning, accompanied by an organ played by the teacher, and a fingernail inspection in order to teach good hygiene, the teacher immediately expressing disapproval if participants had long nails or wore nail polish. The participants also practiced writing letters with chalk on chalkboards. Students were expected to be silent and speak only when spoken to. Any kind of disobedience led to punishment.

The lesson was followed by a debriefing, and participants were able to share their thoughts and feelings inspired by the lesson. Interestingly, the participants – both EDIC teachers and students – indicated that the teaching practices were actually not that different from their own childhood school experience in their home countries across Europe and beyond.

2.2.2 Current Educational Practices

In both Tallinn and Helsinki, field trips to local schools were organised. In Tallinn, the field trip was to Peetri Kindergarten/Primary School, which started out as a kindergarten and has since grown into a primary school with almost 700 pupils. The school's main values and activities are based on Muriel Summers' school improvement model "Leader in Me", which incorporates the main outlines of Stephen R. Covey's book *Seven Habits of Highly Effective People* (Peetri kindergarten-Primary School, 2019). This model is reflected in teachers' practices, classroom decorations, school website etc. The objectives of the model are simple –develop your life principles, take and bear responsibility, know what you are good at and what are your weak points are, and develop good social and collaborative skills (see Leader in Me, 2019). The class observations were enriched with short conversations with teachers and pupils, followed by a spontaneous panel discussion with the school leaders Luule Niinesalu and leading professor of the EDIC+ Estonian team Eve Eisenschmidt.

EXPERIENCING DEMOCRATIC INTERCULTURAL CITIZENSHIP

One of the classes visited was Physical Education, where the IP participants observed pupils learning Estonian national dances. Cultural heritage, folk songs, music, dances and costumes form a very important part of Estonian formal and informal education. Most schools have choirs and dance groups participating in the national Song and Dance festival held every few years. During one of the afternoon sessions at Tallinn University, all the participants of EDIC Tallinn were also invited to learn these Estonian dances. Live music was also provided by an accordion player.

The field trip in Helsinki was to the Helsinki Normal Lyceum (2019), which provides basic education for students between the ages of 13 and 15 (grades 7–9) and upper secondary education for students between the ages of 16 and 18 (years I–III). The Normal Lyceum is also a teacher training school of the University of Helsinki. Every year, a significant number of subject teachers do their teaching practicum at the Normal Lyceum. Student teachers are mentored by the in-service teachers, who are highly educated and experienced, and who can be regarded as exemplars of Finnish teaching with up-to-date knowledge and skills in instruction and in mentoring.

The visits lasted the whole day, and the programme included lectures and roundtables with the EDIC teachers facilitating discussions. During the lectures, participants were given ideas about how and what to observe during the classroom visits. EDIC students were able to choose the subject of the lesson they wished to attend. After lessons, there was time to discuss pedagogical matters with the principal Tapio Lahtero. EDIC students and teachers were able to reflect on what they had seen and heard during the lectures as well as ask questions about the school system and teacher education.

The field trips to Estonian and Finnish schools also included lunch in the school cafeteria with the local pupils. This gave Intensive Programme participants an opportunity to experience one of the main assets and special features of Estonian and Finnish education: every student is provided a warm meal for free (e.g. Tirri & Kuusisto, 2013).

2.2.3   Future of the Schools

The future of the schools – whether schools will be seen as a workplace, a club or a hospital – was discussed with two visionaries from different generations. Professor Ivor Goodson and consultant Marko Rillo represented different generations – baby boomer and generation X, respectively – and were themselves surprised about how similar their views on the future of the school were and how they both emphasised importance of real and meaningful encounters between the students and teachers in both modern and future schools.

3 Methods

During the Intensive Programmes, the aim was to apply multiple teaching and learning methods (see Table 9.1). Traditional *lectures* held by EDIC teachers and visiting lecturers provided deep insights into education for democratic intercultural citizenship by covering such topics as democratic education, intercultural education, citizenship education, and moral education. *Roundtable* sessions were small interactive groups where students had the opportunity to ask questions and discuss with one of the EDIC teachers about the topics of his or her lecture. *Field trips* offered experience-based learning opportunities where participants were able to see, hear, feel, taste, smell and move – in other words, learn with all of their senses, obtain hands-on knowledge and develop emotional connections with the context.

The Intensive Programmes also included *tasks* (see Table 9.2) that were implemented individually or with a group. Before the Intensive Programme commenced, students were asked to prepare a *poster* in which every student was to present him/herself and his/her own research interests. For the Tallinn-Helsinki Intensive Programme, students were asked to introduce the educational practices of their own countries with a *video* or animation, individually or as a group.

During the Intensive Programme, students were expected to write in a learning diary every day; if they were willing, they were asked to send their diaries to Ghazala Bhatti from EDIC UK for research purposes. After the Intensive Programme in Prague, students indicated in their feedback that due to the long days, hectic schedule and active social life, they did not have time to reflect and write their diaries. In Tallinn, time was therefore reserved for the learning diary every morning (Table 9.1).

After the Intensive Programme, students were instructed to write a *reflective essay* in which they considered how the things they had learned during this EDIC Intensive Programme could promote education for democratic intercultural citizenship in their country.

4 Process and Conclusions

This chapter presented two EDIC Intensive Programmes that were held in Prague in 2017 and in Tallinn-Helsinki in 2018. The 10-day programmes included teachers and students from seven European universities and from every continent except Australia. This multinational, multilingual and multicultural

EXPERIENCING DEMOCRATIC INTERCULTURAL CITIZENSHIP   179

TABLE 9.2   Individual and group tasks

Poster Before the IP – IP Prague – IP Tallinn- Helsinki	Goal: With a poster, you present your own study (or your research plan or research interest) relating to your BA/MA/ doctoral thesis. The aim is to teach other participants of the EDIC about your interests. Content: – Title – Your name, contact information, and photo – The poster should explain the following aspects of your study: What is the subject of your study? Why, where, how, and who? If you have results: what is the answer to your research question. – Theoretical framework, research question(s), methods, results or expected results, discussion – Please include pictures, figures and tables to illustrate your work and interests Practical matters: – Print the poster on paper (we will hang all posters on the wall) – Size: A3 (width x height: 297 x 420 mm or 11.7 x 16.5 in) – Font size: 12 or bigger – This is an individual task
Teaching practices in my country Before the IP – IP Tallinn- Helsinki	Goal: Using a digital tool, you present teaching in your country as you have experienced it. In other words: based on your knowledge, illustrate how teachers teach in your country. You may choose your most meaningful teaching experience. The aim is to teach other participants of EDIC about teaching practices in different countries. Content: – Title – Your name and contact information – Share a short story about teaching practices in your country

(cont.)

TABLE 9.2 Individual and group tasks (*cont.*)

	Practical matters: – Use a digital tool to present your experience – Make a script – Record a short video or make an animation or slide show etc. – Length of the presentation: 5 minutes – You may choose to implement this task with students from the same country as a group task, as a pair or individually
Learning diary During the IP – IP Prague – IP Tallinn- Helsinki	Please write down your thoughts each day for about 10 minutes. The following questions are a guide only, you can add to this. After 10 days, please email this to Ghazala at g.bhatti@bathspa. ac.uk. Thank you. Your replies will be treated confidentially. This has been approved by the ethics committee of Bath Spa University. 1. Two things I enjoyed that were different from what I am used to 2. What I found challenging and why 3. What I learned from my peers 4. What I learned about myself as a student and a researcher
Essay After the IP – IP Prague – IP Tallinn- Helsinki	Goal: By writing an essay, you reflect on your learning experience during EDIC IP. Content: – Title – Your name, student ID and contact information – Answer the following question: How can the things you learned during this EDIC Intensive Programme promote education for democratic intercultural citizenship in your country? – Material: lectures, field visits, and discussions, course literature – Minimum of 3 articles referenced – Add list of references at the end of the essay Practical matters: – Length: 1– 2 pages (Font size 11 or 12, double spacing) – APA style in references and list of references (http://www. apastyle.org/learn/tutorials/basics-tutorial.aspx) – Return your essay to the EDIC teachers from your own country

EXPERIENCING DEMOCRATIC INTERCULTURAL CITIZENSHIP

context enabled participants to experience and realise in a holistic manner what it means to be and become a democratic intercultural citizen who shares common European and even global values, such as the acceptance of diversity and critical engagement with matters related to the prevention of violent radicalisation, the fostering of social integration, and the enhancement of intercultural understanding, accepting people with different ethnicities, religions, worldviews and sexual orientations. Intensive Programmes also gave teachers the opportunity to collaborate on a face-to-face basis and to ensure that the EDIC modules are developed based on the principles of shared understanding of aims, values and principles.

The Intensive Programmes were received with gratitude and enthusiasm by the participating students. Building relationships and engaging critically with academic discourse made it possible for all students to make the most of the programme. The fact that each lecturer brought something different from a different EDIC module, together with the emphasis on local issues, was appreciated. Roundtables were highly valued because they provided small group discussions with one academic at a time. Students felt that the programme had something for everyone.

In the Prague Intensive Programme, students appreciated the honesty with which the challenges of the Czech society were shared with the students, both in the trips organised outside the university and the issues discussed in class – such as a country coming to terms with its past and "not being at all afraid to discuss it". In the Tallinn-Helsinki Intensive Programme, the field visits were seen as valuable opportunities to see the education systems of two countries. However, since both of the schools in Tallinn and Helsinki were so-called exemplar schools, some students felt that they had not experienced what "normal" school was like. They would have liked to experience and learn more about the problems the teachers were faced with, for example with special needs children in mainstream classes.

The personal learning process was powerful for the students during the Intensive Programmes. As two students wrote:

> It has required a lot of reflection, thinking and planning, but during this EDIC experience I have come up with ... a very personal and informal plan. I am a caring person. I try to keep myself up to date with the news and why the world works the way it does, but it is difficult to know what to do except complain, mainly when giving up is not an option. I mean, if as educators we do not believe that change can happen, then we are not building any sort of glimmer of light for our pupils.

I struggle to ask questions when I feel they can be sensitive ... being surrounded by these respectful and analytical people, showed me that this is the way to create knowledge. During all lectures I was observing the way my peers where formulating their questions and how they make their points and I think I learnt a lot from them. In a conversation one-to-one with a peer, I was discussing this matter and saying that maybe we were being too critical with the host country, and he replied that part of our ethics as researchers is to be open to criticism and remain as fair as possible when sharing our experiences, and that answer was really significant for me.

Furthermore, although the lectures, roundtables and fieldtrips were instructive, student feedback showed that the most important EDIC lessons were learned through hands-on experiences outside the official programme. Breakfasts, lunches, dinners, after parties, seeing the sights, as well as walking from the hotel to the university and back; this unofficial programme was where the EDIC values were actually practised, as the students became acquainted and eventually established friendships with people from backgrounds which they might not ever have encountered before the Intensive Programme. This was felt to be the most educative and valuable lesson of all. Thus, it can be said that true EDIC courses provide opportunities for both formal and informal learning experiences that make a difference in participants' lives:

> For all of us the [EDIC] experience, intellectually and emotionally, was life-changing! We shall keep the inspiration alive and find ways to deepen our knowledge and skills so that we can transform our daily teaching practice making democratic intercultural citizenship an underlying aspect of our teaching.

Note

1 At the time of writing this chapter, the third intensive program was still to be organized in Thessaloniki in 2019.

References

Antikomplex. (2019). Retrieved February 17, 2019, http://www.antikomplex.cz/de
Centrum Obcanskeho Vzdelavani. (2019). *Civic Education Centre*. Retrieved February 17, 2019, from http://www.obcanskevzdelavani.cz/english-version

EXPERIENCING DEMOCRATIC INTERCULTURAL CITIZENSHIP 183

Helsinki City Museum. (2019). *Children's town*. Retrieved February 21, 2019, from http://www.helsinginkaupunginmuseo.fi/en/exhibitions/childrens-town/

Helsinki Normal Lyceum. (2019). Retrieved February 21, 2019, from https://www.helsinki.fi/en/training-schools/helsinki-normal-lyseum

Leader in Me. (2019). Retrieved February 21, 2019, from https://www.leaderinme.org/what-is-leader-in-me/

Matějka, O. (n.d.). *The Sudetenland – A sociological laboratory (or) Sudeten inspiration on the questions of social capital*. Unpublished article.

Peetri Kindergarten-Primary School. (2019). Retrieved February 21, 2019, from http://www.peetri.edu.ee/pohikool/7-harjumust/liider-minus-endas/

Pragulic. (2019). Retrieved February 21, 2019, from www.pragulic.cz

Rannap, H. (2002). *Eesti kooli ja pedagoogika kronoloogia*. Retrieved February 21, 2019, from https://www.hm.ee/sites/default/files/eesti_kooli_ja_pedagoogika_kronoloogia.pdf

Sarv, E.-S. (2014). A status paper on school teacher training in ESTONIA. *Journal of International Forum of Educational Research, 1*(2), 106–158.

Tirri, K. (2014). The last 40 years in Finnish teacher education. *Journal of Education for Teaching, 40,* 600–609.

Tirri, K., & Kuusisto, E. (2013). How Finland serves gifted and talented pupils. *Journal for the Education of the Gifted, 36* (1), 84–96. doi:10.1177/0162353212468066

Veugelers, W., de Groot, I., & Stolk, V. (2017). *Research for cult committee – Teaching common values in Europe*. Brussels: European Parliament, Policy Department for Structural and Cohesion Policies.

Wikipedia. (2019). *Jáchymov*. Retrieved February 17, 2019, from https://en.wikipedia.org/wiki/J%C3%A1chymov

CHAPTER 10

Students' Experiences in EDIC+ Intensive Programmes

Ghazala Bhatti

Theorising and exploring the meaning of empowerment, social justice, citizenship and democracy in academic papers is one thing. Teaching about it in order to make future teachers and administrators consider policy and practice and facilitate their participation in research is another. The EDIC+ project tried to do both, when Masters and doctoral students came together from seven universities and they worked with academics from their own and other universities. We thought it would be useful to capture student voices and to see what they made of what we were trying to do, and what we could do better next time. Was there something we should do differently, and if so what and how? This teaching and learning experience sought to make students confident learners who could express their views and explore different perspectives in a space which was not their usual place of learning. In addition to other positive experiences, it was hoped that as a consequence of their participation on the EDIC project they would be able to think more critically about their own research projects.

Elspeth Jones (2010) discusses the value in students and their tutors working in ways which underline the importance of international experiences. The idea of the global citizen who is well-informed and capable is a very attractive one. In their research with Erasmus students Golubeva et al. (2018) capture students' views about 'active citizenship'. They report that students' understanding agreed with the definition of the concepts provided in the research literature. The EDIC project made it possible to try two developmental ideas which would feed into the final module. One was IP (Intensive Programme lasting ten days) and the other was a 'try-out' module held once or twice at each university between 2016 and 2019.

Students from seven universities met and studied together for ten days at the Intensive Programmes held between 4th and 14th June 2017 at Charles University, Prague. Then from 14th to 24th May 2018 when 23 students from seven universities met for ten days at the Universities of Tallinn and Helsinki. The final Intensive Programme meeting was held at Aristotle University, Thessaloniki between 13th and 23rd March 2019.

© KONINKLIJKE BRILL NV, LEIDEN, 2019 | DOI: 10.1163/9789004411944_010

This is an open access chapter distributed under the terms of the CC-BY-NC 4.0 License.

STUDENTS' EXPERIENCES IN EDIC+ INTENSIVE PROGRAMMES 185

We obtained ethical clearance from Bath Spa University ethics committee to gather data from participating students. The research with students attending IP on EDIC was optional. There were no strict parameters set on any concepts the students might use, and no predefined outcomes. The questions students were invited to respond to were very open ended. These were:

1. What were 2 things (enjoyable and different) to what I'm used to?
2. What I found challenging and why?
3. What did I learn from my peers?
4. What did I contribute?
5. What did I learn about myself as a student/researcher?

Data was collected mainly through students learning diaries which they were invited to submit to one researcher within one or two weeks of completing the Intensive Programme and in the case of three 'pilot' or 'try out' modules, immediately after completing those modules. The students could structure their answers as they wished. They could use sub headings or illustrations or photographs – anything they wished. They were assured that their identities would not be shared with anyone except the one researcher, nor the full data sets which would identify them and their tutors or their universities. In addition to this, 15 students from one university were prepared to take part in 3 separate focus group discussions, as well as provide data collected through follow-on individual in-depth ethnographic interviews.

When introducing the idea of research and seeking informed consent from the students one of the key readings used in the IP in Charles University Prague was Morwenna Griffith's (2003) essay on empowerment. Other students in subsequent IPs were also informed of this text which would explain *why* their voices were important and how their ideas would be shared. That a ten day Intensive Programme would help this process of 'empowerment' (whatever that means!) was initially met with ambiguity, puzzlement and a vague sort of interest. That this was not a normal 'evaluation of the module' puzzled some students. That it was important to record their views and what they wrote would be taken seriously was made clear to all who took part. After the end of the Intensive Programme or the end of the try out module when students submitted their learning diaries they acknowledged that they had been to quote one student 'on a big journey of change'.

Data was coded and sub categories emerged from the written and spoken (and recorded) texts. What is set out below is based on a selection of what the students said and wrote down to share on two IPs and three try out modules. This is anonymised data from 25 students from a total of 56 students who were invited to take part at different points during the three year duration of the EDIC project.

1 Findings

Overall, students greatly appreciated the opportunity to meet other post graduate students from their own and other universities. Even students from the same university did not sometimes have the opportunity of working closely with their own peers inside their own university until they attended the IP.

1.1 *International Encounters*

The most poignant texts are those which capture what the students shared about their interactions with students from other countries. If these participants become teachers or they train teachers one day, then these shared moments will probably help them to be better informed educators. It is a notable feature of European Universities that they attract post graduate students from across the world, who travel to Europe to study for Masters and doctoral degrees. The nationalities represented during the first two IPs and some try-out modules included students from the seven universities in Finland, Greece Spain, Tallinn, The Czech Republic, The Netherlands, UK, plus students from Columbia, China, Ghana, Iran, Pakistan, Somalia, Switzerland, Syria, Venezuela and Zambia. These are some of the students' words:

> It sounds bad but all I knew about Iran was what the media told me. Some stupid backward things. On TV I see these men and women in black cloaks protesting against the west ...! It was amazing and so wonderful to learn something else, more relevant, more honest, more human from someone who knew so much more about my country than I knew about Iran. I would like to visit Iran. (Interview)

> By the time we got to the end of that talk about what was happening in Venezuela (in 2018) to young people, to children, there was not a single dry eye in the room. What an artificial protected world I have lived in all my life. (Interview)

> Ghana was somewhere in Africa. A dot on the map. But we saw a film about Asanti university and me and my other friends from universities in Europe sat up. What a great campus it was and what an absolutely inspirational guy is leading it! That night when we got talking we thought there has to be a EDIC project set up in Ghana. I think we told her that we will go and help her (the student from Ghana). (Journal notes)

STUDENTS' EXPERIENCES IN EDIC+ INTENSIVE PROGRAMMES 187

China is huge. Before this IP I had not realized what was actually happening in their schools. I have learnt there is so much going on and I know so little about it in the mainland, in Hong Kong. All I know is a bit about my own country's educational policies. (Journal notes)

1.2 *Working in English Language*

Fluent speakers of the English language forget that they must remember some students need a little more time to respond quickly. The *speed* at which words are spoken was mentioned more than once.

I did not feel confident with speaking quickly in English. Same with some other students from other places. But that was only for the first two days. Third day I stopped speaking in my own language to my friends from my university. I wanted to learn about Greece, about China and not just be with my own university friends always, and I didn't care about my English. (Journal notes)

People who speak fast in English including teachers, sometimes leave us behind. But it is not possible to interrupt. That is the main problem I had sometimes. (Journal notes)

I was appalled I was the *only* one in class who could *only* speak English ... Never experienced that before among so many people. I mean even the tutors spoke Dutch, or Spanish or Greek or Finnish ... (Interview)

I was shocked to learn people were talking in English as their third or fourth language. It is frightening how little I know! How few languages I was taught at school. (Interview)

1.3 *Excursions and Off-Campus Visits*

It was really appreciated that students met other people besides their normal teachers and tutors. They found it very educational and useful. It was the element of surprise together with the learning that was commented upon.

Meeting Igor Blazevic in that Laika café was like something out of a nineteenth century novel. We read novels about revolution. We don't meet such people in real life, only in films. This was *so* unexpected, so humbling. I know this changed me somehow – the way he talked about his work, his passion for his country, his idealism. I have *never* met anyone international like that. Thank you to Dana! [Tutor responsible for organizing Prague programme]. (Journal notes)

We stood in the ruins and we wrote poetry in the 'tough Czech north'. It was a strange experience walking through the ruins of the homes the Germans left behind. This was so memorable for me personally including how badly people were treated who worked in the mines. I feel I must read more history. We do not have such places in the Netherlands. (Journal notes)

It was an eventful afternoon strolling the streets of Tallinn's Old City with the high school students who were very knowledgeable about their history and incredible legends. I had never even heard of Tallinn before. (Journal notes)

1.4   *On Learning Together*

The excitement of learning together was shared by more than half of the students. They felt outside their comfort zone but then got used to 'all of us going everywhere together all the time' as one of them noted.

It is not until you are thrown together that you really learn from each other. I am normally not very extrovert, and pushy. I normally follow on. But as the IP was in my country, there I was talking and talking about where to go, what to see! Then in class I could share things easily next day. I have made friends for life. I can't believe it. (Interview)

It is such a gift to have an opportunity to *really* learn together, to be made to think hard and to be honest with each other about what you learn. I feel very privileged. Very fortunate that I was selected to be on this programme. (Journal notes)

I have learnt that each and every one of my peers has taught me something new and important. This can be about themselves, or their value system, or their hopes for the future, or their hopes for education in their country. Some were shy at the very beginning, but not at the end. (Journal notes)

Since I left high school and I went on school trips, I can't remember going on a trip with so many people all together! Hard working trip but also such a very fun trip. In school we were all from same neighbourhood,

STUDENTS' EXPERIENCES IN EDIC+ INTENSIVE PROGRAMMES   189

same country. This is so much more exciting, so amazing, so educational.
Sometimes we don't want to go to sleep- there is so much to talk about.
(Journal notes)

1.5 *On Teachers*

Although direct information was not sought about teachers, about a third of
the students commented on those who taught them.

> We should meet these teachers once a year, every year. I have learnt SO
> much from the 14 teachers who tutored us and were patient with us. It is
> sad we will not meet them again. (Journal notes)

> Each lecturer was so different from the others. Each speaker was add-
> ing and adding to our knowledge and understanding about the subject
> they were so passionate about ... Just by being themselves they were also
> teaching us how to teach, how to be with students and the real value of
> EDIC. (Journal notes)

> This IP was a great learning experience, touching areas that many find
> sensitive or too subjective to address. And the honesty of the professors
> was exemplary. They opened the space up for us to engage with each
> other without being judged. (Journal notes)

> We don't know how to thank our teachers, so we will not be able to do
> that. Ever. (Journal notes)

These are just some of the views students shared. There were not many nega-
tive points. Most students felt fortunate to be part of the project.

2   Discussion

Overall, it is fair to say that this was a productive and valuable learning experience for most student participants. They appreciated the opportunity to work
intensively together for ten whole days. Two students managed to attend two
IPs and found their own additional funding to attend the second IP because
they had enjoyed the first IP so much and because they had learnt so much. For
at least one Masters student, attending the first IP led to writing a PhD proposal
which helped him obtain a fully funded scholarship for three years. For some
the experience of IP and of EDIC was in their own words 'transformational'.

For others it was challenging and to quote two students 'boundary pushing' and 'totally outside my comfort zone'. For another student it was 'beyond my expectations.' No one regretted participating in the Intensive Programmes and no one wanted to leave when it was over. This might indicate that only those students had applied to go on EDIC Intensive Programmes who were willing to take risks and be challenged in the first place. For all teachers it was a great opportunity to network and plan and look forward to the next opportunity of collaborative work, which was academic, educational, social and fulfilling.

References

Golubeva, I., Parra, E., & Mohedano, R. (2018). What does 'active citizenship' mean for Erasmus students? *Intercultural Education, 20*(1), 40–58.

Jones, E. (2010). *Internationalization and the student voice: Higher education perspective*. London: Routledge.

CHAPTER 11

The Future of EDIC+

Wiel Veugelers

Let us take again the list of outcomes we presented in Chapter 2 and describe the progress we made.

1 Outcomes of the Project

1. The joint development of a curriculum for Education for Democratic Intercultural Citizenship (EDIC+), a network structure, and an intensive programme.

Together we developed a curriculum for Education for Democratic Intercultural Citizenship, built a network structure, and designed and trialled an annual intensive programme.

2. The development of one 7.5 ECTS (Master level) module (in English) by each participating university. The seven modules will together constitute the integrated curriculum EDIC+. All material will be published (in an Open-Access book and on the EDIC+ website).

Each university has developed an international module in English and had try-outs of the module or at least crucial parts of it. All universities developed the module in accordance with the content described in our proposal. The intensive dialogues between the participants contributed to a better alignment of the modules with the central theme of Democratic Intercultural Citizenship Education and with a stronger international and comparative methodology. Readers can read about the seven modules in this (Open-Access) book. For further information, interested parties can contact the coordinator of the university involved (www.uvh.nl/edic).

3. The recognition of all seven modules by all EDIC universities. All universities will offer the entire EDIC+ curriculum to their students.

© KONINKLIJKE BRILL NV, LEIDEN, 2019 | DOI: 10.1163/9789004411944_011
This is an open access chapter distributed under the terms of the CC-BY-NC 4.0 License.

192   VEUGELERS

All seven universities have recognised the EDIC+ modules of the other universities. All universities have offered the entire EDIC+ curriculum to their students. For next year this will be done at an earlier stage, and a lot of information about the different modules is now available on the EDIC website and in this book.

> 4. Signing of an agreement by all EDIC universities for student exchange with other participating universities through Erasmus grants.

All EDIC+ universities have now signed mutual agreements with the other EDIC+ universities. Students can use normal Erasmus grants to study at one of the EDIC+ universities, in particular in the area of the presented EDIC+ module. Teachers can use Erasmus grants to attend another EDIC university to teach and to expand cooperation in research.

> 5. Participation of students from these seven universities and students from other universities in these modules. Students can use Erasmus exchange grants for participating in modules at other universities.

There is a growing (but still small) number of students that use or want to use these possibilities in the future. For Master students, the period of three months is quite difficult to fit in. We hope that the new Erasmus programme will make it possible to offer shorter periods for Master students.

> 6. Awarding of an EDIC+ certificate to students after completing two or more modules of the EDIC curriculum. (For students of the EDIC universities this can be a module at their own institute and a module at one of the other universities. The intensive programme can be part of one of the modules.)

We have an EDIC+ certificate including all logos of the participating universities. Universities can use this for their own EDIC+ module. We also use it for participation in an Intensive Programme. When students participate in two EDIC+ modules they receive a certificate signed by the general EDIC+ coordinator.

> 7. All modules will have the following methodological elements:
>
>   a Combination of theory and practice.
>   b Link with civil society institutions (site visits, guest lectures).

THE FUTURE OF EDIC+   193

    c Research and change orientation.

    d International and comparative orientation through the use of data and examples from other countries, in particular the EDIC+ participants.

    e A visiting professor in each module from one of the other EDIC universities to give a lecture and act as a critical friend during the process of curriculum development.

We formulated 5 methodological elements for the modules:

a   All the modules offer a strong combination of theory and practice

b   In all modules there is a link with civil society institutions. Many site-visits are made. Guest lectures by representatives of such organisations are included in the modules.

c   All the modules are linked with research. In the developmental stage of the modules we could benefit from the EU Teaching Common Values project. All the modules are also aimed at educational change, at improving educational practices, and at the professional development of teachers and other educational professionals.

d   The modules became even more international than we expected, as we moved beyond only a European perspective. The participation of students from outside Europe in the modules and in the intensive programmes contributed to this global perspective.

e   The 'critical friend' lecturer who attended the module of another EDIC+ university and gave a lecture in the module was a strong tool in the collaboration. It was a cooperation within the actual educational practice. The EDIC universities wish to continue this form of exchange.

    8. Creation of a team of scholars who can function as experts, co-supervisors or members of a Master or PhD-tribunal in the other participating universities.

The group of lecturers involved in the Intensive Programme and in the modules of the universities are engaged in a growing collaboration in terms of research, publishing, and supervising. People are more aware of each others' competences, are more familiar with each other, and know more about each other's formal and informal institutional cultures.

    9. An academic international e-journal offering students the opportunity to publish their research, their curriculum material and their educational experiences.

We were forced to drop the intended e-journal because an Erasmus strategic partnership does not support this kind of activity. Most of the EDIC teachers are members of editorial boards of academic journals or book series. They showed the students how publishing works and stimulated them to work towards academic publishing.

10. An annual intensive programme (IP) of ten days for students and teachers. After the project period, other resources, such as Erasmus exchange grants, will be used to continue with the IP.

The two Intensive Programmes (IP) were very successful and there was again a lot of interest in the 2019 IP in Thessaloniki. The IPs are important for the (international) learning experiences of the students, the possibility for teachers to present their work to an international audience. Both students and teachers can intensify their contacts in such IP. We hope we can continue them, maybe with the use of normal Erasmus exchange grants.

11. Dissemination of activities in all participating countries; at the European level presentations will be given at leading educational conferences (ECER, EARLI, ATEE).

All universities will organise a multiplier event in May 2019. We already organised symposiums at the annual conferences of the European Conference of Educational Research (ECER) (Bolzano, September 2018) and the Association of Moral Education (AME) (Barcelona, November 2018). At the last conference we saw a lot of interest from universities outside Europe (in particular the US, Mexico, Brazil, China, Taiwan). In the future we will organise more international presentations (e.g. at ATEE, EARLI, AERA).

12. Setting-up of a proper management structure to ensure the sustainability of the EDIC+ curriculum after the EDIC+ project is completed.

The grants for the Strategic Partnership cover the period September 2016–August 2019. We will try to obtain new grants as a consortium but will continue with the EDIC+ structure, at least at this level:
- An annual offer of the seven EDIC+ modules.
- The EDIC+ website.
- Stimulating mutual exchange of students and teachers.
- An annual meeting of the seven EDIC university coordinators to continue the EDIC+ curriculum and to investigate new possibilities of cooperation.
- This annual meeting will be combined with a seminar in which teachers of the EDIC universities present new research and new educational activities.

Printed in the United States
By Bookmasters